PRAISE FO.

Finding Loretta

"In *Finding Loretta*, Diane Wheaton deftly showcases the balancing act all adoptees face when launching a search: displaying loyalty to the only family one has ever known; navigating the closed adoption system; sifting through lies and missing information; staving off fears of rejection; honoring self in the pursuit of truth and identity. The battle between 'right to know' and 'right to privacy' is front and center in Wheaton's gripping personal tale."

—JULIE RYAN MCGUE, author of *Twice a Daughter,*
Belonging Matters, and *Twice a Family*

"Diane Wheaton offers a thoughtful reflection on the realities of adoption for an adopted person. *Finding Loretta* takes an honest look at the complexities of adoptee loyalty and includes many compelling moments from start to finish."

—HALEY RADKE, creator and host of *Adoptees On* podcast

"Most little girls would have felt lucky to have been adopted into a two-parent family in an upper-middle class community by the beach with a stay-at-home mother who kept everything just so. But for Diane Wheaton there was something more she yearned for. Something money or a formally set dinner table couldn't buy. This page-turning memoir is full of twists and turns you won't see coming."

—LAURIE JAMES, author of *Sandwiched*

"*Finding Loretta* opens reader's eyes to the complexity of adoption as Diane Wheaton searches for family and identity while navigating her relationship with her aging adoptive parents and their complicated issues. A moving, personal story of loss, love, and coming home to self."

—ANNE HEFFRON, author of *You Don't Look Adopted* and
To Be Real

"In clear, well-paced prose, Diane Wheaton offers gentle insight into the effects of infant relinquishment on an adopted person's life. *Finding Loretta* is an emotionally honest portrayal of the author's choice to recover what was lost to her in adoption. Five Stars!"

—MARY ELLEN GAMBUTTI, author of *I Must Have Wandered*

"In *Finding Loretta*, Diane Wheaton offers a glimpse behind the veil separating fallacies from the shattered fantasies that guide her life as an adoptee. Mixed emotions color complicated relationships as she begins her brave journey toward self-discovery. Wheaton courageously rises after every fall, piecing together fragments of *who am I* and *where did I come from*, while risking abandonment and betrayal in turns of events readers will least expect. Every word of *Finding Loretta* is true; a rare opportunity to view adoption from multiple angles."

—JUDITH CASSIS, book coach and author of
Where Do I Go From Here?

"*Finding Loretta* unfolds like a good mystery, but it is so much more. It is a love story and a hero's journey. Memoirs tend to be vulnerable to either of two pitfalls; one is the story of 'poor me'; the other is the story that ends with a neatly gift wrapped resolution. *Finding Loretta* is neither one. Wheaton has written a captivating memoir that does justice to the complexities of real people and real life. I found it to be a moving story and a satisfying read."

—LEAH FISHER, author of *My Marriage Sabbatical*

"One of the best books on adoption. This is groundbreaking work, far beyond a memoir. There is much that can be gleamed from *Finding Loretta*."

—NICOLE NEUMAN, cultural consultant and psychologist

Finding Loretta

AN
ADOPTED DAUGHTER'S
SEARCH TO
DEFINE FAMILY

Diane Wheaton

SHE WRITES PRESS

Published 2025
Printed in the United States of America
Print ISBN: 978-1-64742-796-2
E-ISBN: 978-1-64742-797-9
Library of Congress Control Number: 2024918848

For information, address:
She Writes Press
1569 Solano Ave #546
Berkeley, CA 94707

Interior design by Stacey Aaronson

She Writes Press is a division of SparkPoint Studio, LLC.

For my children, Heather and Travis

And for my granddaughters, Alaina and Olivia
And all my future grandchildren

AUTHOR'S NOTE

This is a work of nonfiction. I relied upon my personal journals, researched facts, and called upon my memory of events and times in my life. I have changed the names of most of the people mentioned in this book, but not all. I have modified identifying details in order to respect and protect the privacy of others. There are no composite characters or events in this book. Occasionally, I omitted people and events, but only when the omission had no impact on the substance of the story.

Prologue

I'M LINING UP WITH OTHER GIRLS MY AGE TO WALK onstage. We're dressed in freshly cleaned, pressed Junior Girl Scout uniforms. White gloves. Patrol cords. Badge sashes proudly parading across our chests. I'm holding a large poster board in my hand. I'm the tallest girl in line. I'm always the tallest girl in line—and the tallest in my class. My heart pounds as I think about having to walk across the slippery pine floor of the school stage to stand in my designated spot. I'm ten years old. We're exhibiting our ethnicity for a badge, of some sort, to an evening audience of parents and family members from several different Girl Scout troops. We're to stand onstage, hold up our decorated signs, and declare where our ancestors came from before immigrating to America. We're told to add stories of our family history when it's our turn to speak.

I'm old enough to know that what I'm about to share won't be my truth. It'll be my adoptive mother's history, not mine. I have to take on her truth because I don't know my own. My adoptive parents, Stan and Madge, have told me that I am Northern European, like they are. Whatever that means. That's all I really know.

I only have my parents' stories to fill in for mine. My father was the first person in his family to be born in the United States. His family emigrated from Krakow, Poland. My mother was second generation, born in Fargo, North Dakota, into a large family of immigrants from Norway.

I don't know my ethnicity. I could've been born under a rock or on another planet. Looking out at the audience, I feel bad that I'll be lying to so many people. I feel like an impostor, pretending to be someone I'm not.

But standing on the stage, holding the sign in large blue, handwritten letters—NORWAY—would make my mother happy and proud, like when I'd use Sun-In to lighten my brown hair to blonde, like hers, like mine used to be when I was little. I want to make my mother proud of me. And so, I smile and tell her story because I don't have my own to tell.

Part One

In all of us there is a hunger, marrow-deep, to know
our heritage—to know who we are and where we have
come from. Without this enriching knowledge, there is
a hollow yearning. No matter what our attainments in
life, there is still a vacuum, an emptiness, and the
most disquieting loneliness.

—Alex Haley, author of *Roots*

Chapter One

IT WAS 1961, AND WE HAD RECENTLY MOVED FROM VIRGINIA to settle for a few years in San Diego, California. My adoptive father, Stan, a naval officer, had been transferred from working at the Pentagon in Washington, DC, to the Naval Amphibious Base on Coronado Island. We rented a redbrick, ranch-style home in the Sunset Cliffs section that had floor-to-ceiling living room windows that overlooked the Pacific Ocean. I loved this house. I walked to kindergarten from this house. It was where I learned how to ride a bike without training wheels, lost my first tooth, got my first Barbie from my grandmother, and started swim lessons from Navy chiefs. Moving back to Southern California meant that we were again living near my grandparents, whom I adored. I made many fond memories living there, but probably the most profound was when my mother told me what adoption meant. I can still remember that day.

Sunlight streamed through the prism of the kitchen windows, offering a rainbow to offset the black-and-white tile floor. My adoptive mother, Madge, wearing navy capris and a white oxford shirt, was ironing. She asked me to sit on the barstool, up at the counter. She wanted to talk to me. I was between five and six years old.

Dangling my legs, I waited.

My mother put the iron upright and stood still. Finally, she asked me a question. "Diane, do you know what the word 'adoption' means?"

"No, but I know I'm adopted."

"Yes, yes, you're right. You are adopted. But it means something. I think you're old enough to know what that word really means."

I began to swing my legs under the counter, curious as to what this word might mean.

"Adoption means that you were born from another woman's tummy. You didn't grow in my tummy. You grew in another woman's tummy."

"I did?"

"Yes. Just like your brother, John. You know, he's adopted too. He didn't grow in my tummy either. Both of you grew in other tummies. Remember when we went to the orphanage and met John for the first time? We got to pick him out from all the other babies that were there?"

"Yes."

"Well, we did the same thing with you. We got to pick you out from all these other babies, and we chose you. We loved you from the first moment we saw you."

I'm not sure if I asked about my birth mother or not. I don't know if in this moment I realized, really understood, I had another mother out there, somewhere in the world. I do remember crying inconsolably because I didn't come from my adoptive mother. I didn't want to be different, though I already was. I wanted to be like my little friends and come from my mother's tummy like they had come from their mothers. I knew where babies grew. How could I have come from a stranger? I wanted to be connected to the only mother I knew, not some other lady.

Looking back, I realize she told me the usual story told to adopted children—that we were chosen—but in reality, nothing could be further from the truth. Years later, I'd find a copy of their actual request form that said they wanted a "Nordic" baby with blonde hair and blue eyes. My parents didn't *choose* me; they put in their request for a white baby. And they didn't choose *me*; I just happened to be the next blonde, blue-eyed baby in line.

As a five-year-old, it was too difficult to grasp the concept that my mother could have given me away. Instead, I settled for the absurd abstraction on offer—I was chosen by new parents who were the ones who really wanted me, more than my mother. It was a pretty good salve to cover the primal wound and add confusion—at least for a few decades in my case, and for some, a lifetime.

What I now know about what really happened is this: My adoptive parents, Stan and Madge, had to wait twenty-four hours after signing legal papers to adopt me before they could take me home. When they finally had me in their arms, there was no fanfare. After thirteen years of trying to have a biological child and losing six babies, my parents had no crib waiting for me that first night. There had been too many letdowns trying to adopt to keep a crib around, a constant reminder of their unintentionally empty nest. A crib would have only reminded them of their disappointment, their grief and pain, the loss they'd already experienced.

It was a cautious beginning for all of us. They borrowed a bassinet from friends. Nobody threw a baby shower to celebrate my arrival or their long-awaited parenthood.

I was born a secret, and before my adoptive parents brought

me home with them, I had spent the first ten weeks of my life in foster care somewhere in Alameda County, California. I have no idea who took care of me or how well I was cared for. I don't know if I was ever cuddled and comforted, and I don't know how many different foster homes or cribs I slept in.

I was curious about my beginnings. Over the years, up until around age ten, I asked my mother questions. I was told my birth mother was twenty-one, not married, and couldn't keep me. Supposedly, she was engaged to my father, but he didn't like my mother's family, which was why they never married. All I knew growing up was that my parents were Northern European, my father was an artist, and my mother had auburn hair and blue eyes. Later, I'd find out that half of this information was untrue.

As I grew older, it became more difficult to talk or ask my mother questions about my adoption. I could tell from her wincing and tears when I asked if my interest in my birth mother upset her. I didn't want to upset her so I stopped asking questions around the age of ten—that's when I began to fantasize to give myself my own answers.

When I was ten, my father retired from the Navy after serving twenty-four years. We moved into a new home and a settled life in Palos Verdes, a coastal suburb in Los Angeles County. It was rural, on the southern side of the peninsula. From the back of our house, we had a panoramic view of the Pacific Ocean, Catalina Island, and the cascading cliffs that welcomed kelp beds that calmed the waves so they gently splashed upon rocky beaches. It was here that my most memorable childhood fantasy arose, centered, understandably, on the nautical.

I pretended I was a mermaid. Not just any mermaid, but a

mermaid cursed to live my life on land during the day with my human family who had adopted me. At midnight, I'd embark as in a trance, on my starlit journey down to the cliffs to home, to my "real" parents and family, who lived in the sea. I wouldn't remember anything about my visit because that was part of the curse given to me. I only remembered vague things, so I'd know where I came from and that I was cursed.

Yes, I had a vivid imagination at ten years old. And the mermaid fantasy satisfied me, because it gave me the answers I needed as to why I was given up for adoption. For a while, I could believe it wasn't my biological family's desire to ever lose me—it was a curse that had separated us.

It certainly was a childish answer to serious questions, but it was the answer I needed at the time, something my adoptive parents couldn't or wouldn't give me because of their own issues. And as I grew older and understood more, it became too hard for any of us to talk about my adoption at all.

Eventually, of course, I grew out of my mermaid fantasy phase and put adoption in the back of my mind. Life was busy and growing up was hard; trying to figure out and understand why my birth mother couldn't keep me would have been emotional overload.

So I simplified the story in my mind: The truth was she didn't keep me. That must have meant she was a bad woman. She gave me away. Who does that? Who gives away their child? And if she was bad, wasn't I also? Since I came from her, wasn't I just like her? I was born in shame and grew up in shame. I was formed by it.

I was also doomed to never know anything about my past or who my biological parents were. I was born in the Baby Scoop Era (1943–1973), in a closed adoption, and this was just the way it was. The Baby Scoop Era was a period in American history characterized by a surge in premarital pregnancies along with a higher rate of newborns being surrendered by unmarried mothers. For decades, looking into the bathroom mirror, I'd wonder who I inherited my facial features from. My fine hair? My nose? My blue eyes stared back in the mirror, offering no answers.

I think I've always been wondering and searching. My mother told me that when I was little, I would go up to strangers and say, "I'm lost." Those two words were profound. I *was* lost. I had features of unknown ghosts from the past. I wanted—needed—to know where I came from because maybe by knowing my history and my beginnings, I'd find myself and, with that knowledge, I'd be grounded enough to find my way home.

Chapter Two

I WAS SIXTEEN YEARS OLD WHEN, ONE NIGHT, MY FATHER had a rare evening when he had too much to drink. He drank every night, stopping on his way home from work at the 7-Eleven to pick up a bottle of sherry. Over the years, my mother had become quite good at limiting his drinking by having dinner nearly ready when he got home. That way, he didn't have much time to drink and get too woozy before dinner, which was served promptly at five o'clock.

Growing up, I hated being the only one of my friends who had to leave at four thirty in the afternoon to go home and set the dinner table. Our ambience at dinner wasn't like my friends' either. It was formal, with sterling silver candlesticks, china, and cloth napkins folded neatly into engraved sterling silver napkin rings.

My brother and I, for the most part, kept quiet at dinner while we listened to my parents talk about their day. Sometimes they asked us about schoolwork or school activities. I look back and find it interesting my parents had coffee every night with dinner. I wonder now if that was my mother's way of trying to keep my father sober after his bottle of afternoon sherry.

On this particular night, my father, who now worked as a project manager for an aerospace corporation, came home earlier than expected, which he sometimes did, so he had time to move on from sherry to Scotch whiskey, landing after dinner on the couch in his den to sleep it off.

I was sitting on the floor in my parents' bedroom, across the hall from his den. The bedroom door was closed. I was using their phone for privacy, talking to one of my girlfriends, Ellen, when my father awoke from his drunken slumber.

I only heard the door slam against the bedroom wall as he clumsily and mightily threw it open, yelling, "Get off the goddamn phone." I turned my head to see my father standing in the doorway, looking like a grizzly ready to attack. His stance said everything.

"Hold on, Ellen," I said, as I put my hand over the receiver.

"I said to get off the goddamn phone! Now!"

"Okay. I will, Dad. Just give me a minute to say goodbye and hang up with Ellen."

"Now!" he roared.

I jumped back. He was even louder than before.

Before I knew what was happening, I felt the rush of him charging toward me. He grabbed the phone from my hand and slammed it down on the base. Horrified, I quickly stood up and ran out of the room.

"I told you to get off the goddamn phone and you didn't listen to me!" he yelled after me.

I angrily yelled back, "You didn't give me a chance! I was going to hang up!"

He didn't like that. We weren't allowed to "talk back" to our parents. But he ticked me off and embarrassed me in front of my friend. He was unreasonable. Charging at me, like a bear! I ran toward the other side of the house, but he caught up with me in the hallway.

He pushed me against the wall, banged my head into it, and swung his fist at me. Soon, he was using both arms to punch. I put my arms up to protect my face, frightened by his wild behavior. He reeked of alcohol.

I screamed, "Dad, stop! Dad!"

He yelled, "You're a goddamn fucking mistake! A goddamn fucking mistake! You were never meant to be born!"

I burst out crying. Those words sank into my brain.

My mother and brother showed up. My mother yelled, "Stan, stop this!"

He stood back and stared at her. I ducked out and ran upstairs to my bedroom and locked my door. I fell on my bed sobbing. My arms hurt, and worse, my whole idea of who my dad was and our relationship was in tatters on the floor.

How could my father have said that to me? Did he really think that? Is that what he truly believed, that I was a mistake and should've never been born?

I sat up on my bed and wiped my face. My father had hit me before, but always with a belt for punishment and not often. He'd never slugged me, and he was so much stronger than I was. It was wrong.

A few minutes later, I secretly used the upstairs phone to call Ellen back and tell her what happened. Ellen told her mother, who offered me a place to stay. I loved Ellen's mother, and she'd always been warm and kind to me. I accepted her offer. I packed a few bags of clothes and my schoolbooks and waited for one of Ellen's older sisters to pick me up. I told my mother on my way out the door that I was leaving to stay for a few days at Ellen's house. I needed a break and some time to think about what happened with Dad. She didn't try to stop me.

I went to school and carried on as usual living at Ellen's ranch house with her mother, three sisters, and an array of cats, dogs, and horses. She seemed to like me, and once when we were alone, she fixed me hot tea and taught me how to paint my nails the way a manicurist would.

Their home was always busy and staying there felt like freedom, but in my downtime, I felt alone. My mother didn't check on me and that hurt my feelings—didn't she care what happened to me? I had more support from my friends and their parents than my own family. *Why didn't they check on me? Why didn't they call to see how I was and to say how sorry they were this happened?*

I knew I wasn't at fault in this. My father had brought this on. He should have taken the high ground. He was the one who hit me and said those horrible words. I refused to come home until he apologized. He called once, insisting he never touched me. Maybe he honestly didn't remember, but my mother knew, and I told him that I had bruises to prove it.

My father's words were hurtful. As an adoptee, to be told I was never meant to be born, that I was a fucking mistake, cut deep. Adoptees already know we're unplanned or unwanted and many of us already feel we're a mistake. Abandoned. Lost. Disconnected from our roots. My father's words cut to my core and haunted me for years because I thought this was how he really felt about me.

One week later, he called again.

"Hi." His voice seemed to crackle a bit. We were both nervous.

"Hi, Dad." I held the phone to my ear with one hand while my other hand waved to Ellen and two of her sisters who were standing in the kitchen, staring at me. I knew they were wondering what was going to happen. I silently mouthed, *Oh my gosh*, as I widened my eyes.

"Are you doing okay?" he asked.

"Yeah, I'm fine."

"Well, I think it's time you come home."

"I'll come home when you apologize for hitting me."

"That never happened. I never hit you."

"Ah, yes, you did, Dad. I had bruises. You hit me hard that night. Mom and John were there too. You also said some pretty horrible words to me. You probably don't remember because you were drunk."

"I don't remember saying anything mean to you or hitting you."

"Well, you did and I'm not coming home until you apologize for it."

There was silence on the other end of the phone.

His voice was low. "I'm sorry if I hurt you. I'm sorry I hit you and said some hurtful things."

I couldn't believe it. He did it. I heaved a big sigh.

He picked me up in his Cadillac several hours later, waiting in Ellen's driveway for me to climb into the front seat. We drove home in silence.

When I woke up the next day, breakfast was served as usual. My father went to work early in the morning like he always did and my brother and mother acted as if nothing had ever happened. I didn't say much. It would take me some time to feel comfortable, to feel at home again.

I was still hurting from everything that had happened. I knew my parents weren't going to talk about it, and I was afraid to bring anything up. Besides, I wasn't sure I could handle talking to them either.

I was glad that at least I had some good friends at school I could talk with. It helped, but still, we were so young and inexperienced. I was on my own to cope. My brother and I were raised not to bring up conflicts, and we were not allowed to argue with our parents. It just wasn't tolerated. They ran a tight ship. So, I had no choice but to move on, thinking my father, and possibly my mother as well, felt I was a mistake and perhaps that they thought it had been a mistake they had even adopted me.

At sixteen, I felt alone beyond the normal teen angst, but my belief and faith got me through some tough thoughts about myself. I believed in God, and in the possibility of fate, and so I believed that since I had been born, I was meant to be here. I had to believe this. I was thankful for my high school girlfriends, for the boys I dated who fulfilled my need for affection and intimacy, and for my determined and independent nature gifted me from my unknown birth parents.

Chapter Three

LIKE MANY ADOPTEES, I WONDERED WHAT IT WOULD BE like if I found my birth mother. I wondered where she was and wondered about my birth father too. *Who were these people?* They had to be living somewhere on this planet. I knew they saw the same sun, moon, and stars that I did, but without anything tangible to go on, it seemed impossible that I'd ever find them. *Did other adoptees wonder where they came from?* I didn't grow up knowing any other adoptees except for my younger brother John, who wasn't interested in talking about being adopted or in finding his birth mother, so I didn't know.

I did learn more as a teenager, though it wasn't much, just a small sliver of truth I discovered accidentally. As I've gotten older, I have come to consider this moment of truth a gift and have learned over the years to be grateful for what I found; it was special enough that it changed my thoughts about my beginnings and my relationship, in my mind, to my birth mother.

It was the summer of my nineteenth year and I was rummaging through my mother's bottom dresser drawer in her bedroom, looking for a scarf to borrow. She was out running errands that morning. It wasn't a big deal to borrow one of her scarves. As my hands parted layered fabrics of colored scarves, looking for that perfect match to my outfit, something odd brushed against my fingertips. Something that didn't belong among silk, cotton, and polyester.

I lifted the scarves and saw, resting comfortably on the bottom of the drawer, an old, worn-looking manila envelope. *What's an envelope doing here?* My parents were organized people. Paperwork belonged in my father's den or in my mother's desk, not in her dresser drawer.

I pulled the bulky envelope from its hiding place and sat down on my parents' bed. Pushing my hair behind my ears, I wiggled into a comfortable sitting position. The envelope was typed, addressed to an armed forces college on an Army base in Washington, DC, which was odd because we were Navy. The return address was the same as the addressee. I unfastened the rusted clasp that held whatever treasure was inside.

A batch of papers fell out. A small booklet tumbled from the top—it was titled *Your Adopted Child*, and featured artwork reminiscent of the 1950s. Several yellowed newspaper clippings on adoption from Dear Abby slipped out too. As I unfolded the papers on my lap, I saw articles geared toward helping your adopted child understand adoption, offering advice about how to tell your child they're adopted and at what age.

I also found several handwritten letters tucked carefully inside a white envelope. They were addressed "To Whom It May Concern" and dated 1955, the year before I was born. I felt my pulse rise along with my curiosity. The letters were perfectly written on formal stationery, praising my parents as kind, caring people who would make wonderful parents to some lucky child. It was strange to see letters from people I didn't know who seemed to know my parents well enough to be character witnesses. I wondered how well they knew them and assumed they were friends from the Navy.

The last set of papers was different. There were three documents, folded into thirds, each copy with light blue construction paper as the bottom layer. Unfolding the papers, I knew right away they were legal documents because of the delicate, onion-type paper, plus there was an attorney's office and address at the top. My heart began to pound. *What is this? Was this about John? Or me?*

My parents' names were typed in capital letters in the header. Next to them was an unfamiliar female name. The document was about custody of a female child. Well, this couldn't be about me because my name wasn't mentioned. It wasn't about John either.

Turning to the second page, I stopped short after reading the first paragraph. My mouth dropped open. Gasping at the sight of my birth date and the city where I was born, I began to slowly comprehend what I was reading. *Oh my God.* My mind spun wildly, realizing what this meant; this document *was* about me. I quickly turned back to the first page and stared at the strange name at the top of the document. The name *Loretta Annette Stewart* stared back at me, a witness to my past, to my truth, to myself.

It only took an instant for me to know my birth mother had seen me. I had grown up thinking she never saw me because they, the doctors or whoever, wouldn't let her or maybe she didn't care. *She gave me away, didn't she? Why would she name me? She didn't want me. She let me go.* There was no mention of my birth mother in the document.

I was stunned. This was such a revelation, such a turning point in my adoptee psyche. *She named me. She saw me.* A deep sense of relief poured over me as I sat on my parents' bed. No longer would I wonder if she ever knew if I was born a boy or girl. I was sure she had held me. Tears welled up and fell down my cheeks. *She knew me. And now, so did I.*

I put everything back in the manila envelope, just as I had found it, except for one copy of the document. Not thinking my mother would notice one missing document, I hid my stolen copy in the bottom of my desk and left to share my miraculous news with my friend Ellen. Upon returning home that evening, I checked my desk drawer and it was gone. *Crap.*

Obviously, my mother had noticed the missing document and went searching for it in my room. Years later, I thought she might have purposefully left the envelope in her drawer for me to find because it was never there before and I never saw it again. *Why was she hesitant to share it with me in person? What was she afraid of? Was it just too difficult to talk about?* Even though it was long overdue and a possible passive act on her part, I'm grateful.

In all the years we were together—decades—my adoptive mother and I never said anything to each other about this incident. She knew that I knew, and I knew that she knew. We were both fearful and insecure about our relationship with each other, so we chose silence. I guess it was safer that way.

It was all so secretive. I hated that secrecy as I grew up, but I was raised to be caught up in her dance, and not to question her decisions. All these years later, I feel sad we could never talk about the truth of who I was with each other, and I certainly couldn't talk about any of this with my father.

I never found the documents over the years I looked for them. I figured my mother had thrown them away, or better yet, burned them. Finding my birth name was a gift, my secret treasure. I thought my birth name beautiful. It hinted of Southern roots and a Scottish ancestry.

I now felt different knowing my birth mother had named me, whoever she was. No matter what her circumstances were, that name was her message across time, telling me that she once had loved me enough to have named me before sending me on my journey in life without her. This was the only gift she could give me. Loretta Annette Stewart was who I had once been, and who I could've been. At nineteen, this ghost name became etched on my heart and became my own, a private secret. I felt love from an unknown woman from the distant past before my memory was ever formed.

Chapter Four

I MARRIED MY HUSBAND, MICHAEL, IN THE SUMMER OF my twenty-eighth year. Fifteen months prior, we had met at a friend's wedding. He knew the groom and I knew the bride.

Two weeks after we met, we had our magical first date. Michael brought me flowers—long-stem, white carnations—and had the evening planned: pre-dinner drinks overlooking the marina in Redondo Beach, then dinner at the Bottle Inn, in Hermosa Beach, known to be the best Italian restaurant in South Bay. We were the last couple to leave that night.

I remember going into the restaurant bathroom that evening, looking into the mirror, and thinking, *There's something different about tonight, about Michael.* By our third date, I knew he was the one. Three months later, wildly in love, Michael asked me to marry him and I said yes.

As I got to know Michael, he stood out from the types of guys I usually had been involved with. I was intrigued by his genuineness, his generosity and kindness, and down-to-earth manner. I usually dated much older men—older men who were successful business-wise, but complicated with commitment issues, self-absorbed, and somewhat shallow. But thanks to my ongoing therapy, I was making different choices. Michael was an anomaly. He was an electrician at the same aerospace company my father, brother, and I worked at. He had a great job and was ambitious. He was thirty years old, still attending college, and was just a few classes shy of an associate's degree in electrical science.

We had a lot in common. We both loved sailing, hiking, camping, and bike riding. We liked the same music and attending concerts. Michael grew up two blocks from the beach in Hermosa Beach, a Los Angeles South Bay suburb, and like me, enjoyed anything to do with the beach and ocean, something I desired in a life partner.

When I met Michael, he had blond hair that hung loosely to his shoulders and the bluest and kindest eyes. It impressed me that he had a young golden retriever named Shelby that he adored. And I was in awe of his open affection for his family, especially his parents. He couldn't wait for me to meet them, and for them to meet me, whereas I rarely, if ever, brought home anyone I was dating.

It was difficult for me to know how to approach my parents about the feelings I had for Michael. I lived a private life because they never seemed interested in meeting anyone, nor did they ever seem to like anyone I brought home, whether it was someone I was dating or one of my friends.

I figured Michael wasn't the type they'd warmly embrace, either, but I was falling in love and wanted them to be a part of my happiness. I mean, they were my parents and I thought they should know I was becoming serious about him.

When they first met him, at their invitation for dinner on a Sunday night, I think they tolerated him, silently hoping this wouldn't last long. Michael didn't do anything wrong. They were just snobby people. They were polite to him, because they were polite people even when they didn't like or approve of you.

A few weeks later, when I was over at my parents' for another Sunday night dinner, my father caught me off guard walking past his den, announcing, "I don't care to hear about your love affair with this guy you're dating. We have nothing in common with him or his family."

I was shocked. My mouth felt as though it dropped to the floor. *How could he say this to me?* His words stung. My father was shutting me down.

"Well, Dad, that will be hard to do because I'm getting serious about him," I answered. "It's not just an affair. It's more than that."

My father looked up at me, snickering. He said, "This is not going to go anywhere. We have nothing in common with those people." He turned back to the book he was reading, a signal that our short conversation was over.

When I left that night, I felt alone, and sad that I couldn't share my excitement and fondness for Michael with my parents. I couldn't believe they had already made up their minds. Sure, his parents were different but they weren't horrible people. They were down-to-earth, raised-at-the-beach people who didn't care about status or making a lot of money. They cared about family and enjoying life.

After my father's pronouncement, it was hard to invite Michael over for dinner or for anything, so I kept him at a distance from them, which I'm sure made my parents happy and hopeful I would soon come to my senses.

On the other hand, keeping Michael away didn't help our situation. Looking back, it would have been better for all of us had I continued inviting him up to my parents' house so they could get to know him better. It was all so uncomfortable and complicated. My brother John really liked Michael, and they got on well together and had a lot in common. John couldn't figure out why my parents felt the way they did about him either.

When Michael and I became engaged so quickly, we didn't know how to tell my parents. It was easy to share our good news with Michael's parents. They were elated. But with mine, it was going to be difficult to navigate around their already suspicious and adamant feelings toward him.

I decided it would be best to go by myself to show off my unconventional aquamarine engagement ring, and thus share my happy news. My brother agreed. Michael wanted to go with me, but I told him no, because I wasn't sure how my parents would react. I expected a nasty, unforgiving scene.

They proved me right. They were taken aback by my news and weren't excited. My mother ignored any kind of wedding talk, and my father left the room. I left their house listening to sad songs in my car when I should've been listening to uplifting, happy ones.

Thank God I was in therapy. I was slowly learning to stand firm in my own decisions and this was one of them—a testament to how much I loved Michael. I was determined not to give up on my chance for happiness and a good relationship because my parents didn't approve. Heck, they didn't seem to ever approve of anything I did. They were impossible to please.

Two weeks later, my father surprised me by calling me at work.

"Say, your mother and I were wondering if you and Michael wanted to come up this Sunday night for dinner?"

It was my turn to be taken aback, but I was pleased. "Sure, we'd like that. What time should we be over?"

"Why don't you come up around four o'clock?" He sounded upbeat, which made me suspicious.

"Okay, thanks, Dad. We'll see you in a few days." I hung up the phone and wondered what prompted this change of heart.

We arrived a little after four o'clock, both of us nervous and curious. My father barbecued his signature T-bone steaks, and we shared friendly, polite conversation over dinner. I don't remember any talk of our engagement or of any wedding plans, but there must've been some because the next day, my father took the day off from work and went around to various wedding venues. This warmed my heart. Sometimes, my father could be sweet and thoughtful. In this moment, he was.

Several days later, he asked me to meet him after work at my favorite wedding venue, La Venta Inn, in Palos Verdes Estates. La Venta Inn was built in the 1920s, as a Spanish-style inn overlooking the South Bay beaches all the way to Malibu. That afternoon, after talking with the wedding coordinator at La Venta, my father put a deposit down on a wedding date for the following spring, in March. I was thrilled that my parents were accepting Michael, which meant they were accepting me too. I felt validated, happily engaged. All was well with the world. We could announce our wedding date and start planning our lives together.

The calm didn't last. One month later, I received an unsettling letter from my mother. She was big on writing notes, especially when she was upset. The note revealed that my mother had suddenly become paranoid about Michael. Everything had been going along just fine, but for some unknown reason, she had convinced herself that Michael was using me to get money, though I had none, and that he was going to "dump me to the curb" just days before our wedding. It didn't make sense, but then crazy doesn't.

She informed me in her letter that she and my father would not be attending our wedding, but that they'd still pay for it.

What? Not attend our wedding? What the hell? But they'd pay for it? She wouldn't answer my phone calls and took the phone off the hook for hours every day. She told me my father and brother would be coming over to my apartment the following Friday after work to pick up personal items she had loaned me: purses, jewelry, belts, scarves, dishes, and my grandparents' antique coffee table I loved, which I was using in my tiny beach apartment living room. She didn't want Michael or his family to have anything of hers. I was shocked, sickened, and embarrassed by her sudden paranoid outburst. This time, her crazy righteous rage affected not only me, but Michael and his family.

I was ticked. *My mother was having a tantrum, but why? Why was she suddenly paranoid?* I had finally found someone who was a decent, good person. Someone I loved, who loved me back, and cared about me. If she and my father were going to be weird about it, that was their problem. I was marrying Michael no matter what they said or did. My mother's childish stomping wasn't going to change my mind.

Geez, I was nearly thirty years old, had a career as an administrative assistant at a large corporation, and had been living on my own for years. Michael and I were adults. There was nothing wrong with Michael or myself. He wasn't a criminal or a jerk.

I wrote back, refusing their payment, saying, "I want your love, not your money," and asked them to reconsider attending our wedding and getting to know Michael better. Michael and I contacted La Venta Inn and postponed our wedding in order to give my parents some more time to accept Michael and our decision to marry.

When I saw my brother a few weeks later, he told me my mother had twisted my words, telling him that I had said I "wanted their money, not their love." I shook my head. *My mother seemed to be stirring the pot, but why?*

They never thought Michael was good enough. His level of education and what he did for a living didn't meet their expectations. I probably didn't meet theirs either. Michael wasn't an executive like my father and brother were. He hadn't graduated from Stanford or the University of Southern California. Michael was, as my mother called him, with an air of disdain in her voice, "a blue collar worker." Never mind that *I* dropped out of college, but then, I could've compensated by marrying up—which I wouldn't be doing if I married Michael.

Michael had ambition. He was a trusted, hard worker, who worked and studied his way to middle management, eventually becoming a project manager at an aerospace company, and working there for nearly forty years.

But my parents didn't approve of him, and on reflection, it was clear they didn't approve of me either. It was lonely not being able to share my joy with my parents. After my mother's letter, my father and brother reluctantly picked up the items she wanted, causing a rift between me and all of them. I felt abandoned by them. There was little communication between us.

About a month later, on a crisp, fall day in October after a therapy session, I took the day off from work and surprised my mother by showing up unannounced at her house. I wanted to talk with her, and that day, I felt strong enough to bring up our conflict.

I stood in the family room, looking down at my mother who was perched on the love seat, looking bored, and said, "I just want to tell you that I'm going to marry Michael. I love him and he loves me and we see a future together. But we've decided to wait until after the first of the year to make any firm plans for our wedding so that you and Dad can get to know him better and see that he's not going to be dumping me on any curb before our wedding. He's not like that, Mom. He's not whatever it is you think he is. You need to get to know him. And, his parents may not be as educated or as worldly as you and Dad, but they're good and kind people."

"Well, I'm going to need some time to think things over," she replied. "I also need to talk to your father about this before I can say we've changed our minds about our decision. We'll let you know what we decide."

My mother seemed to have softened a bit, which gave me some encouragement. I left with a glimmer of hope that my parents might change their minds about coming to our wedding and also a sense of strength—I had stood up for myself. But I was still unsure how things would be between us in the future.

I didn't hear from either of my parents after talking with my mother. I still couldn't get hold of my mother on the phone because she had the damn phone off the hook for weeks, and I was too uncomfortable to call my dad at work. Michael and I both felt their silence was their answer.

I wanted a wedding. We wanted a wedding. Not anything big or showy, but we wanted a beautiful day and ceremony celebrating our marriage with family and friends and making a meaningful memory. I was hurt, which made me angry. *How could my parents deny me this special day? They weren't even trying to give Michael and his family a chance!*

My anger was justified, but not helpful. Things didn't move an inch with my parents over the following month. They had their heels dug in.

Fortunately, at one of my therapy sessions, my therapist, Dr. Goldman, challenged me with this question: "So, how long are you going to wait for your parents' approval until you get married? Ten years? Twenty?"

He made a good point. *How long was I going to wait for them to finally come around?* The right answer was no longer! And so Michael and I decided to pay for our own wedding, to stop this nonsense, to gain control over our lives. But in order to make it work, I needed to move in with Michael so we could save my paycheck to pay for our wedding and honeymoon.

So, I moved in with Michael, into a house he rented from one childhood friend and shared with another. I really liked Tim and the house was large enough so that the three of us could live together and still have privacy. Besides, he was hardly ever there, as he worked several jobs as a swim instructor by day and a waiter by night. It helped us out financially too.

I wrote to my parents, telling them Michael and I had decided to pay for our own wedding and since that would cost some money, I had left my beach apartment and moved in with Michael and his friend Tim to save my paycheck toward our wedding and honeymoon. We told them the date wasn't set because we still hoped they would change their minds.

The news didn't go over well. Instead, it gave my parents the ammunition they sought to justify their position. My mother wrote me a short note saying, "You have really done it now, Diane. This is a slap in our face. Now we really won't be going to your wedding as we don't approve of anyone living with someone before marriage. Please don't ask us to attend your wedding anymore."

I felt the familiar feeling of being alone settle in the pit of my stomach. The sense that I had let my parents down once again. I couldn't seem to get anything right with them. On the other hand, I doubted they would have ever changed their minds. I knew all along that refusing their money, taking the circumstances into my own hands, standing up for myself, and paying for my own wedding would tick them off. My moving in with Michael was the icing on the cake they needed so they had an excuse not to ever go. I had sealed my fate, and theirs.

In January, Michael and I put a deposit down on a date at La Venta Inn for a Sunday morning in July.

I didn't get to plan my wedding with my mother as I had always hoped. She had no interest in anything to do with it. I picked out my wedding dress by myself. I still couldn't understand how my parents could be so stubborn, so righteous. *It just didn't make any sense. Who wouldn't want to attend or be involved with their only daughter's wedding?*

Mad as I was, though, I still wanted them there.

So I kept trying to convince my parents that Michael was good enough. I went up every Sunday night—alone, because Michael was no longer welcome in their house—and ate Sunday dinner with them. I talked a good game, playing up the teachers and executives of Michael's extended family, and saying how happy I was. I'd even had my mother invited to my family bridal shower to be given poolside at the home of one of Michael's aunts. My mother ended up throwing the invitation at me, yelling, "I don't know who the hell this woman is and I don't care." None of it mattered to them.

I still couldn't quite believe that my parents didn't want to know Michael or meet his parents or any of his family. But clearly, they weren't interested in socializing with any of the people in my life and I couldn't wait for their approval anymore. I was heartbroken, but I knew I had to move on with my own life if I wanted to be happy, and being with Michael made me happy. He was good for me. If I let him go in order to please my parents, I wasn't sure I'd ever find again what I had with him.

On a midsummer morning in July, my brother John and I walked, arm in arm, down the stone steps toward Michael, who was waiting for me under a white gazebo covered with white and pink roses. We said our vows at La Venta Inn in Palos Verdes, surrounded by family and close friends. The sun broke through the morning clouds, revealing the wide, sandy beaches we grew up on from Palos Verdes to Malibu. The ocean glistened like diamonds in the sun.

We had a wonderful day. It was perfect, meaningful, and beautiful. I didn't think too much about my parents that day. My sadness was behind me. My parents and I lost out on being together this day but I didn't let them ruin my hope or my happiness. I was grateful to my brother for being there with me and for me. He was the only family I had at my wedding.

My parents never met my in-laws—not one time—in all the years to come. My parents didn't attend family birthdays or holiday celebrations, even when we had our children. They held their own court. They were a tough regime.

Chapter Five

I WAS FOUR-AND-A-HALF YEARS OLD WHEN MY PARENTS adopted my brother John. Because of my father's naval career, we were living in Fairfax, Virginia, as he was working in Washington, DC, the city where John was born. My mother used to kid my brother that he was probably a senator's son. He was the cutest, chubbiest baby boy with blond hair and vivid green eyes. I was thrilled to be a big sister and no longer an only child. I enjoyed making him laugh and adored him throughout his life, always feeling motherly toward him.

I remember my mother telling us when we were young that they had no idea where John had been living the first six months of his life. He had been called Patrick when we met him. Social services matched his ethnicity to mine, whatever that was, I guess hoping we'd all look similar in some way to each other—you know, like a "real" family.

Growing up, John was the golden child, my mother's favorite. They formed a close bond when he was a baby. My brother was painfully shy and had to be held back a year starting with kindergarten, as he was too traumatized separating from my mother. He needed another year before he could be away from her. I think my mother secretly loved that he needed her so much.

Perhaps his shyness and fear didn't come from genetics, but rather from his adoption experience—whatever happened the first six months of his life could have triggered deep-seated feelings of abandonment. We knew he had been taken away from his birth mother. And how many different foster care cribs did he sleep in? We had no idea and it seemed like social services didn't either.

As we grew up, I always felt protective of John. He was my baby brother. We weren't best friends because of our age difference, but we definitely had a close bond. We played together as children, and probably my favorite memory was setting up Matchbox villages. Using pencils and pens to designate roads, and shoeboxes and books for buildings, we designed elaborate villages. We would play for hours over several days until my mother couldn't stand the mess anymore and made us put our towns away.

Sometimes, but not too often, John and I talked about being adopted. He wasn't as curious as I was. I remember asking him when we were both teenagers, "Would you want to ever find your real mother?" (I used the word "real" because I wasn't aware of another term to use at the time.)

John, who was sitting on his bed, looked over at me, and shrugged half-heartedly, expressionless, responding in a flat voice, "No. She didn't want me so why would I want to find her?"

"But how do you know she didn't want you?" I asked in earnest.

"Because I'm here." John turned away and looked out the window.

"Well, I'd like to find my mother one day," I whispered, leaning forward on the queen-size bed. "But I don't see how I can ever find her."

"We can't. Hey, I don't want to talk about this, okay?" John leaned back against his headboard, closed his eyes, and waved me out of his room.

My brother body-rocked and head-banged himself to sleep until he was in high school. I know this can be normal behavior for some children, but it usually goes away by the time they reach elementary school. I attribute John's need for self-soothing to those first six months. I don't think that need ever went away; in fact, I attribute his decision to end his life at age twenty-five to a deep, unconscious trigger, a familiar, primal feeling of abandonment that he'd experienced as an infant. I now know that adoptees are four times more likely to attempt suicide than nonadoptees.

The last time I spoke to my brother was two days before he committed suicide. We were talking on the phone when he told me his girlfriend, Alyce, had broken up with him.

"Oh my gosh, John, are you doing okay?" I asked. He'd been dating Alyce for the past nine months. I knew he was smitten with her. I was sad to hear she'd broken up with him.

"Yeah, I'm okay. I'll tell you more about it later."

We had a standing lunch date every other Friday, but this coming Friday wasn't our day. I figured we'd talk about it over the weekend. I didn't want to pressure him to talk if he wasn't ready yet.

"Okay. That sounds good. I hope you're doing all right. Call me if you want to talk before then."

"I will." We hung up. That would be the last time I heard his voice.

That October Friday, John cleaned his desk out at work and wrote a note to my parents, leaving it in his bottom dresser drawer to be found later. At lunchtime, he drove just a few miles to the Redondo Beach townhouse he shared with two childhood friends. He took one of his roommates' rifles, which were kept in the garage—unlocked in those days—and went upstairs to his bedroom, leaving his uneaten lunch on the kitchen table. One of his roommates found him later that afternoon when he got home from work.

Michael and I were out that night with friends, having dinner and seeing a Kenny Loggins concert in Orange County, arriving home around one in the morning. When we pulled into the driveway, we saw Tim's bedroom light on. I said to Michael, "How odd that Tim is still up this late. I hope he's not sick or anything."

The first thing I did after getting out of the car was greet our Shelby, in the backyard, then head to the bathroom.

Coming out of the bathroom, I saw Michael standing in the doorway to our bedroom. The color in his face had disappeared, and he was now the color of ash. Something had happened.

"What's the matter?" I asked, afraid to know why he looked so shaken.

"It's John."

I noticed Tim standing behind him.

"What? Did something happen to John?" I had to ask, looking between Michael and Tim for answers. By the silent looks on both of their faces, I could tell whatever it was that happened to John was probably serious. I wasn't sure I wanted to know.

"John's gone," Michael said in a low voice.

I couldn't decipher his words. "What?"

"John. He's gone, hon. I'm so sorry. Your brother is gone." Tears gathered in Michael's blue eyes.

"What do you mean, he's gone?"

"He died this afternoon."

"Oh no! Was it a car accident?"

Slowly, Michael said, "No, John killed himself."

"What? No! No way!" I couldn't put my mind around those words. "He wouldn't have done that. I don't believe it. John would never have done anything like that. That's wrong. Why would he have done that?"

It seemed impossible. I had just spoken to him two days ago. Everything was okay, or at least not bad enough to kill yourself.

"I'm so sorry, hon." His spoken words were ever so slowly sinking into my mind, like mud. I was trying to comprehend so many things at once that I couldn't quite understand or accept. I didn't even know how I was feeling in that moment. It all unfolded in slow motion.

Michael came over and gave me a tight bear hug, wrapping both his arms around me, enveloping me. Tim joined in. The three of us stood there in silence, holding onto each other, trying to grasp the tragedy that lay before us.

John had his whole life before him. Why would he have done such a thing as this?

Tim made me hot tea while we sat in the living room as he told us what had happened while we were gone. My brother's roommates couldn't remember my married surname, but they had remembered we had been married at La Venta Inn, so that's how they found me. Don, one of John's roommates, came by that night to tell me about John. When he found out I wasn't home until late that night, he told Tim what had happened, and since I was the only available family member, I was to call the Redondo Beach police in the morning.

"I have no idea where my parents are," I said, looking over at Michael and Tim. Michael had just come from my closet with my red down parka. He urged me to wear it, because I was shivering uncontrollably.

I learned from John's roommates that he was supposed to pick up my parents from the airport Sunday night, but nobody knew what flight. All they knew was that they were flying home from Greece.

We spent the good part of that weekend at Michael's parents' home in Hermosa Beach. I hung out in sweats, slippers, and my down parka. I couldn't sleep. My sweet mother-in-law, Betty, made comfort food and coffee to keep me warm. Ellen came over, too, and hung out with all of us. So did her sisters. I felt supported and loved. They were, indeed, family.

All I could think about those first two days was how much my brother must've been hurting to commit suicide and how I hadn't known he was suffering so much. It was heart-wrenching to think of him in his last moments of life. I couldn't get away from the pain and the hurt I felt knowing he left us by his own hand.

My parents and I were still somewhat estranged, but since our first anniversary, they had made attempts to reconcile by inviting us up to their home and serving us champagne and hors d'oeuvres. I saw this as their truce, their white flag. They seemed ready to accept Michael or at least try to accept our marriage, although we never spoke about it, which was typical.

After our honeymoon on Kauai and Maui, I wrote a letter putting the ball in their court. I told them we'd be interested in moving on, but only if they'd accept us as a couple. If they wanted to see me, they would see us. We waited months for a response. Thankfully, I was still in therapy so I could vent my frustration and hurt, working through it, little by little. It took them a year to finally come around. I think they waited to see if we'd make it that long.

After our first awkward visit, sipping champagne, pretending everything was okay between us, my parents invited us to Thanksgiving dinner at the Naval Officer's Club on Terminal Island, near Long Beach. Even though the holiday was several months away, it was their special place; the invitation was an honor. This seemed like good news to my brother and me. They were trying and Michael and I would sweep the hurt away in order to have a relationship with them.

John told me he felt my parents were in the wrong about Michael and he was bothered by the way they acted toward both of us. He stood up for me throughout my engagement and got dressed in his ivory tux for our wedding, all while still living at home with my parents. I loved my brother so much for walking me down the aisle, for standing up to my parents in his own way. It couldn't have been easy.

We had only seen my parents once since getting married, and now I had to pick them up at the airport and tell them about John.

On Sunday night, Michael and I drove together to LAX. My hunch had been right—they were flying home on a Greek airline. The airline helped me find their names. They would be expecting John to pick them up. I figured they'd know just by seeing us that something had happened to John. I only hoped I could get them into our car before they started asking too many questions.

We pulled up to Aegean Airlines. I hopped out to meet them inside after baggage claim. I stuck my ice cold hands into my parka's pockets to warm them and stood, waiting to spot my parents.

I saw the surprised look on their faces when they recognized me. My heart sank for the sorrow the news was about to bring them.

"What are you doing here?" my dad asked, his thick, white eyebrows scrunching up under his black glasses.

I gave him a hug and said, "John's not able to pick you up, so Michael and I are here." I tried to sound matter-of-fact, like it was no big deal, but I knew I probably looked like shit.

"Michael's here?" my mother asked, looking around. I gave my mom a hug and a kiss on her soft, warm cheek.

"Yes, he's waiting out front in our car. Can I take one of your bags to help you, Mom?" She passed me a shopping bag to carry and slowly followed me out the door.

Michael was standing beside our Jeep Cherokee. He waved, flagging us down, and popped open the back of the car.

"Hi," Michael said, hurriedly, smiling at both of my parents, trying to act normal.

My father seemed flustered as he handed over his luggage to Michael, then silently got into the back seat of the car. My mother followed suit.

After about five minutes of silence riding in the car, my mother said in a firm tone, "I don't understand why John wasn't able to pick us up tonight."

I turned around and looked at her. She looked tired. *Hell, she'd just flown how many hours on a plane to get home after a two- or three-week vacation?* I so wished I could tell them what happened at home, but I knew they weren't going to wait another thirty minutes. My mother, tired as she was, was determined to find out why.

"He wasn't able to, Mom." I gave a vague reply, trying to delay the blow.

"Something happened to him, right?"

She isn't going to let this go. "Yes," I answered. Then, slowly, I added, "Something happened to John." I didn't want to lie, but I didn't want to tell them the truth either.

"Is he dead?"

Wow. She just came out with it. Why was she so blunt? This was going to be hard. I turned back around, and looked at both of my exhausted parents sitting in the back seat.

I knew that once I told them the horrific news about John, their lives would never be the same.

"I'm so sorry, Dad and Mom." My eyes filled with tears. "But John isn't here with us anymore. He died on Friday." My bottom lip began quivering. *Get a grip, Diane. Be strong.*

My mother immediately looked away, out toward the evening lights where life was still vibrant, in motion, and alive. My father sat perfectly still. His eyes stared ahead. He looked like stone as I saw his face lose its color. He sat motionless. Emotionless. He became numb, like me.

A few minutes later, breaking the horrible silence that filled our car, my mother quietly asked, "How? How did he die? A car accident?"

John loved cars. Always had. Some of his first words were "wheels off." He had been a dirt bike rider since the age of six when my parents bought him his first dirt bike to ride in the quarry and hills near our house. He learned how to take bikes apart and put them back together. He had a good reputation for fixing things in the neighborhood. He started racing motocross when he was thirteen. John had trophies lined up in his room for winning races. It was his passion and he was good at it, but John had been in a bad motorcycle street accident before, so that's why we all jumped to the conclusion that he had been in an accident of some sort. But this wasn't a car accident; it was much worse.

"Maybe we should wait until we get home."

"No, I'd like to know now."

I couldn't blame her. This was her son and she wanted to know how he died but I didn't want to tell them.

I paused before I said anything.

"John killed himself."

"How? How did he kill himself?" I hardly had taken a breath when she asked this.

"With Don's rifle." Don was one of John's two roommates. He had been the one who found him.

"Geezus," my father answered, shaking his head. Those were the last words I heard my father say that night. My mother looked out the car window for the rest of the ride home. Nobody said another word until we were inside their house. We didn't stay long. Just long enough to help them with their luggage, and then my mother asked us to leave. My parents, ever private, even to me.

Three days later, more than three hundred people attended John's memorial. It was standing room only, with many standing outside of the chapel. At first, my parents didn't want to do anything, but there were so many friends and coworkers calling to find out when his service would be that my parents gave in to the pressure and hosted a memorial.

We were dealing with such grief and shock that we didn't prepare anything. There were no photos of him in the chapel. No special speakers. No casket either, because he had been cremated. Flowers from John's friends and mine lined the altar and scented the air with sweetness. My parents had stopped going to church years before, so they had no pastor either. They used the cemetery's pastor, a kind man who said generic, comforting words—but he didn't know John, or us. We were so numb, we were just going through the motions. It was all we could do.

Afterward, a receiving line spontaneously formed in front of us. It just happened. Nothing was planned. I remember thinking how strange it was to see my parents, who were standing beside me, receive all these people who came to shake our hands, to give us a hug while sharing their sorrow and condolences, without shedding one tear themselves. They greeted everyone kindly and appreciatively, but they stood stoic.

I, on the other hand, was a basket case. I couldn't stop the tears from flowing even if I tried. Michael was crying too. Everyone was. I don't know how you couldn't be emotional that day, but my parents weren't capable of showing it.

John's ashes were given to the deep. As far as I know, my parents didn't attend his burial at sea. Maybe they did but never told me. I found John's paperwork from his burial, complete with longitude and latitude off Marina del Rey, after my parents passed. I don't know if the papers were mailed to them or not.

I do know my mother was sorry they didn't bury John traditionally at the cemetery where her parents were. I think she missed having a place to be able to visit him.

All these years since, I've missed my brother for most of my adult life. There was so much to look forward to. John was with us for such a short time. I wish he could have talked to me about whatever it was that was making him hurt so much, what made him feel so hopeless and in such despair that he couldn't find a way out, but he just couldn't.

I have a photo of John, taken at our wedding, sitting on my bookshelf in my office in a gold heart-shaped frame. He's smiling, looking handsome in his ivory tuxedo. My brother was so tall and handsome. I can now fondly look at him, remembering that happy day he gifted me by standing by me, walking arm in arm down the aisle together as brother and sister. At least we had each other in childhood. As adopted children, we hadn't been alone. Now, even though I had Michael and his family, I felt alone with my parents. John was gone forever and I was left standing on my own with them.

Chapter Six

LIFE IS CHANGE, AN INFINITE ROLLER COASTER, FULL OF UPS and downs, with curves that take you to unknown places. In the midst of this ride of life, there are calm spaces where you can catch your breath and enjoy the ride, taking in the beauty and wonder of it all. Breathe. Let life move you forward.

After passing through the unforeseen, dark curves of losing my brother, I thought I'd never be happy or smile again. It's true what they say, though: time heals. When John died, I allowed the waves of grief to rush over me, waves of deep blueness that enveloped my emotions, my psyche, until I felt the world calling me back, to live life, and be happy again. With the healing balm of time, the waves of grief rolled in less often and I learned to carry John's memories in my mind and heart.

After John's passing, my parents asked me to handle his belongings. I wanted to help my parents in their silent grief, so I answered like the good daughter I hoped to be, saying, "Yes, we can do that."

Michael and I set ourselves to the task of gathering the remnants of my brother's young life. We sold his car, John's pride and joy—a beautiful black 1969 Chevrolet El Camino SS. We gave away his bedroom furniture, his clothes, and his weight equipment. I closed his bank accounts and canceled his gym membership. Each step of the way was another step in saying goodbye, steeped in sadness. I felt the burden of it and accepted the responsibility that fell on my shoulders.

One of the hardest tasks was retrieving John's personal belongings from the Los Angeles County coroner. My parents received a phone call from the Redondo Beach Police that the coroner had personal items of John's. If we wanted them, we needed to go downtown to pick them up. I didn't know what they might be, but anything personal of John's seemed precious, so I took the day off from work and drove downtown. Driving to Los Angeles was uncomfortable, as I had to drive in an area I wasn't familiar with; still, driving there would be the easy part of the day.

Walking through the automatic door, I felt the rush of cold air. The air conditioner was blowing so that the wire in the walls hummed a mysterious, sad song. Everything around me was sad then. The crowded waiting room was cold to my eyes as well as my skin. I signed in at the reception desk and found a seat, where the steel and plastic chairs stood guard against the stark, white walls. I looked around the room and wondered why these people were there. Had they just experienced a violent death of a family member too? Probably; police officers were everywhere.

Fortunately, I didn't have to wait long until a young police officer opened the door and called my name. "Diane Wheaton?" He inspected the room until our eyes met. "Follow me," he said firmly, as he turned around, taking me down a narrow, dark hallway. "Officer Menendez will help you from here." He nodded, turned, and walked away.

I was left staring at a small office, secured by metal bars and a large glass window, its only opening at the bottom, like a bank teller's window, only with a larger space to pass things under.

Nobody was inside. I looked around the room and noticed bags and boxes with tags on them sitting on the counter. It was sobering to be there. Suddenly, a middle-aged police officer walked into the room, letting the steel door slam loudly behind him, which shook my senses. He was carrying a rifle and a brown bag in his arms.

"I'm Officer Menendez. I have your deceased family member's personal belongings." He sounded so matter-of-fact as he set the rifle down on the counter directly in front of me. I cringed. I knew immediately what this was. I quickly turned away. I couldn't hold my tears back and my chin began quivering. I knew I was going to lose it. *I wasn't expecting to see this.* I don't know what I expected to pick up, but it certainly wasn't this. Tears were now freely flowing down my cheeks. I had lost control. Seeing the rifle was just too much.

"I'm so sorry," Officer Menendez said, looking through the glass at me. "I know it's hard. If you don't want the rifle, we can destroy it for you. You just need to sign the release right here."

No, I don't want the damn rifle.

He pointed out where I needed to sign and handed me a clipboard under the protective glass. Through clouded eyes, I could barely read what I was signing.

Officer Menendez removed the rifle to the other side of the room. He came back to the window and said in a softer, kind voice, "It'll all be taken care of."

I nodded my head up and down as I tried to blot my tears with my hands, instead rubbing them into my makeup, into my skin. *Crap, Diane. Stop crying.*

"Thank you." Whispering, I could barely get the words out.

"I understand, but you may want these." He picked up a small brown bag and pushed it toward me.

"What's this?" I asked, looking up at him, silently pleading with him by meeting his eyes to not give me anything I couldn't handle.

"It's personal items that were found on the body. You'll probably want these." He added the final push on the bag as it reached my tentative, shaky hands.

"Thank you," I said again, stone-faced, unable to muster up any smile to thank him for his graciousness.

Officer Menendez, who had probably dealt with hundreds of mourning people such as myself, nodded his head in silence as I turned and walked toward the exit, carrying the small brown bag under my arm.

A few minutes later, I was sitting in my car. I sat there staring at the brown bag, uncertain of its contents and whether I should open it or not. I pulled apart the stapled bag and saw that it was John's wallet and his set of car keys. *He hadn't even taken his wallet or his keys out of his pocket.* I tenderly fondled the used leather, trying to feel the shadow of his hands under my own. I found the courage to open it, and there was his license photo staring back at me. His beautiful face I'd never see or kiss again. I couldn't stop my tears. John was really gone.

One weekend afternoon, after Michael and I finished erasing my brother's presence in this world, I paid a visit to my mother for a few hours. We were upstairs in my childhood room, where the walls still proudly displayed the pink and white striped wallpaper I put up as a teenager. Looking out the window, I saw a large, rusted screw still clinging to the eve where I used to hang the ceramic wind chime I'd made in my high school ceramics class. My mother hadn't changed or painted my room since I moved out at age twenty-three. I liked seeing these vestiges of the past. But today they were harder than usual to see. Seeing things from the past only reminded me that life had changed, that there was now a marker in our lives—before John died, and after.

My mother now used my empty closets and dresser to store things. Today, she wanted to purge. We were busy looking through bags and boxes, when all of a sudden, my mother turned toward me and said with tears in her eyes, "Diane, I just want to tell you how grateful we are for Michael. I don't know how we could've done what we had to do without him. He was a huge help to us, and his friend Tim too."

My eyes grew wide as I stood perfectly still before answering her. "Oh, yeah, Mom. Michael was more than happy to help you and Dad out. Tim too. We all were. It was a hard thing for sure. Michael and Tim were definitely a huge help."

"We're really grateful for it." Her green eyes were now full of tears.

I wanted to hug my mom but I knew that it would've been too emotional, too much for either of us in that moment. So, I just said, "Of course, Mom. It's been a tough time for all of us." I looked down and started opening up another box, inwardly shocked by her statement, yet thankful that my mother, my parents, could finally see what I had seen in Michael all along—a good, kind person. It warmed my heart. Michael and Tim were so deserving of my parents' gratitude.

Michael and Tim had been the ones brave enough to have gone into John's bedroom, which had been closed off with yellow police tape. I wasn't capable of going upstairs to his room, so they were the ones who brought his dresser drawers down, one at a time, so I could go through them. They moved his bed and bedroom furniture, called Goodwill for the pickup, and put his mattress out for the trash.

Two months after John's passing, a week or so before Christmas, my parents had Michael and me over for a holiday dinner. It seemed a good sign that my parents were doing better. Dad was barbecuing steak like he used to. He and Michael were sitting on the couch, talking work-talk, and I sat on a stool at the kitchen counter chatting with my mom while she put together side dishes. It all felt pretty normal.

Then my mother put the cover on the green beans to steam and looked over at my dad. "Stan, do you think we should tell them now?"

"Tell us what now?" I asked, turning around to look at my father, who was sitting cross-legged in his comfy white shorts and light blue polo shirt, barefoot as usual. His home uniform.

"Now?" He looked over at my mother who was grinning.

"I think now is good." She wiped her hands on a flowered green kitchen towel and turned toward all of us. *What was going on?*

"Well, we know it's hard to save money for a house these days, so your dad and I were thinking we'd like to help you two out. We'd like to help you with a down payment on your first house."

"Oh my gosh, what?" I yelled out, nearly falling off the stool. *Were they kidding us?*

"Wow, that's really nice," said Michael, who looked stunned. His eyes had a blank stare to them.

"Really, Dad and Mom?" I looked at my father. His face was lit up, smiling. My mom was too. I thought, *It makes them happy to help us.* After all we'd been through the past couple of months, we could now share a degree of happiness in this moment. I went over to my mother and gave her a kiss on her velvet cheek, and said, "Thank you so much, Mom. This will mean so much to us."

I then walked over to where my dad was sitting and, leaning over him, kissed his forehead and gave him an awkward hug on the couch while he patted my arm.

"Thank you, Dad. This means so much. I can't believe it." His blue eyes twinkled while mine teared up. This was such a surprise. A great gift. I also knew this was my parents' way of showing their gratitude and their affection. *We have to say yes.*

Driving home that night, Michael and I both remarked how taken aback we were by my parents' generous offer.

"I don't know. I mean, I'm thrilled, but I wonder if it's too soon?" I asked Michael.

"What do you mean too soon?" He glanced at me, his blond eyebrows furrowed, questioning.

I looked out the car window at the passing lights and answered, "Is it too soon to look forward to something as wonderful as a new home?"

Michael paused before he answered. "No, I don't think so. I think it gives all of us something good in our lives. It gives us all something to look forward to."

I looked over at him with the passing car lights on the freeway silhouetting his profile in the dark. *He's right. This is a good thing. Try to be happy again, Diane.*

We spent the first month of the new year visiting different areas, looking at all sorts of homes, old and new. My parents encouraged us to move out of town, to move away from the beach area we loved. They felt it would be better to raise a family in a slower-paced, smaller community. Besides, it was expensive to buy where we wanted and if we moved away from the beach area, we could get a larger home, even a brand-new one with a nice-sized yard. We thought about it and decided it was probably better financially if we moved away, plus it meant that when we had children, there was a greater possibility I could stay home with them, at least when they were little.

So, we landed in the Santa Clarita Valley, which at the time was a new, rural community only forty-five minutes from work. It was beginning to be built up, promoting itself as a great place to raise a family. We had friends from work who lived here, too, who loved living here. We loved the mountains that surrounded the valley as well as all the open spaces that had yet to be developed. We also liked that we weren't too far from Ventura Beach. It seemed a good spot.

The next month we found a brand-new, Cape Cod–style model home we liked and picked out a grassy lot with cows grazing on it, signed the papers, and put down a deposit to become homeowners.

Over the next eight months, while our house was being built, my parents enjoyed giving advice and helping us pick out tile, carpet, and furniture for our new home. I felt closer to them. Since they didn't participate in our wedding plans, this was satisfying and comforting.

My mother was an avid gardener, a Martha Stewart type. My father didn't do much yard work and wasn't handy around the house. He was geared toward intellectual endeavors while my mother mowed the lawn, designed and worked our yard, and put up Christmas lights. She could fix a minor plumbing problem as easily as she sewed a lined ballgown. One year, she painted the outside of our two-story house. She was something—a strong, independent woman I admired in many ways.

I grew up watching my mother and learned to love gardening from her. It was one of the things we enjoyed doing together, so talking to her about our new yard and asking her advice made me feel like she cared about me, my life, and our well-being.

Early every Saturday, Michael and I drove up to see how our house was coming along. Once a month, my parents joined us. The four of us would picnic, sitting in beach chairs in the half-built house, eating egg salad sandwiches and drinking sodas, talking about our week and the plans we had. Life was turning a corner, and it looked like smooth sailing for a change. I was feeling happier inside and genuinely smiling on the outside. I think my parents were too. We had a lot to look forward to, even though I knew that, privately, we were all still learning to live without John. Finally, we moved into our new home in late summer. After settling in, we added a kitten named Zachary to our family, along with our first Alaskan malamute puppy, Timber, thereby giving Shelby some company while we were away at work during the day.

I had loved anything Alaskan since I'd been a little girl, especially Alaskan malamutes. I didn't know it then, but my love for Alaska would have significance down the road.

For now, it was enough that life was good. We were living in that calm space, enjoying the ride, catching our breath.

Chapter Seven

IT WAS NOW OVER A YEAR SINCE JOHN LEFT US AND SIX MONTHS since we moved into our new home. Michael and I felt life moving forward. After we both celebrated birthdays in January, we had decided to start our family. I got pregnant right away.

Ten weeks later, on a Saturday morning, we were driving to have breakfast with my parents to tell them our exciting news. We wanted my parents to be the first to know so there wouldn't be any hurt feelings.

Walking into the family room, I smelled the freshly brewed coffee and heard the familiar repetitive circling of my dad's spoon being stirred in his coffee cup. He was sitting in his robe at the kitchen-dining table while my mother, who was always impeccably dressed and fully made up before breakfast, was standing in the kitchen, putting the finishing touches on a smorgasbord of breakfast croissants, sweet rolls, and muffins. She was wearing a cotton turquoise shirt, tan polyester pants, comfortable-looking brown flats, and the gold ankh necklace she always wore, the one my father bought her when they were touring Egypt. Her blonde hair, as always, was perfectly coiffed. She looked up when she heard Michael close the oak front door behind him and saw me standing in the doorway.

"Good morning, Mom and Dad," I said, beaming inside, trying not to be too obvious on the outside. I stood far enough away so they could get a good glimpse of my newly acquired light pink T-shirt that read in large, black letters, BABY UNDER CONSTRUCTION.

"What's this?" my mother asked, setting the inviting breakfast plate on the kitchen table. "What does this mean?" She waved her index finger back and forth toward me with a slight grin. Her green eyes opened wide underneath her gold, wire-rimmed glasses.

"What do you mean, Mom?" I smiled back at her while using both hands to display my T-shirt, as if I were a game host.

"Are you pregnant?"

"Yes! We're pregnant!" I clapped my hands together like a cheerleader and quickly looked at my father to see if he was paying attention to our conversation.

"What?" My father put his coffee cup down on the china saucer and looked at me, his white eyebrows rising above his glasses as he slowly read my shirt.

"Congratulations, Dad! You and Mom are going to be grandparents!"

Michael announced, "We're due October 28. Hope it's not a Halloween baby!" He grinned as we both laughed out loud at the horrid thought of our child forever cursed by orange and black decorations on their birthday.

"Oh yeah," I answered. "But don't worry, no Halloween baby—I'm shooting for November 1."

"Well, congratulations! I'm happy for you both. This is certainly some unexpected news," my mother said politely as she sat down at the table, placing her napkin in her lap.

Was that it? No hugs? No happy tears?

I was taken aback by their lack of displayed emotion but had learned their reactions were almost always different from my expectations. I never said anything to question or challenge their behavior. It just wasn't done.

"Wow!" my dad joined in. "A baby, huh?" He dabbed his cloth napkin on his mouth and carefully chose a bear claw from the blue and white china.

What kind of a reaction is this?

"Yeah, Dad, can you believe it?" I plopped down in my designated chair, the one I had always sat in since I was ten. It was the seat closest to the window and the kitchen, where I used to talk about boys and girlfriend troubles to my mother while she fixed dinner. I looked over at my father, sipping his coffee and enjoying his bear claw. He was quiet. It was as if he didn't know what else to say to us. Neither of them.

I'm having my first baby, their first grandchild—isn't that cause for more heartfelt emotion? I guess we really surprised them.

We stayed a couple of hours, visiting after breakfast in the family room, sitting casually on the couches talking about work, the new house, and our pets' antics. When we were standing in the driveway, getting ready to get in our car to leave, my mother gave us both a hug.

Smiling, she said, "Congratulations again! This is great news." My father, standing next to her, now dressed for the day in sweats, a flannel shirt, and slippers, nodded in agreement and smiled, and gave us both quick hugs.

"Thanks, Dad and Mom. We're pretty excited. I can't wait to start shopping!" *Better to joke and act like nothing is bothering me.*

We waved goodbye from our car as we pulled out of the driveway, as we usually did, but I couldn't help but feel disappointed and tried not to take their cool reaction personally.

Our next stop was at Michael's parents' home. His mother

was fixing us lunch. We parked outside their beach house and walked into the ground-floor apartment. Betty was casually dressed in a white sweatshirt and jeans, sitting barefoot at the dining table working on paperwork, while Gary, Michael's dad, was watching golf on TV from his recliner in the living room.

Betty looked up as we walked into the cozy, well-lived living room, and right away, she noticed my pink T-shirt.

"What's this? You're kidding me!" Betty screamed so loud I thought their neighbors might be concerned.

She jumped out of her chair and ran across the room in her signature shuffle to hug me with tears welling up.

Now this is more like it.

"No, not kidding, Mom! We're pregnant, due in October," Michael answered, winking at me.

Gary got up out of his chair, stood up and stretched from sitting too long, and said, "Well, it's about damn time!" Gary shook Michael's hand and then slapped him on the back in a fun, congratulatory guy gesture. Our parents, in many ways, could not have been more different from each other.

In the beginning, I shared with my mother how I was feeling as my pregnancy progressed, and how my doctor appointments were going. I wanted to include her and convinced myself that surely she'd be interested in my health as well as her grandchild's. *I mean, won't she be interested because I am her only daughter, her only living child, and the baby will be her soon-to-be first grandchild?* I hoped we'd become closer.

At three months, I was gaining weight and beginning to show. I couldn't wait to wear maternity clothes and begin buying baby items. I was more than ready for motherhood. As an avid reader, I had a stack of books about parenting cluttering my nightstand. My favorite book was the classic *What to Expect When You're Expecting*, by Heidi Murkoff, which I devoutly read each evening.

Things were going so well that I was oblivious to how my mother was acting, but soon, I became aware she just wasn't that interested in my pregnancy. Sure, she'd listen to me talk for a bit, but then she'd change the subject. She seemed indifferent. Aloof. I couldn't understand at first, but then remembered several years before that John had told me our mother had said she'd lost six babies. *Maybe that's why she seems so cool?* Losing six babies is a lot. That's a lot of grief and trauma. I wondered why she never confided in me. It hurt my feelings that she didn't, but I knew better than to bring up the subject. I had no idea how far along she was when she lost the babies, and neither did John. I always knew she had lost a baby, maybe two, but certainly not six. I can only imagine the heartbreak and disappointment my parents must have gone through each time they lost a baby.

Reflecting on this made me realize my pregnancy was another milestone in my life that we wouldn't be sharing. It wasn't anyone's fault. It just was. My mother still carried her grief, which affected our relationship; how much was from the grief, I had no idea at the time.

Midway through my pregnancy, I stopped sharing with her. I didn't want to trigger her or cause any trouble between us, especially since it was beginning to bother me she didn't seem to care. I never asked her if she wanted to feel the baby kick, and she never asked. My father was just as detached. When I saw them, they both acted as if I weren't pregnant. It made for strange visits with unspoken resentment and confusion on my part.

It was during this time that I started wondering more about my birth mother. She had been living in the back of my mind for years, safely kept for my private musings. I knew we shared this experience of being pregnant through an ethereal tether, something I wasn't able to share with my adoptive mother, although I wished I could have. When I felt my baby kick, I began to think of her and how she had once felt me in the same way.

How can you miss someone you don't know?

During pregnancy you're asked by your physicians how your mother's pregnancy had been. Adoptees are pretty adept at answering these empty medical questions that have no answers. We've learned to say, "I have no idea about my medical history. I'm adopted." And, "I have no idea how my mother's pregnancy was." Those of us from the Baby Scoop Era grew up not knowing any medical history. No medical information was ever provided, nor thought needed. We were given away with nothing. Not even our given names would accompany us on our solo journey living with strangers.

My mother was invited to attend the family baby shower given by Michael's aunt. I knew she wouldn't go and she didn't, but this time she didn't throw the invitation in my face. I didn't make an issue of it. To be fair, nobody from my family attended. My beloved grandparents, my mother's parents, had passed away years ago. The rest of my mother's family lived in North Dakota and my father's lived in Massachusetts. I hardly knew any of them, so it didn't really matter. They didn't even know I was pregnant.

When I entered the latter part of my third trimester, the baby suddenly became real to my parents. All of a sudden, they became excited about the baby, even insisting on buying the nursery furniture we had picked out, and diligently stocking up on newborn diapers and wipes for us. They wanted to know the hospital's protocol for visits. I was happy they were finally excited and showing it, but I didn't have the time or the energy to think too much about why they suddenly came around. I had recently left work on maternity leave and was too busy and too tired getting ready for our baby's arrival. I just took their coming around as a good omen and let it be.

I used to always think my parents' reactions to things were because they weren't happy with me, that I had done something to offend them or something they didn't approve of. With the grace of time, I can look back and see their reaction in this situation had nothing to do with me. It wasn't that they weren't happy that I was having a baby—they were happy for us—but perhaps they were a bit fearful because they never could carry to term their own baby that they so desperately desired. Perhaps their distance had more to do with their own grief than anything about me—grief from so many years ago. I was just the catalyst. Their reminder. I wish I had been aware of this at the time but I just wasn't.

Two years and two weeks after John's passing, our first child, our daughter Heather, was born in the middle of a stormy night on Halloween. She didn't wait until November. We were overwhelmed with joy and love toward her. I remember seeing her little, pink, cherub-like face when the doctor placed her beside me. She was wide awake, looking around the new world she found herself in with her dark blue eyes. Her face was heart-shaped. She was the first person on this planet who I had ever seen who was blood-related to me. I was thirty-one years old.

Chapter Eight

WHILE I RECUPERATED IN THE HOSPITAL, THE DAYS FLOATED by as if I were dreaming. I was happily processing the fact that I was now a mother. Our daughter was here and I was mesmerized by her. My whole world had changed.

We had lots of visits from family and friends coming by to congratulate Michael and me and to meet Heather. Even my parents showed up that first day, eager to meet and hold their first grandchild. It was so out of character for them, risky even, with the possibility of running into Michael's parents, but they did it anyway, which made me feel loved. Though they never saw his parents, they did accidentally run into my sister-in-law Tara and my two-year-old niece Megan as they were leaving. It was the only time my parents ever met anyone from Michael's family.

The big storm was still moving through Southern California, with the rain punching hard against my hospital window. After visiting hours, sitting in bed in the dim light and quiet of my hospital room, I held and rocked Heather in my arms. She was curled up, swaddled tight, sleeping peacefully, her breath a melody. I was overwhelmed with feelings of fullness and joy. This beautiful little baby girl before me wasn't connected to me by legalities and paperwork. She was the first person in my life connected by love, blood, and history. I wasn't alone anymore.

Holding Heather in those tender moments, I reflected on the mysteries of my own birth. There was no hospital listed on my birth certificate. *Where was I born?* Supposedly, I had been born in a Navy hospital in Oakland but I didn't really know. I pictured my biological mother giving birth in such a place, alone, and thought how awful and lonely that must have been. I doubt anyone came to visit either one of us; I don't imagine anyone bringing flowers and good wishes, for I was not a welcomed baby in this world. I was more like an accident my birth mother had to deal with, just like my father had told me when I was sixteen. *A goddamn mistake.*

I had so many questions. *Did my birth mother ever hold me? Did she rock and cuddle me or was I just handed over to strangers at birth?* The only thing that comforted me about my birth was that she had named me. That much I knew, but there were no answers for my other questions and there probably never would be. I had to just let these thoughts float away, as if they were leaves on the wind, holding on to the only tangible truth I had— my birth name. Loretta Annette Stewart.

I was fortunate to be able to be home to take care of our daughter. I had planned on returning to work after taking a few months off, until we crunched numbers and figured out I could actually stay home. It would be tight but we could do it.

Heather was growing fast, and watching her grow, my mind sometimes wandered back to my situation at her age, wondering where I'd been the first few months before I was adopted. *Who cuddled me? Was I comforted when I cried and fed when I was hungry? Was I held when given a bottle, or was it propped up? Where was I?* More questions without answers. I didn't know a thing about my beginnings in life. There are no pictures of me as a newborn.

It is such a strange way to handle things. After all, most of us wait weeks before we adopt a pet because we know the importance of letting a kitten or puppy stay with its mother and not weaning them too early. Why don't we do this for human babies? I know why—it would be too difficult to separate human babies and mothers from each other. Too many mothers would say no, as many wanted to before they were coerced into giving up their babies. That wouldn't go over well with adoption businesses and privileged, childless people with money. Instead, we humans take the baby away from their mother at birth, hand them over to strangers, sometimes within minutes of their first few breaths. We seem to treat our pets with more dignity and empathy.

My parents drove up to visit once or twice a month. They were always generous, bringing with them formula, diapers, and wipes to help out, which Michael and I greatly appreciated. I had hoped that my mother might stay and help me a few days, especially the first few days when Michael went back to work, but she never offered and I didn't ask. I couldn't ask my mother-in-law to help because she worked and also because I knew that would have caused major issues if my mother ever found out. So that was completely out of the question, even though Betty would have been more than happy to have helped me with her new granddaughter.

One time when my parents were visiting, with Heather in her swing in the family room and me in the kitchen taking a casserole out of the oven for lunch, I looked over with hot pads in my hands to see my mother pull a small, white box out of her purse.

My mother was standing at the end of the kitchen counter, wearing a beige silk blouse and black pants, and smiling through her red lipstick. "I thought you might like to have this," she said and held out the box toward me. I put down the hot pads and wiped my hands on my pants.

"What's this, Mom?"

"It's for Heather."

I looked at my mother, tilting my head to one side, wondering what this was, as I took the box from her outstretched hand.

Slowly, I lifted the lid off the box to find inside a tiny gold bracelet and next to it an even smaller gold ring.

"Oh my, Mom," I said, as I lifted the tiny bracelet, holding it up in the sunlight that streamed into the kitchen from the bay window. I turned it over and saw that the inside of the bracelet had been engraved with my mother's name, Madge Lois Gundersen.

"I thought Heather could wear this bracelet the next time you took her for pictures. My grandmother had this made for me when I was born."

Her paternal grandmother, my (adopted) grandfather's mother. I had adored both of my grandparents. They had lived close by, in Santa Monica, and were the only relatives I grew up with. I loved them both dearly.

I knew from my mother's family stories that my grandfather's parents had moved from Norway to Minnesota, a young married couple ready to make a new life in America. Everyone in my adoptive family was proud of their ancestry and talked often about it. My grandfather had been the youngest of ten children. My mother grew up with lots of aunts and uncles and cousins in a huge family back in North Dakota and Minnesota. My father, the oldest of four children, grew up surrounded by extended family from Poland. I loved their stories, but they left me feeling sad, too, because I knew their ancestry wasn't mine.

"Don't forget this too," my mother said, pointing to the box.

"Oh yes, the baby ring! It's so little! This was yours too, Mom?" I picked up the tiniest little gold ring and saw her initials engraved on the top.

"Yes. She had them both made for me. I think Heather can wear them both right now."

I smiled at my mother. "Thank you, Mom. This is really special. I love it."

She nodded her head. I went over and hugged her. She hugged me in return.

"Let's see if this fits, Heather!" I smiled back at her while I placed the little ring and bracelet on my daughter's little pudgy finger and wrist. They fit perfectly.

That evening while falling asleep, I thought about my mother's gift. I knew it meant a lot to her to give it to me, to pass it on to Heather. It was hers. I thought about ancestors, family trees, and how, really, I wasn't a part of my mother's family tree, nor my father's. As much as they wanted it to be that way and we all pretended it was so, myself included at times, it wasn't the truth. Eventually, I'd be lost, written out, erased by their family. Most of them didn't know me and I had no relationship with them. I doubted if anyone would include John and me in their family tree because, heck, we were adopted. I knew they felt this way because one of my aunts (my father's sister) had once encouraged me to date her son, my adoptive first cousin, by saying, "Well, you're not related to each other anyway, so why not?"

It made me kind of sad but it was reality. The truth was that I was lost to my own blood relatives and wasn't connected to my adopted family. I did so love the meaningful and sentimental gift, though. What mattered in this moment was that my mother had offered something very special to Heather, her granddaughter.

I had the beginnings of my own family now and would make

it as special as I could; I would appreciate the sentiment my mother offered today—wishing the truth were different from what it really was.

Heather had now turned one year old. We hosted a first birthday party in our backyard, which included family, close friends, and neighbors, but not my parents. It was a great day even though I was still trying to get used to the idea that my parents would never be here to take part in this. They preferred to do their own thing, having us over for lunch and celebrating quietly in their home, in their own way.

Four months later, I found out I was pregnant again. This time, my parents were excited from the beginning and reacted with interest and more support than the first time. Being pregnant the second time was easier only because I'd been there before. Of course, I was busier too. I had two dogs, a cat, a house, a yard, a husband, and a toddler to take care of. I also had to plan for taking care of another little human in the midst of my busy life.

Halfway through my pregnancy, I received a call from our obstetrician's office that I had tested positive on a particular blood test that screens for Down syndrome. My doctor convinced Michael and me that we needed genetic counseling and amniocentesis.

It was scary to think we might be the parents of a special needs child. For two nerve-racking months, we waited for the results from the painful procedure. I was concerned that I knew nothing of my medical history. There could be something lurking in my genes that we would only find out about if it reared its head in one of my children—a frightening and worrisome thought.

Finally, the phone call came and it was good news. Our second baby was perfectly healthy. I heaved a deep sigh of relief. *Our baby was okay.* We wouldn't have ended the pregnancy anyway—our doctor had encouraged us to go through with the tests because it would be good to know, to be able to prepare ahead of time, just in case our baby had any issues. We had done it more for peace of mind and knowledge.

The silver lining inside all the worry of the past two months was that we'd now be able to know if we were going to have a boy or girl, if we wanted to know. I'm a planner so I liked the idea of knowing. I was home when I got the phone call from the nurse.

"Okay, Diane, are you ready?" the nurse asked me, a skip in her tone of voice.

This is probably one of the phone calls she enjoys making. "Yes, I am." My heart pounded with anticipation.

"Okay!" She paused for a few seconds, like a drumroll, before announcing, "You're having a boy!"

"Oh my gosh! You're kidding me!" My hand went directly to my heart. I loved hearing this news that our baby would be a little boy.

"No, I'm not kidding you!" She laughed. "Congratulations!"

"Thank you so much. This is so exciting!" I hung up and just stood there, in the kitchen, thinking how great it was going to be to have a little son. We'd have a daughter and a son. I was thrilled.

I desperately wanted to call Michael at work to tell him the news, but instead decided to surprise him the next day, which was Saturday. I could only hold off on this exciting news one day. Tomorrow I'd make it a moment.

The next afternoon, Michael was swimming with Heather in our neighbor's pool while I went grocery shopping, then made a quick trip to the party store to pick up a bouquet of blue balloons. The Mylar balloon at the center announced: "It's a boy."

Arriving home, after putting the groceries away, I walked into our neighbor's backyard and stood silently on the grass by the patio, holding the blue bouquet, waiting for Michael or Heather to notice me.

Heather was first, floating in her tube and calling out, "Mommy!"

Michael turned around in the pool, and gave me a dazed look. "Well, hello there!"

"Hi," I said to our neighbor Todd, a Los Angeles police officer who happened to be sitting in his whirlpool tub.

Todd nodded his suntanned head and smiled. "Hi, Diane." He saw the bouquet. *He knows.* I laughed to myself because Michael hadn't comprehended yet.

"Ba-yoons, Mommy!" Heather squealed with delight.

"Yes, Mommy has balloons for you. Has Daddy figured it out yet?"

"They're all blue," Michael said, as he pushed Heather toward me in her float.

"Yes, they're all blue," I answered, trying not to smile too much. *How long will this take him?*

Mike put his hand to his chin in the water. "Blue balloons. Wait. What does that balloon say? What? Oh geez. You got the call. It's a boy?"

"Yup. Surprise!" I yelled. I could now smile all I wanted to.

I couldn't see Michael's eyes hidden under his sunglasses but he slapped the water hard enough that it made a good splash.

"Yes!" he yelled out.

"Congratulations, you guys," Todd added. "That's some great news."

"Heather, you're going to have a baby brother!"

I remembered being told at four-and-a-half years old that I was going to be a big sister to a baby brother who was soon going to come live with us. I thought back to shopping with my mother in a department store in Washington, DC, where I had chosen a light blue rattle to give to my brother. I can still remember the plastic smell of that rattle. I looked forward to watching Heather be a big sister to this baby, like I was to my brother. I liked that our children would be closer in age than my brother and I were.

It was exciting to know ahead of time that we were having a boy. I liked knowing and felt bonded to our son before he was even born. We chose a name right away—Travis John—and I loved rocking him to sleep at night in my rocking chair, singing to him and calling him by name. We couldn't wait to meet him.

Two years and three weeks after Heather's birthday, on Thanksgiving eve, we welcomed our beautiful, healthy son into the world. Travis John looked a lot like Heather did when she was born, except that Travis had blond hair. He had the same dark blue eyes and heart-shaped face as his sister. He was already loved deeply, like Heather, from the first moment we saw him. Our baby boy. I now had two little people on my journey beside me who were blood relatives of mine. I felt full of joy and had peace in my heart. Our family felt complete.

Chapter Nine

HEATHER'S FINE, GOLDEN HAIR SLIPPED THROUGH MY FINGERS easily as I fumbled with French braids on an autumn morning in 1992, five years after she was born.

"Are you done yet, Mommy?" Heather asked, looking at me through the bathroom mirror.

"Almost." I smiled.

"Mommy?"

"Yes?" My fingers moved quickly, weaving the last segment of hair and wrapping it carefully with an elastic hair tie around her blonde tips. I looked up, clasped my hands together, and said with a grin of triumph, "There. All done."

"Thanks, Mommy," Heather said as she checked out her braids in the mirror, moving her head side to side. I handed her a small hand mirror from the counter so she could get a better glimpse of my handiwork.

"We better get going, Sweet Pea. We have to leave pretty soon."

Heather paused. As she put down the hand mirror, she turned around and asked in the softest voice, "Mommy, did you come out of Grandmother's tummy like I came out of yours?"

I jerked, and felt my forehead tense. Bending down toward my daughter, I asked, "What in the world are you asking me? What did you say?"

"Did you come out of Grandmother's tummy like I came out of yours?" Heather's blue eyes were wide, awaiting my reply.

I didn't know what to say. I'd promised myself I'd always be honest with my children about my being adopted, but I hadn't planned on talking about the subject anytime soon. I thought this conversation would happen when she was older, when I could explain my story, what adoption meant, when she'd be better equipped to understand it. I certainly didn't expect my five-year-old daughter to ask me out of the blue like this.

Heather wasn't asking where babies come from. She already knew. Heather was specifically asking if *I* came from my adoptive mother, the same way she came from me. I cleared my throat, and sighed deeply. *I don't want to lie.*

She just wanted to know how it all worked. Generationally speaking, I suppose. The circle of life. It was an innocent question from a five-year-old that deserved an answer. I took another deep breath.

"No, honey, I didn't come out of Grandmother's tummy like you came out of mine. I came from another lady's tummy."

"You did?" Heather's eyes widened and her little mouth dropped open.

"Yes," I said, nodding my head. "Grandmother couldn't have babies. She tried, but she couldn't carry them. Sometimes that happens. Grandmother and Grandfather wanted a family, so they chose me to be their first baby."

"She couldn't have any babies?"

"No, honey, she couldn't," I said, making a sad face in the mirror. I wanted to change direction. I didn't want to upset Heather before school so I said, "Say, we need to get your sweater on and get going for school." I playfully patted her on the bum.

"Where's the lady who grew you in her tummy?" Heather followed me into her pink and white wicker bedroom.

I picked out a navy blue sweater from her closet before turning around to kiss her forehead, telling her, "I don't know who the lady was, Sweet Pea. I never knew her. I don't remember her. All I know is that she couldn't raise me so she had to find people who could, which was Grandmother and Grandfather." I stuck my head out the bedroom door and yelled down the hall toward the family room, "Travis! We're leaving in five minutes to take Heather to school!" It was his five-minute warning watching morning TV. I looked over at Heather, who wore a blank stare. *What is she thinking?*

Several seconds later, I panicked, realizing we were seeing my parents in a few days. *Oh shit.* A feeling of dread rose up in my chest. My little talk with Heather could never get back to my parents. They'd freak knowing I was talking about my being adopted. Adoption was the forbidden word.

I leaned down toward my daughter and took both her little hands in mine. "You know you can always talk to me and about this, sweetheart," I said. "I'm always here if you have questions. But you know who we can never talk to about this? Your grandparents." I looked into her eyes, and with my thumb rubbed the top of her small, soft hands. I hoped I was making my point seem serious.

"We can't?"

"No, honey. I'm sorry. We can't say anything to them about this. This is just between you, me, and Daddy. Okay?"

"Why?"

"Because it'll make Grandmother sad."

"Why will it make her sad?"

"Because she lost her babies, Sweet Pea."

Heather looked as if she were about to cry. I pulled her close to me and hugged her tightly.

"It's okay, sweetheart. Everything is okay. Really, it is.

Grandmother and Grandfather are okay too. This was all a very, long, long time ago. You don't need to worry or be sad because it all turned out just fine. Grandmother and Grandfather got their babies; they got me and my brother John." I tried to lighten the moment. I looked down at the watch on my wrist and said, "Oh boy. I don't want to run late. We've got to get you to school."

"Okay, Mommy." Heather hugged me back, and then as children do, she quickly turned her attention and ran down the hallway toward her brother. *Thank goodness that's over.*

Looking back, why didn't I wait another day or until the following week to talk to Heather? I could've given her question a better answer with more considered thought. I should have, but at the time, I thought I handled it well by being honest. I didn't want to keep secrets from my children as my parents had with me. Heather seemed fine after school that day and the next. I naively assumed she'd been satisfied with the answers I gave her, so I chose not to give our conversation any more room in our busy lives before seeing my parents that weekend.

Several days later, on a sunny Saturday morning, I was driving down to my parents' home with Heather and Travis in the back seat. By habit, I turned the music down as I exited the end of the freeway in San Pedro. I always felt that if I had to, I could drive around this small seaport town blindfolded. San Pedro was known as Little San Francisco, which now feels more like a coincidence knowing how tangled up my history would be with San Francisco and the Bay Area.

San Pedro was a quaint, small town built on a hill overlooking the Port of Los Angeles with its steep, hilly streets, a fisherman's wharf, and rich cultural diversity. The town had a bridge that resembled the Golden Gate, but on a smaller scale, painted sea green rather than the sunlit orange-red of its larger, sister bridge. Spanish-style homes with red-tiled roofs nestled on top of the hill, allowing views to Newport Beach, the San Gabriel Mountains, and downtown Los Angeles.

It was one of the gateway cities to the Palos Verdes Peninsula, the town where my parents bought their first home several months after I was adopted. San Pedro was across the bridge from Long Beach and the now defunct US Navy base on Terminal Island, where my father had been stationed several times. My parents loved the small, seacoast town—that's why they bought their first home up on the hill.

San Pedro is fairly close to Santa Monica where my grandparents lived. My parents were glad to set down some sort of roots even though they ended up renting their first home to military families for six years while the Navy took us to Hawaii, Japan, Virginia, and San Diego. They said they were glad to know they had a house they owned, in a town they loved, to come back to once my father was near retirement.

Right before I turned ten years old, my parents sold the San Pedro home where we had been living during my third-grade year. My father was planning to retire after twenty-four years in the Navy and was ready to settle down and make a permanent home at last. We didn't settle down far, just around to the south side of the peninsula where it was rural. Our new home, hugged by cliffs, overlooked the Pacific Ocean, open fields, and Catalina Island, one of eight in the Channel Islands archipelago.

It was a beautiful place to grow up. I was a beach girl who grew up playing in and loving the ocean. I felt magic in the water whether I was snorkeling, boogie boarding, or making a futile attempt at surfing. Being near the ocean has always felt like home.

Driving down Main Street in San Pedro, I was greeted by

shops so familiar they felt like old friends. I turned toward the coastal route, past Ft. MacArthur, a once grand Army base from World War II that now served as a bustling marina that still held onto remnants of its military past. Palm trees on Paseo del Mar waved me past the well-kept California bungalows, sentinels to the tumultuous ocean below the ragged cliffs. I turned the music up and rolled the windows down so the kids and I could inhale the sweet smell of the salty ocean air. The cool wind whistled through our hair.

"Wheeeeee," Travis sang in his car seat behind me.

I looked in my rearview mirror and saw both kids smiling with their eyes closed and their hair whipping around their faces in the wind. They loved this sense of wildness, like me. To my left was the rocky beach Royal Palms, where memories of high school came alive. I remembered when my girlfriends and I would drive down in colorful VW buses to smoke a quick joint at lunchtime—it was the early seventies. It's where I'd sit listening to Joni Mitchell, Led Zeppelin's "Stairway to Heaven," and Crosby, Stills & Nash on cassette tapes while waiting for surfing boyfriends. I drove past the apartment where I bought my first car, a used, cream-colored 1964 German-imported Volkswagen Karmann Ghia, complete with an electric sunroof and Porsche engine. How I had loved that car.

It was a clear morning with no fog. The ocean shimmered like crystals in the sun. Leaving San Pedro, we turned onto the winding, two-lane country road. Coming around the bend, we were greeted with green rolling hills, plateauing to cliffs that stood strong and tall as aged defenses to the never-ending force of the ocean.

As a child, I'd watched men walking two-by-two here, carrying shotguns and wearing camouflage—pheasant hunting. On the roadside, peanut farmers used to sell hot peanuts in their one-man stands, while Japanese farmers displayed their beautiful strawberries and flowers in weathered, wooden, open-air shops.

As kids, we walked the weedy dirt paths through fields of tall wildflowers to rocky and sand beaches at the bottom of the craggy cliffs. Today, the acres of fields have been tamed, and the wild weeds and hills have become manicured greens at the Los Angeles Trump National Golf Club. It was here, above the golf course, that I turned right, up the hill toward my childhood home.

Heather, Travis, and I were going to have lunch and spend the afternoon with my parents. Mike was working overtime that day. I still hadn't mentioned anything more to Heather since our conversation the other day. I didn't want to bring attention to it as she was so young to talk about something as important as this was to me.

"Hello, sweethearts," my mother greeted us in the driveway, her warm smile carrying the aroma of Shalimar perfume, her signature scent of sweet, smoky vanilla and musk, which wafted in the morning breeze.

We usually visited my parents once a month. With Heather now in school, visits were relegated to weekends but we tried to make the most of our time together. My parents played board games with the kids and we walked around the yard noticing raccoon tracks and the new flowers my mother had recently planted. We sat out on the back patio for lunch. It was a beautiful day. Heather and Travis played croquet on the back lawn.

When it was time to go, we said our goodbyes to my parents in the usual way: Heather and Travis blew kisses to them from the car as they waved goodbye to us from their driveway. The day was nothing short of ordinary; in fact, we had a very pleasant visit.

The following Wednesday, I received a letter in the mail from my mother. She was always prompt, writing thank-you notes after our visits, so I thought nothing of it. Standing in the kitchen, feeling the warmth of the afternoon sun through the greenhouse window, I began reading the handwritten note.

"What?" I said out loud. I took a step backward, putting the letter up to my chest. *Oh geez. Heather said something to my mother.*

We'd only had a few minor issues between us since Heather was born. I'd hoped we were over our troubles. But no, it seemed my mother had found her dark place again and was on the warpath. She was angry I had spoken to Heather about my being adopted, and I had been foolish to think a five-year-old could keep a secret. Of course Heather would not have understood why I had asked her not to say anything.

I immediately tried to call my mother but their phone was busy. After several hours of trying, I realized she'd taken their phone off the hook, a typical thing she used to do when she was angry and didn't want to talk with me. She didn't make it easy to work things out.

As I felt anxiety grip my stomach, I thought about the last time she went crazy, before Heather was born. She had accused me of keeping her large Hawaiian-monkeypod appetizer tray. She didn't speak to me for six months because of it—until she found it in her own home, hidden somewhere different than her usual spot. She never apologized for her accusation or her cutoff. She wrote a letter to tell me she found it.

But in today's letter, my mother blamed Michael for everything. She said that he told Heather to ask me how I was born, and then encouraged Heather to say something to my mother when we visited. She went on to say that Michael did this intentionally to hurt her; he wanted to make sure Heather and Travis would never feel as close to my parents or love them like they would Michael's parents because they would grow up knowing his parents are their blood grandparents and they weren't.

She knew Michael set this whole thing up because Heather never would have thought to ask those questions on her own. She wrote that Heather had been very upset and near tears, telling her how sad she was that my mother had lost some babies.

I can't believe this. I read and reread the letter, shaking my head, feeling the tension build up in my neck. *This is not good. She is super ticked.*

Since I couldn't talk to them, I wrote my parents the next day, which was my usual mode responding to my mother's craziness. It was often the only way I could communicate with them when they were on a tirade. I told them there was no way Michael had anything to do with prompting Heather to ask me a question or to say anything to her. They should know by now that Michael wasn't a deceitful or spiteful person. I told them Heather was simply at an age where she's trying to figure things out, and I told her the truth. Of course, the children loved them dearly and might have even felt closer to them than to Michael's parents.

I began wondering if my parents felt that way about their grandchildren not loving them as much compared to "blood" relatives, then what exactly did that say about their love for me? Or mine for them? Were they saying that love isn't as good in an adoptive family, that if you are blood family, the love is more meaningful? *Is that how they feel?*

Days turned into weeks that turned into months. They never responded to any of my letters. I continued to randomly call but either the phone would be off the hook or they didn't answer. I could've driven down to try to talk with them in person, but I didn't. I had become hurt, frustrated, and angry and hated how they withdrew from me, refusing to talk and try to work things out. Besides, I knew if they saw me at their front door, they wouldn't answer; they'd act like they weren't home, and I didn't have a key to their house. They'd said I didn't need one. I had to knock on the door or ring the doorbell just like anyone else. It would be easy for them to hide.

I wondered if they missed us. And I wondered why I didn't at least hear from my father. In years past, when my mother would be on one of her rampages, he'd call from work or from the peninsula public library, secretly, to check on us. But not this time. He was silent. *Did my parents expect me to never tell my children that I was adopted?*

Several months later, I found a new therapist closer to home, a middle-aged, soft-spoken man who kindly encouraged me to "grieve the loss of the relationship I had with my mother."

I grieved for my mother for months privately, usually when driving. I didn't want to be upset about my parents in front of Heather and Travis. Eventually, I had no more tears left for either of my parents, only a remnant of sadness and confusion.

My therapist continued counseling me, saying, "It could be very healing for you to become the mother you always wanted, to your own children." This, I strived hard to do.

Therapy and grieving my mother helped a lot that summer. I was heartbroken my mother was acting this way again and that my father was going along with her. I knew something had to change, so I listened carefully to the last words of advice my therapist gave me: "Stop dancing the dance with your mother." Of course, this was easier said than done. I knew it would be hard to ignore her tantrums, but I was so tired of going through these antics with her, trying always to defend myself or Michael or his family. I didn't want to dance anymore. It was exhausting.

And yet, here we were again. *Honestly*, I thought, *what do I have to lose?* She wasn't around or involved in my life much. It was really all about the grandchildren at this point. And yet, I was terrified of losing my mother, losing my parents, being shunned and shut out—as if I weren't already experiencing this. *Isn't she already gone?*

For the sake of my family and for my own mental health, I had to let go and move on with my life. Act normal. Remember that we didn't do anything wrong. Adoption had reared its head once again, triggering my mother's pain and loss, projecting itself onto us. Her fear of losing us was her own undoing. I couldn't imagine how this conflict would come to its end.

The longer our estrangement went on, the easier I found it was to daydream about my birth mother, wondering if she would treat me this way, effortlessly cutting me out of her life as my adoptive parents seemed capable of doing. Would she love me unconditionally, when my parents seemed incapable of doing so? But there were no answers, and since I had no clue who or where she even was, I assumed there never would be, so I let my wondering thoughts drift away as on a river as quickly as they came to mind. It was easier that way.

Chapter Ten

THE CORDLESS PHONE RANG AN UNFAMILIAR NUMBER. I waited for the voice recording to hear who it was. "This is Dad. Are you there?"

Tentatively, I picked up the receiver. "Hello, Dad?"

"Hi. I'm glad you picked up."

"Is everything all right?"

"Yes. Everything's fine but I need to talk with you about a few things. Do you have a few minutes?"

"Yeah, I've got some time. Wow, I'm surprised to hear from you." It had been eleven months since we'd spoken to each other.

"I bet. We've actually been waiting for you to call."

"What do you mean—waiting for me?" I raked my hand through my hair as heart palpitations rose up along with the hair on my neck.

"We've been waiting to hear from you for a long time." He sounded annoyed, which annoyed me in turn.

"Well, Dad, that's funny because I've been waiting to hear from you and Mom. I've tried calling you for weeks, if not months, but the phone was either off the hook or nobody answered. I wrote several times and never heard anything from you or Mom. I finally gave up trying."

"Well, I don't know about any of that, but I can tell you your mother is still pretty upset with what happened."

"So am I, Dad."

"She doesn't know I'm calling you today. I've got some words of wisdom for you," he went on. "If you don't call your mother soon to apologize, we're going to assume you don't want anything more to do with us and we'll be forced to write you out of our will."

I paused for a few seconds. *Who says this? Does he really mean this?* I knew my father wasn't home and was calling from the public library at Peninsula Center, standing in the phone booth, secretly calling me like he had so many other times. This time he called to give me fair warning of their nefarious plot to erase me from their lives.

"What? I'm supposed to apologize? For what?"

"For what happened when Michael told Heather to ask those questions the last time you were here, when Heather asked Mom about losing babies. I think she wrote and told you what happened, right?"

I took a deep breath and rubbed my eyes. *I can't believe I'm going to have to deal with this ridiculousness.* "Oh my gosh, Dad. Michael never said or did anything like that to hurt Mom. He didn't have anything to do with what happened. You both should know he is not like that. We would never do such a thing. I wrote and told Mom all of this months ago."

"Well, she doesn't believe it."

"I guess not. I think she wants to find something to be mad at Michael for, or me? I don't know anymore. I've tried but she just doesn't want to hear or believe what I have to say."

"That's why I'm calling. The only way out of this is if you apologize. You need to do it soon before it's too late."

"Too late? I have a deadline before you and Mom are going to cut me off? Wow. I just can't believe this."

"We don't want to. That'll be up to you."

"So this whole estrangement is my fault? And Michael's?"

He ignored my question. "The only way to resolve this is if you apologize. Before I hang up, I want you to know we've been worried about the children. Are they doing okay? Are they healthy?"

"They're fine, Dad. We're all good. We're all healthy." I could feel fire growing within me from anger and frustration of the situation. Even my lips felt hot.

"I'm glad to hear everyone is healthy. Call your mother this week." And with that, he hung up.

I stood in silence for about five minutes in the bedroom, gripping the phone tightly in my hand. Tears of anger and hurt stung my cheeks. I sat down on my bed, grabbed a tissue from my nightstand, and dabbed my face. Looking out the French doors into the backyard, I watched the pine trees waving in the wind on our back hill. I sat, staring outside, thinking about the phone call with my dad. *I can't believe they expect me to apologize.* But didn't they always? This was part of the dance, my mother's drama game.

I had no more dance cards left.

I couldn't fathom that they could write me and their grand-children so easily out of their lives, as if we were chess pieces on a game board. It seemed so easy for them. It scared me and hurt so much, making me wonder if they really even cared about me and Heather and Travis.

They wanted an apology to restore our relationship. My father sounded serious about his threat, but I didn't think he wanted our current estrangement to be permanent. It was a strange way to show it, but I thought he was worried they might have to go through with their promise. That's why he called. He cared—at least it seemed he did.

Later that evening, Michael and I sat down after dinner to

talk privately. Heather and Travis were in our bedroom watching TV.

"I don't know what to do," I said, tapping my glass of wine, a nervous habit of mine.

"This is what they do," Michael said calmly. "It isn't different from any other time. Your mother reacts dramatically, can't accept responsibility, and puts it all on you. Her problem becomes your fault. It's called gaslighting, and your father goes right along with her."

"Yup. You're right." I sighed deeply. I looked over at Michael sitting cross-legged on the floor across from me in his blue sweats and lived-in, surf T-shirt. Michael was a soft-spoken man of few words who could focus on what I was saying and help put my thoughts together in a thoughtful, comprehensive way.

"So, what do you want?" he asked.

"Well, I don't want this estrangement. I don't want to lose my parents, to be cut off from them or from their will either. I know it must sound odd, but I miss them. It would be hard not to ever see them again. I can't believe they're making it so that it all comes down to me."

"I know you miss your parents, and so do the kids. Can you do it?"

"You mean apologize?"

"Yes, just in order to keep the peace. We know what really happened and that's what matters."

"Yeah. I think I can—for that reason, to keep the peace and the door open between us. I wasn't going to get sucked into my mother's drama anymore, but here I am. Maybe the best thing to do is just apologize and end this craziness. Enough is enough."

Falling asleep that night, I felt sad I had to give in again to my mother's untrue crazy thoughts. I wondered if I was metaphorically asking for her hand on the dance floor one more time. Maybe so, but I convinced myself this was the only way to preserve our relationship. We had gone almost a year not speaking to each other. It needed to stop before something happened that made us unable to ever restore our family, and it seemed that this was up to me. I held the cards in this precarious game of ours.

The following Wednesday seemed a good day to call my mother. I was sitting at our kitchen table with a fresh mug of coffee. Hot drinks always soothed me. Still, it took me a few tries to actually dial the familiar number.

I dialed and let the phone ring. Someone picked it up after the third ring, and then, silence. I knew it was my mother who answered because she never says hello. She waits to know who's calling before she says anything. As long as I can remember, my mother had been like this: suspicious, worried about prank phone calls, concerned that someone might be after her for some unknown, strange reason. I sometimes used to wonder if she was worried my biological parents might be trying to find me and that's why we always had unlisted phone numbers and addresses. Or maybe she was just paranoid.

I could hear her breathing. "Hello, Mom?"

"Oh, hello," she answered, matter-of-factly, like nothing was the matter. It was kind of funny except this was a serious phone call.

"Mom, can we talk?"

"Sure. I'm surprised to hear from you. Why are you calling?"

Is she really surprised? Or did my dad cave and tell her he called me and that she should be expecting my call? Is that why she finally answered? It was hard to trust them. I took a sip of coffee and closed my eyes, trying to center myself before I continued.

"Well, yes, it's been a long time, hasn't it? I think not talking to each other has just gone on too long." I wanted to tell her I was glad she answered the phone this time, but I didn't want to start anything.

"I think it's gone on far too long as well," she said, curtly.

"I hope we can work things out, Mom. I know I'd like to. So, first, let me apologize for hurting you the last time we saw you. I'm sorry. I never meant to hurt you in any way, and Michael certainly didn't intend to hurt you either. I hope you can accept that. There wasn't anything nefarious going on, but anyway, I hope you can accept my apology." *Please say yes and do not expect more from me. Do not move the bar up to something else.* I took another deep breath.

She paused, then answered, "Well, thank you, Diane. I accept your apology."

"That's really good to hear, Mom." Why was she so formal with me? I hated that. There seemed such a high wall between us. "I hope we can move forward from this. The kids miss you and Dad." I didn't say anything about myself. It felt too vulnerable.

"I think we can—in time. We miss them too," my mom answered politely.

Does she miss me? I didn't think she did.

"Okay, well that sounds good." Tears filled my eyes and I could feel my bottom lip quivering. It was finally over between us. Eventually, we'd be okay again but I couldn't help but feel sad about our inability to communicate our feelings. I had missed them both this past year. At times, it was heart-wrenching to think they might never have come around again. I'm sure they missed us, too, but we'd never talk about it. We'd never cry about it with each other and express real feelings. As usual, our misunderstanding and the year without a relationship was swept under the carpet and life would go on.

It took several months before we were back to regular visits with my parents, still acting as if nothing ever happened. There was never a discussion of our longest estrangement or what had happened, and there certainly was no discussion of adoption.

Not long after I apologized to my mother, my father called and asked, "Your mother and I want to have Dave be the executor of our will and trust we recently drew up with our attorney. Dave has agreed to do this, but on one condition—if you were okay with this. So, I'm asking if you will be okay with this?"

Dave was the husband of a former childhood friend of mine, named Joanne. Over the years, my parents had become close with Dave and Joanne. Joanne, especially, had won my mother's heart over the years. She had known my parents since she was nine years old, when we lived in the same neighborhood before my father retired from the Navy.

She idolized my parents and thought they were glamorous. No other mothers in the neighborhood were seen wearing evening gowns, elbow-length white gloves, and rhinestone tiaras and pearl necklaces topped off with sparkling evening bags and wraparound mink stoles. My mother looked like royalty walking out the door with her husband, dressed in military white-tie and tails, and driving away in their aqua Cadillac DeVille sedan to an evening of cocktails and grown-up conversation over dinner.

Joanne was three years older than me and always seemed mature beyond her years. After my father retired from the Navy and we had moved to the south side of the peninsula, she still came over, supposedly to play and hang out with me, but she always preferred my mother's company over mine. As we grew older, we went our separate ways but Joanne and my mother remained close. Joanne seemed to do everything I didn't.

She went away to college at Mount Holyoke in Massachusetts, received her degree in history, then came home, met and married Dave, a dentist, in a beautiful wedding my parents attended several years before I met Michael. I was in her wedding party although we weren't close anymore.

My parents and Dave and Joanne seemed to have a lot in common and lived near each other in the same city. Dave and Joanne had twin daughters, Caroline and Catherine, who were Travis's age. Photos of Caroline and Catherine embellished my parents' home just as much, or more, than pictures of Heather and Travis, which always bothered me. I gave Joanne a nickname—*the daughter my parents always wanted.*

My dad continued, defending his plan, saying, "I don't want to burden you with the tasks that'll need to be done. Dave knows how to handle these things since he was executor for his mother's estate and did a good job, but he said he'd only take it on if you'd agree. Are you all right with this?" My dad sounded nervous.

I felt like I didn't have a choice in the matter, so I answered, "Sure, that's fine."

It made sense that my parents were updating their will and trust, now that our estrangement was over. They never discussed it with me beyond saying they wanted Dave to be their executor. I never thought about it again.

There wasn't time for daydreams during the busy years raising children in school and sports and after-school activities. Michael and I were both active with the kids, volunteering as American Youth Soccer Organization (AYSO) coaches and referees, Girl Scout leaders, cheerleading coaches, field trip chaperones, and more. As far as fantasizing about biological parents, I was done;

I had come to terms with the fact that I'd never find them. It was what it was—impossible.

Every so often, though, I'd still wonder about my invisible parents. I'd wonder when I saw someone on TV or in a store who resembled me or my children—*Can we somehow be related?* I was like the baby bird in the children's book *Are You My Mother?*, looking for clues in every face I saw, although I never said anything out loud. The wondering was just a part of my inner life, ever present and always a secret, much as it had been since I was a little girl.

The only way I figured I'd find someone related to me would be by the whims of the powers that be. It wasn't likely, but it could happen. After all, there was that odd meeting when I was twenty years old and still living at home, when I thought I had come close to finding my birth mother.

It had been a warm, sunny Saturday morning, and out of character for both my mom and me, we decided spur-of-the-moment to go to a local dog show. I had always loved Alaskan malamutes and was hoping to be able to see my favorite breed in person. I don't know when I began to love the beautiful, wolflike breed, but I think I fell in love with these dogs from the first moment I laid eyes on them. I loved that they seemed wild and were the oldest, Indigenous, Native American dog breed. For some reason, I was fond of anything that had to do with Alaska.

After watching the different breeds and seeing the malamutes, and how big and gorgeous they were, my mom and I walked the show grounds until we found the shopping area. My mom went off to look at something on her own. While I was looking at some items at one place, an older woman with short cropped white hair, wearing a blue print dress, looked over at me and smiled, then cocked her head and marched toward me, her blue eyes twinkling with determination as she approached.

"I know your mother," she said in a thick Scottish brogue, while pointing a bony finger at me.

I was taken aback. She sounded so sure of herself. *What does this mean? Does she?* It was so out of the blue, but I answered earnestly, because she seemed to truly know, "You do?"

The spry little woman said, "Yes, I do. What's yer mother's name?"

My eyes darted around, looking for the whereabouts of my mom. I didn't see her anywhere. She couldn't hear this conversation. I became excited and thought that I must look so much like my birth mother that this woman immediately recognized our long-lost relationship. I desperately wanted to ask her who my mother was, how she thought she knew her, but within seconds my mom came up behind me and I had to answer, "This is my mother, Madge." All hope was then lost.

For years afterward, I wondered if that Scottish woman really did know my birth mother and if that had been the one and only chance the universe would give me to find her. As an adoptee, I was always wondering who could be lurking on the television set or around the corner, or at the mall, who might be a blood relative of mine.

But for a long time to come, my dreams and wishes to find my biological family were just that—dreams and wishes. Then, in 1997, when Heather was nine and Travis was seven, we bought our first home computer. The internet, and what it could do, was becoming a reality for many people. The internet promised it would change the world. Little did I know how much it would change mine.

Part Two

Hope is a waking dream.

—Aristotle

Chapter Eleven

SITTING AT MY DESK, ALONE, LATE AT NIGHT IN THE family room, I stared at the computer screen, reading adoptee search stories online in private chat rooms. It was now March 2003, and I was forty-seven years old. It had been ten years since my parents and I had our yearlong estrangement. They were in their early eighties, and I was looking at a milestone birthday in just a few years myself.

By this time, the internet and the World Wide Web had infiltrated everyday life, appearing in people's homes and opening up opportunities for all sorts of searchers, including thousands of adoptees who now had before them a tool that allowed them to search online for their biological families. Websites started by people wanting to help other adoptees begin their search sprang up like wildfire on windswept plains. Search angels, as they were called, were eager to help and had access to state birth databases and census records. (This was long before services like Ancestry and DNA testing became available.)

I loved reading the stories of adoptees finding their families of origin and spent hours immersing myself in their lives. Most stories were heartwarming rather than heartbreaking. *The Oprah Winfrey Show* and other weekly television talk shows shared adoptees' reunion stories. I wept as I pictured myself in their position, and imagined how wonderful it must have felt to discover and meet a blood relative. The important thing for me was that it *was* happening—and by seeing that, I saw that I could use these new resources too.

All my life I'd yearned to know people who looked like me, who had my blood, but I still found it difficult to envision my biological parents as real people who had jobs. People who lived somewhere, and, like ordinary people, ran everyday errands. I hardly dared to imagine my birth parents might have married and had other children. Siblings? I had to banish that thought—it carried too much hope.

The passing of years didn't bring any resolution with the mother who raised me. And now, at age eighty-two, my mother had been having health issues. Both of my adoptive parents were aging and weren't as strong and healthy as they once had been. The previous Christmas, Michael and the kids and I spent the day taking my dad, now in a wheelchair, to visit her in the hospital. She'd been in the ICU, having had heart issues and surgery for a pacemaker.

It scared me to think of losing them—after all, they were the only parents I had known. Just the thought of them gone made my heart step up its beat; it was silent on the outside, but sounded like Lakota drums on the inside. At the time, I didn't realize that what I was feeling was familiar or that I had been triggered. I eventually realized that it was the familiar subconscious feeling of fear of losing my parents, and that became the catalyst that prompted me to begin searching for my birth mother.

For the past several years, I had played around on the internet, casually placing my birth name on various adoptee search sites hoping someone might be looking for me, but no one had responded. That night in March, feeling discouraged by my passive endeavors the past few years on the search sites and worried about my mother's failing health, I thought it time to step up my game. Reading successful, happy stories in the chat rooms made it seem possible. *Why can't this happen to me?*

The question was: *How do I begin?*

I decided to step out and post my question in a California adoptee chat room. Hesitantly, I typed, "How do you begin to search?"

To my surprise, within minutes, someone responded to my question, a search angel named Judy.

"It depends," she said. "What information do you have?"

"I don't have much, only my birth name," I replied.

Judy answered quickly, "That's a good start. Do you know your birth mother's maiden name?"

"No, but I'm guessing it's the same as my birth surname?"

"Has anyone ever looked up your name on the California Birth Index?"

"No. I don't even know what that is."

"The California Birth Index is a database from the California Office of Health Information and Research. The index contains the birth records of all registered births in California between 1905 and 1995. I'd be happy to look up your name and try to find your birth mother's maiden name for you—if you want?"

I sat up straighter in my chair. *What? She can find my birth mother's maiden name?* I was all in for this.

"I'd love that. Yes, please." I typed as fast as I could.

"I need your birth name and your full amended name—you know, the name your adoptive parents gave you. I also need your city of birth and birth date."

I sent my information.

"Give me ten minutes and I'll be back with your mother's maiden name."

I felt my heart, or maybe it was my whole body, rev up with

anticipation. I needed some chamomile tea to calm my nerves. I walked into the kitchen to put the teakettle on and pulled out a mug. It seemed like forever but as soon as I was done making tea, I heard my computer chirp, announcing a message. Judy was back.

"Success! I found you, Diane. Was your mother married to your father?"

Responding, I said, "I have no idea."

"The reason I ask is that you have a different surname from your mother. You must have your father's. It's unusual for an adoptee to have their father's surname unless they were married."

"Oh really?" *This is interesting.*

"So, Stewart is probably your father's surname. Your mother's maiden name is Douglas. Down the road, you might want to check into this to see if your birth parents were ever married."

"Wow. Thank you so much."

I couldn't believe it. I sat at my desk staring at my birth mother's surname. It reminded me of when I was nineteen and found my birth name, how one clue, one name, can change your perspective on your identity. *Douglas.* I felt a bit dazed trying to comprehend that I now knew both of my parents' surnames. Stewart and Douglas—both names were very Scottish.

I was thrilled. Ecstatic. I thanked Judy again for this information, this gift. She said she was more than happy to have helped and encouraged me to join a private, online group exclusively for adoptees born in California. It had a good reputation in the adoptee community for finding people. She gave me the information, and as we said our goodbyes, I heard footsteps in the hallway. It was Michael walking toward me, barefoot, wearing his red plaid, flannel pj's. He must have fallen asleep watching television in our bedroom and had woken up wondering where I was.

Michael shook his head, giving me a sly smile while he grabbed a glass of water in the kitchen.

"Playing on the computer? When are you coming to bed?"

"Soon," I answered, putting my mug on the desk. I smiled up at him and said, "You won't believe this, but I just found out my birth mother's maiden name."

"What?" His mouth fell open as he clumsily clanked his glass down on the counter.

"Yup." I smiled, feeling smug, nodding.

"Is that what you've been doing? How did you find that out?"

"Well, you don't know this, but for years I've been putting my name on adoptee search sites hoping to find someone related to me. And tonight, I reached out to a search angel who was able to find my birth mother's maiden name! She matched my amended birth certificate number to my original birth certificate on this California Birth Index she has access to, and there was my mother's maiden name. Isn't that something?"

"It sounds complicated."

"Well, it didn't seem like it was. It happened within minutes. So . . . my birth mother's maiden name is Douglas. And," I went on, "my surname of Stewart is more than likely my father's. She said they might have been married, which is why I have his surname and not hers."

"Really?" Michael was listening intently now.

"I'm shocked I could find this out so quickly. Shocked and thrilled. This should be a helpful clue toward finding her."

"That's amazing. Douglas? Wow. Oh, wait a minute. What are you doing? Are you thinking of searching for your birth mother?"

"Yes, I am. I think it's time." I hadn't shared with Michael that I had been putting my name on search boards. My thoughts and wonderings about finding my biological family were my own secret thoughts.

"Why in the world do you want to do that?" He looked at me with a puzzled expression.

"Because I know nothing about who I am, where I came from. I'm forty-seven years old and I don't even know what ethnicity I am. I don't know any medical history, which sometimes worries me. I want to know more, not only for myself, but for the kids, because they're missing half of their heritage and history too. Right now, I don't know what could be waiting down the road for any of us. And tonight is like, wow, I mean, I just learned my mother's maiden name. It happened so fast."

Michael walked behind me and stood looking at the computer screen and said in a cautious tone, "I'm not so sure about doing this. You could be opening up Pandora's box. You don't know what or who you're going to find. I get that you want to know your medical history, but I'm not so sure about searching and actually meeting someone."

"I hear you, but rest assured, I may never find her. Just because I got lucky tonight doesn't mean I'll ever find her, or anyone. I still have so little information, this may not really be feasible anyway."

"I don't know," Michael hesitated. "You know you can never let your parents find out you're doing this."

"Oh, believe me, I know that. There's no way I'm ever telling them I'm doing this."

"Good, because that would be the end of your relationship with your parents."

"Don't worry, I'll be careful. It's not like I'm going to find anyone next week. This could take years—if it ever goes anywhere. I just want to try to see how far I can get."

"Okay," Michael answered, finishing off his glass of water.

He shrugged his shoulders and shook his head. "Well, I'm not sure about this, but one thing I do know is that I don't want to deal with your parents. That would not be good." He turned toward the hallway. Looking back, he asked, "Are you coming to bed soon?"

"Yeah, I'll be there in about fifteen minutes." I watched him walk out of the room. He didn't get it, but I didn't care. I knew what I had to do.

The next day I applied for membership into the private, online group the search angel Judy had recommended. I was accepted later that day. The two mentors who monitored the group, Kathi and Dawn, introduced themselves and then assigned me homework. They said they couldn't help me until I had my NID—non-identifying information—from the county I was adopted in. I had never heard of an NID before. Apparently, every adoptee is eligible to receive non-identifying information—information about the situation and/or the parents that don't identify who they are.

I told Kathi and Dawn it had been a private adoption, but they told me that from now on I was to only rely on facts, not what my adopted parents had told me. I thought that sounded a bit harsh, but went along with their rules. Since I didn't know the attorney's name or where my adoption had taken place, my first task was to find out where I had been adopted and what type of adoption had occurred. They told me to start my search by requesting information directly from the state of California's social services offices in Sacramento.

A few days later, I thought about what Michael had said. I understood his concerns about opening up Pandora's box and what would happen if my parents found out. I wouldn't—I couldn't—let that happen. But I needed to move forward. I calculated my birth mother was probably around sixty-eight years old. I wasn't getting any younger and neither was she.

Even though I appreciated Michael trying to be empathetic toward me, he would never truly understand what it felt like to be an adoptee, simply because he wasn't adopted. Michael never had to secretly wonder who he might be related to, and actually, neither did my children. Heather and Travis had experienced family mirroring while growing up, something I never had. So, even though they didn't know half of their ethnicity, they knew their parents, where they came from, and how they came to be in the world. They grew up with extended family who told them who they laughed like, where their hair color came from, or how they danced just like their grandmother Betty.

Never mind that Michael was nervous about my searching. This wasn't about him. This was about me. I needed to know more about myself; I needed to discover my history, find my ethnicity, and acquire the self-knowledge and truth that would help me feel more grounded in the world. I wanted to pass my side of history down to my children and future grandchildren. The clock was ticking. It was now or never.

I chose now.

Chapter Twelve

IT TOOK ONE MONTH TO RECEIVE A RESPONSE IN THE mail from the Sacramento Department of Social Services. I ripped the envelope open like a madwoman.

The first paragraph stated, "Our records indicate this was an agency or relinquishment adoption maintained by the adoption agency that arranged the adoption. We are returning your original request so that you may send it to them for the requested service. The adoption agency name and address is Alameda County, Social Services Agency."

"What? You're kidding me," I said aloud. "So, I wasn't a private adoption? Wow."

In the quiet of the afternoon kitchen, it was stunning to see my first truth, realizing that what my parents had told me had been a lie. I had been a county adoption, not a private one. I laughed to myself—of course my parents tried to make my adoption sound better by telling me I had been a private adoption. To them, that sounded more prestigious than a county adoption.

The next day I sent the same letter to Alameda County requesting my NID. I waited another month before I heard from them. This time, the letter said they received my request

for my non-identifying information but asked me to be pre-
pared to wait three more months before receiving a response.
The letter was signed by my assigned caseworker, Shannon
Walker. I was discouraged to hear about the wait, but I figured
I had already waited forty-seven years. What was three more
months in the scheme of things?

While I languished in limbo, Dawn and Kathi encouraged
me to study the group members who had found their biological
families and were now in the midst of reunion. Kathi suggested
several books, and since I was an avid reader, I devoured them
all. The one that touched me the most was *The Primal Wound,
Understanding the Adopted Child*, by Nancy Newton Verrier. I
highlighted and dog-eared the heck out of that book.

The author was not an adoptee, but a parent of two daughters, one who was adopted and one who was not. She held a master's degree in clinical psychology and had a private counseling
practice in Northern California. I had never read a book about
the adoptee psyche before, so it was eye-opening for me. Her
words resonated, articulating things I'd felt inside but had been
silent about for years. I had no idea I shared these same desires
and feelings with other adoptees. I never knew that much of the
angst, fear, and anxiety I had toward losing my adoptive parents
was due in large part because I had already experienced losing
my birth mother as a newborn—hence the term "the primal
wound."

This new information accounted for a lot of my nervousness
in childhood—it got so bad that my mother had to paint my legs
and in between my fingers with calamine lotion because I had
Dyshidrosis, a form of eczema. She also had to paint the inside
of my mouth with iodine because I would bite my mouth raw.
Obviously, I had been quite a quietly nervous child.

And why? As Nancy Newton Verrier wrote, because ". . . the

primal experience for an adopted child is abandonment which begets core issues of loss, and fear of further abandonment. The adopted child copes in whatever way he/she can, manifesting in behavior that often is misunderstood." This book opened a door to feelings of belonging and gave me an opportunity to heal and better understand my journey in life as an adoptee.

It was during this phase of my journey that I discovered what the term "coming out of the fog" meant for adoptees. In the adoptee community, "coming out of the fog" refers to adoptees coming to terms with their feelings and emotions that have been suppressed over time, arriving at their own realizations on how adoption and their own adoption experience has affected them.

I was "coming out of the fog" and it felt good. I was awakening to the fact that my beginnings had been kept secret by several entities: the government, society, and my parents. It was infuriating. It wasn't fair that all of these people kept me from knowing who or where I came from. Life isn't always fair; I get that. But I had been denied a basic human civil right that is taken for granted by almost everyone else on the planet, and I was still being denied. Even at my age, I was still treated by the government like a perpetual child, not allowed to know about my birth, parents, ethnicity, or history. The only way I could possibly gain access to my original birth certificate in California was through a court order and that was nearly impossible to obtain, even for medical information. Worse, there was no end in sight—I could easily turn eighty, long after my adoptive and birth parents were gone, and *still* not be allowed to obtain my original birth certificate.

Ever so slowly, through hard-fought years of legislation, this situation is changing; some states are opening up their restrictions and allowing adoptees access to their original birth certificates. Currently, only twelve states allow unrestricted access, while other states maintain complicated restrictions that require adoptees to jump through hoops of hope. As of this writing, California is one of twenty-four states that are still fully closed for adoption records.

I became angry at a system that held me hostage. I was stripped of my personal rights by people and a system that cared more about protecting my birth and adoptive parents than me, the actual victim in this situation. Decisions were made for me entirely without my input, long before I had a voice. I was born into secrecy and torn away from my original family and the many future generations to follow.

The system had erased my past by amending my original birth certificate and changing my given name so that I could never be legally connected to my birth family, and neither would my children and grandchildren. Even if I legally changed my name to my birth name, California records would always list me as Diane Carol Mason and my adoptive parents as my "original" parents, the ones who bore me—a lie.

So, I tied my boots tighter for the uneasy road ahead. Dawn and Kathi promised me that receiving my NID would give us clues we could work with to find my biological family, but they admitted it wouldn't be an easy search with two surnames as common as Douglas and Stewart.

And so I waited.

It took five long months for my NID to arrive. It came in the mail, without fanfare, on Friday, September 5, which, coincidentally, I'd later find out was my birth mother's birthday.

I wasn't thinking about my NID the day it arrived. I stood casually in the kitchen, leafing through the daily mail. Stuffed in between advertisements and bills was a letter-size manila envelope. The return address read: SHANNON WALKER, SOCIAL SERVICES, ALAMEDA.

As I stood in the empty house and stared at the envelope, the only sound I could hear was the grandmother clock, ticking time away on the wall. *Is this it?* By the weight of the envelope in my excited, shaky hands, I guessed it held more than just a few pages. I bit my lip and looked around the room. I was home alone. Michael and the kids wouldn't be home for hours. There was no way I could wait for them. My patience had run out, especially now that I was holding the golden prize in my hands.

What I needed was someone to share this moment with. I called my friend Mary, but there was no answer, then I remembered she was down South visiting her sister. *Darn.* Who could I call that I'd be comfortable with? Robyn. Robyn was another good friend who lived a few houses across the street. I opened up the garage and saw her white van parked in their driveway.

My fingers shook as I punched in her phone number.

"Hello," Robyn answered in her upbeat voice.

"Oh, good," I said, relieved. "You're home. Oh my gosh, Robyn. I just got my NID in the mail."

"What? You did?"

"Yup, I'm pretty sure I'm holding the envelope in my hand. I haven't opened it yet. It's from my caseworker in Alameda County, so this has to be it. I don't want to read it alone and I can't wait for Michael and the kids to get home. I was wondering if you have some time to come over and read it with me?"

"Diane, I'll be right over."

"Oh, thanks so much, Robyn. I'll put a pot of coffee on for us."

It was hard to concentrate, even to measure out the coffee that I made on a daily basis. My adrenaline had been shot to sky-high, or beyond.

Several minutes later, Robyn, a somewhat shy woman in her late thirties, entered through the wooden screen door in the garage reserved for family and friends.

"Diane, I'm so excited for you. You've certainly waited long enough for this to arrive." Robyn's hazel eyes seemed to twinkle with the same excitement I was feeling.

"I know, right? Here it is." I showed Robyn the envelope, handling it gingerly, as I would a family treasure. Her eyes widened.

"Well, then, let's get this party started!" she exclaimed excitedly.

"Have a seat. I'll get our coffee."

Smiling, I grabbed our mugs and then pulled out a chair for her to sit at the dining table. With my heart pumping loudly in my chest, I took my brass whale letter opener, the one Michael and I had bought when we were first married, and held the envelope up in the air. With a flourish, I cut a triumphant slit on the back of the envelope.

"Here we go," I said, looking at Robyn's freckled, smiling face as I sat down.

There was no cover letter. On the first page, the basic personal information for both of my birth parents was laid out in a chart. What I saw first was that both of my birth parents were born in the South. My father was born in Alabama and my mother in Tennessee. My mouth dropped open. I didn't expect to see information on both of my birth parents, but I was thrilled my father was included.

"Wow. They're both from the South," I said, shaking my head in disbelief. "I guess I should've known by my birth name, Loretta."

"This is really something, Diane." Robyn was huddled close to me, our chairs touching. I was glad she was there.

Smiling at Robyn, I said, amused, "Geez, they're both Confederates."

"So, you didn't know where they were born, right?" Robyn asked over her mug of coffee, the steam rising along with her blonde eyebrows.

"No, I don't know anything." I stared at the information in a kind of daze.

"I know you didn't know much, but wow, there seems to be a lot of information here. How many pages are there?"

Robyn began counting. There were eight typed pages of non-identifying information. This was incredible. Not many people in my group received as many pages. Most received maybe two or three. Surely, Dawn and Kathi would be able to gather some sort of clues from all of this.

Reading on, I learned that my mother was tall, very tall. She wasn't five foot seven as I had been led to believe; she was five foot eleven and a half inches—nearly six feet tall. And she didn't have blue eyes either. Her eyes were green. Apparently, I had my father's blue eyes. My NID stated my father was also tall. He worked as a commercial artist while my mother worked at a phone company. Both were high school graduates. My father was twenty-six when I was born and was already divorced, which I found interesting. My mother was twenty-three when she had me, not twenty-one as I'd been told. It was surreal to read about these strangers, my biological parents.

After the first page, my caseworker recounted the story told by my mother years before. My maternal grandparents were both alive when I was born, and my mother was the middle of three children. That meant I had an aunt and uncle somewhere, probably in Tennessee.

Shannon described my young mother from notes social workers had taken long ago: "A tall, attractive girl. Her skin was very fair, her hair light brown and her eyes a greenish-blue. She carried herself well as if she were proud of her height. She came to the interview well-groomed and tastefully dressed. She had a rather slender oval face and a sweet mouth. She was a gentle and friendly girl, sweet, sensitive, and devoted to her mother and father and her two siblings."

"This is unreal, Diane," Robyn said with tears in her eyes.

"It is, isn't it?" I looked over at Robyn, then up at the ceiling to take a break from the incredible but overwhelming news. I took several deep breaths, closing my eyes while Robyn took charge, refilling our coffee mugs, before continuing.

A few paragraphs later were words never dreamed or considered.

"This pregnancy was your mother's second out-of-wedlock pregnancy. You were the second child she felt compelled to relinquish. Your half sister was born in 1954."

I gasped. She had another baby before me. *I had a sister.*

Robyn and I looked at each other in disbelief. I pushed my body away from the table and then came back again, trying to absorb what we had just read.

"Oh, Diane." Robyn let her mouth drop open as she grabbed my arm.

"I can't believe this. Oh, wow." It was all I could say, and all I could think was that I had a sister out there somewhere and how sad it was that we were separated.

Robyn echoed my thoughts. "Diane, you have a sister," she whispered gently.

My head felt heavy. I looked at Robyn as I raised my arms and moved to support my neck. I was processing. I was not my mother's firstborn child. All my life I assumed I was. Never in my wildest thoughts did I imagine I wasn't.

Shannon Walker continued writing: "Your mother placed

her in foster care, paying for it out of her own earnings from work. She tried to be the best mother she could while hoping the father would marry her. In early 1955, it became apparent he had no intention of marrying her so she relinquished her daughter. It was very difficult for her to do as she had come to love her very much."

I learned my maternal grandfather tried to help my mother financially so she could keep her baby, which touched my heart, but it wasn't easy to be a single mother in the 1950s, especially in the conservative culture of the South.

Not long after my mother relinquished her firstborn, she met my father. After dating for a while, my father left for California to find work. I suspect he left rather quickly after reading that the Federal Bureau of Investigation came looking for him where my mother lived with her grandmother. My mother found out she was pregnant when my father was in California. He told her to keep the baby and that he would send her money to join him. She was concerned about the FBI looking for him, but he must have soothed her worries because she then became the one sending him money to help him get established in California before she went to the Bay Area, presumably following him, where she ended up living with her pregnant sister and her family. A few months later, she went to live at the Salvation Army's Booth Memorial Hospital for unwed mothers in Oakland, California, where I was born.

"What? I wasn't born at Oakland Naval Hospital?" I asked out loud. Another truth revealed.

My NID said my mother felt "foolish" for getting pregnant a second time. She hated that she had to make this decision all over again. But this time would be different because she knew she couldn't take care of me. She is quoted as saying, "Above all, I can't bear to repeat the painful experience I had bonding to a child and relinquishing again." Because of this, she decided she didn't want to see me or name me. It was too hard for her after what she'd been through with my older sister.

Shannon Walker wrote that eventually she changed her mind and named me. She probably saw me as well. Maybe she even held me.

Somehow, it seemed my mother must have still been in contact with my father when I was born because my caseworker stated he knew about me, never denied paternity, but didn't want the responsibility of raising me; yet his name is on my birth certificate, which is why I had his surname, Stewart.

"I still just wonder"—I glanced over at Robyn, rubbing the back of my neck—"if they were married like the search angel had said."

Eight pages about my birth parents, my mother's relationship to her uncles and her siblings, and her relationship to my father was a lot to process. Yet there was more to come.

Two weeks after I was born, my mother sat at the social worker's desk and sobbed for over an hour before signing papers relinquishing me. She had told social services that she was going to return home to Tennessee.

My eyes filled with tears. For her. For me. For both of us. How difficult it must have been for my young mother to relinquish two babies within two years. I couldn't imagine giving up either of my children and saying goodbye to them forever, never knowing what happened to them. She was young and it seemed she had minimal support going through all of this. *Where was her mother, my grandmother? Was she supportive? Were they talking?*

Reading about my birth mother made me more determined than ever to find her. I desperately wanted to tell her I was okay, that I'd had a good life. I was happy and healthy. She had grandchildren. More than wanting medical information, I wanted to hug her and feel her body next to mine.

I felt an overwhelming sense of gratefulness finally knowing it wasn't just a guess or a hope anymore—my first mother loved me. She loved me enough to have named me. Enough to have cried over relinquishing me. The truth poured over me in a rush of healing warmth.

The last page of my NID was bittersweet. It contained notes from the social worker about when my adopted parents first saw me. The detailed notes from March 1956 said my parents were "accepting of the information given and were eager to see me." It went on to say, "They made up their mind immediately and couldn't wait to take her home but had to wait the perfunctory twenty-four hours, which they did, and then left with the child in her mother's arms to start new lives together."

I couldn't help but cry. It was all so mixed up. I loved my adoptive parents yet I discovered I also loved these ghosts, these strangers who were a part of me. I wondered how I could love people I had never met, but I did. I desperately wanted to call my adoptive parents and tell them what I had found out about myself. I hated keeping this secret from them but I knew I had to, at least for now, if I wanted a relationship with them.

It felt satisfying to finally know some of the truths about where I came from and who I was. I had a Scots-Irish heritage, and crazy as it seemed, I had an aunt and uncle—and a sister!—out there somewhere. Yet, with all this valuable information, I still had no names or birth dates. I didn't know what cities in Tennessee or Alabama my parents were from. That was still a secret.

But maybe not for long. In her last paragraph, Shannon Walker said it was fortunate that I had been born in a Salvation Army hospital, for they were now helping adoptees who had been born in their hospitals find their biological families. She gave me the name and number of a woman who was a Salvation Army caseworker who could help me find my mother.

Chapter Thirteen

MY SALVATION ARMY CASEWORKER'S NAME WAS PHYLLIS. I contacted her by phone the day after I read my NID. She seemed friendly and promptly mailed me an agreement form. Before she could legally begin searching for my birth mother and requesting her medical file from the Booth Memorial Hospital records, she needed my notarized signature.

Phyllis seemed optimistic; she told me to expect her to find my birth mother. My mentor Kathi, however, felt differently about Phyllis. She had worked with her on and off for the past several years and found her difficult, too black and white, and not empathetic enough toward adoptees. She said, "Phyllis is more concerned about protecting birth parents." Kathi tried to warn me, but I was too caught up in the hope of the moment and wanted to trust Phyllis as much as I trusted Dawn and Kathi.

One week after sending Phyllis my notarized agreement, she called while I was in the middle of fixing dinner. I wiped my hands on a dish towel and answered the phone in the kitchen.

"Hi, Diane, it's Phyllis." She sounded chipper. "Do you have a few minutes to talk?"

"Yeah, I've got some time before I have to pick my kids up. What's up?"

"Well, I have some good news. I found your mother right away. She popped right up."

"Oh my gosh. You're kidding me."

Phyllis laughed and said, "No, I'm not kidding you. She was very easy to find."

"I can't believe this. So, she's still alive?" My voice sounded shaky, betraying my hope that her answer was a yes.

"Oh, yes. She's alive."

I shuffled back a few steps until I found a dining chair to sit in. The news was incredible.

"I can't believe how quickly this has happened."

"I'm sure, Diane, that this must come as a big surprise to you but it can happen fast when you have the right information on people. I'm really happy your mother is still alive. It's hard when they're not. This means you have a good chance to connect with her."

"Oh yeah, I think I'm in some sort of shock here. What a relief to know she's alive and that you've found her." I sat still, glued to the dining chair, trying to digest Phyllis's words.

"The next step that will be done is that I'll be sending a letter to your mother, telling her that I'm in contact with someone who is looking for her. I don't mention names or who is looking for her. Sometimes, these mothers don't know what to do when they find out the child they gave up for adoption is looking for them. Some don't want to be found, so we don't tell them right away who's looking for them. The hope is that if I can talk to them, and if they are tentative at first, I can usually ease them into agreeing to making contact. That's our goal. Let's hope your mother answers my letter right away. So . . ." she said, pausing before asking. "Are you ready for this?"

It seemed so sudden. *Didn't I need some more time to process this? I couldn't say no to Phyllis—wasn't I the one who asked her to find my mother? Wasn't this what I wanted?*

"Yes, I'm ready, Phyllis. Let's do this." I took a deep breath. "Let's hope she answers right away."

"Okay, then. I'll send the letter by the end of the week. I'll email you when it's been sent."

I took another deep breath, trying to take this all in.

"Oh, there's one more thing, Diane. I need a short note or letter, just a few paragraphs on one page from you to your mother, so when she calls, I'll read it to her over the phone. Don't make it too deep—we don't want to scare her off. But—do consider that this could be your one chance to say something to her, so write from your heart. Tell her a little about yourself and how you feel about getting in touch with her. Remember, just a few paragraphs on one page."

"Ohhh. You need this when?"

"I'd like to have it at least by next Tuesday so if she calls right away, I can read it to her."

"Okay. I'll work on this and email it to you on Monday."

"Thanks, Diane. Again, I'm happy your mother is alive and that she was such an easy find. Have a nice evening."

I thanked Phyllis for finding my mother. It was surreal to know she was alive, that she was a real person somewhere. Remembering what my NID had said about her returning to Tennessee, I assumed she was living there. It was difficult to imagine that I could be talking to her in a week or so. Despite the long months of waiting, I didn't feel prepared for this sudden success, and I didn't think that writing a few paragraphs would let me express all my feelings.

Over the next few days, I couldn't help but think I already knew my mother and imagined that she would be as elated to hear from me as I would be to hear from my long-lost child. I also understood what Phyllis was saying: the goal was getting her to call and making her feel relaxed enough to make contact with me.

The upcoming weekend we had camping reservations at one of our favorite spots, Camp James, along the stunning Kern River in Sequoia National Park. I decided it would be there, up in the mountains, that I would write my letter to my mother.

I sat on a well-worn wooden picnic bench next to the Kern River. Birds chirped secret messages to each other while woodpeckers kept busy hammering their territories as the wind sang a wild tune through the pine trees. I struggled under the cover of pine bough canopies to find the right words. Nature wasn't acting as my muse that day.

At least half a dozen crumpled pieces of paper lay tossed aside on the old table waiting for their final destination, the trash can. This was hard. *What do I say to this stranger, my mother, in just a few paragraphs? So much was riding on this. I felt pressure to convince her to make contact with me. I needed to plead and beg her in a nice way, but I couldn't come on too strong. Heck, I didn't even know her name.*

Looking up toward the cloudless sky, I closed my eyes and allowed the sun that peeked through the trees to embrace me and warm my face and tanned, bare shoulders. I slowly inhaled the pine scent on the breeze and tried hard to relax. *I just needed to write her how I was feeling in that moment. I needed to tell her this was the most important letter I had ever written*—which was true.

I thanked her for the opportunity to reach out to her after all these years apart and told her who I was. I told her how I found my name at nineteen and that it had always meant a lot knowing she loved me enough to name me. I told her my adoptive parents loved me and gave me a good life. I wrote that I had wondered about her as far back as I could remember and that I had always felt there were pieces of myself missing.

Then, I said that I'd love to have contact with her, of some kind, and if a reunion was possible, I would welcome the opportunity with open arms and a grateful heart. I let her know that if she wasn't ready for this, I'd be disappointed, but would accept her decision, though I would hope that sometime in the future, when the time was right for her, we could one day meet. I decided to sign by the name she'd know me by: Loretta.

Taking a deep breath, I finally felt pleased with what had just poured out of me. *This was it.* I knew it. I was done. Hopefully soon, Phyllis would read this to my mother and she'd be receptive to my words. *The cards were no longer in my hands, but then again, they never were.*

I returned home, ready to embrace whatever lay ahead. I did some calculations: Phyllis had my letter, so she was ready to read it to my mother when she called. Which could be any day now. If she was living in Tennessee, she'd receive the letter within four to five days, which took us to Thursday. Then I thought she might be like me, not always picking up her mail promptly. In that case, it might be a few more days until she received it, so I added another week to my timeline. Then another, because maybe she was out of town, on vacation somewhere, which could last a couple of weeks.

I was trying to give her the time she needed, but after a month went by, I began to feel a heaviness. A sinking feeling, like weights connected to my core. She wasn't calling. *Maybe she didn't get the letter? Maybe it got lost in the mail? Maybe somebody else read the letter and hid it from her?* The truth was I didn't know.

I called and asked Phyllis if there was any way she might have the wrong address.

"Oh no, Diane. I definitely have the current address of your mother. I'm so sorry she hasn't answered yet. Sometimes it takes time for them to build up the courage to call."

"Can you send another letter, but send it certified—to guarantee she receives it?"

"Oh no, I'm sorry. I can't send her another letter for a while now. We just have to be patient and give her time."

That seemed odd.

"Why can't you send another letter for a while? How long will it be until another letter is sent?"

I was surprised by how brusque Phyllis's reply was. "I can't send another letter until after the holidays. It's just too questionable. We don't know what her life is like or what is going on with her. We don't want to make the holidays difficult for her. I won't send another letter until early next year. I'm sorry."

This was early November. I suddenly felt sick to my stomach, frustrated that I was being told I had to wait another two months or more before she sent a second letter. Phyllis sounded as though she didn't care. She sounded distant, maybe even a bit cold, and made it clear she wasn't going to budge on her decision.

I hung up the phone and slumped on the family room couch, pulling a soft cotton quilt around me like a cocoon. I lay there for maybe half an hour, feeling the most disheartened I'd felt since receiving my NID. *There wasn't anything I could do. Phyllis was in control.* I tried to accept it, but my body was heavy with disappointment and grief. *Why did this have to be so difficult?*

Kathi and Dawn were frustrated, too, but not surprised by Phyllis's heel digging. They had several ideas to keep me busy while I waited for the new year. They were going to go over my NID again, digging deeper for any clue that might help us find the city where my mother was from. Kathi suggested I get some maps and look for all the towns close to the military bases associated with the first baby's father. A few days later, I was laying out maps of Tennessee and Alabama on our dining table.

Trying to find where my father was from in Alabama was impossible. There weren't enough clues in my NID and there were too many Stewarts in Alabama, plus I didn't know his first name. I folded the Alabama map up fairly quickly.

I didn't give up on my research, though. Another thing I needed to do on my truth check list was to find out if there really was an Oakland Naval Hospital, as my parents had said. I searched the internet and found that there had been one that opened during World War II (1942), but it was built exclusively for the purpose of treating American military personnel who were wounded in the Pacific theater. Later, it was used for veterans wounded in the Korean and Vietnam Wars. There was no maternity ward.

Kathi told me adoptive parents could pay to take the hospital where their adopted baby had been born off the amended birth certificate, so that must have been what my parents did. It was difficult to imagine my parents had actually paid to hide the name of the hospital where I had been born. It was Booth Memorial Hospital, but there's just a blank space on my certificate, so my parents had free rein to say anything they wanted as long as their fantasy hospital was in Oakland, California.

I had never thought to check on what they had told me until now, but I was coming out of the fog and no longer believed everything they had told me when I was a little girl. It made me sad to think they kept important things about my beginnings to themselves. I was forty-seven years old, and they still had never made an attempt to talk about my birth name or where I had actually been born. *What else did they know and were keeping from me?*

After several attempts to make progress, Kathi and Dawn hit a wall in my search. There just weren't enough clues to let us pinpoint where my mother was born and raised, and presumably, was currently living. They did, however, find photos of an old home once owned by a Douglas family in Nashville. *Had this been my great-grandparents' house?* Maybe, but there was no way to verify it. (It turned out that it was my great-grandparents' place. Kathi and Dawn were great sleuths but we just didn't know it then.)

Frustrated, I decided I needed more help, and from someone other than Phyllis. I began researching a search angel in Tennessee. She had good credentials and a great track record. She was also an adoptee who had found and reunited with her birth family. I liked that. I called her one evening at the number listed on her website. Her name was Deborah.

I cleared my throat while her phone rang.

"Hello," said a strong, husky woman's voice on the other end. I introduced myself and told her where I was in my search, which didn't seem to deter her.

"Oh, I think I can help you," Deborah said, encouragingly. "I have access to records, and for those that I don't, I know people who do. But I just want to say it's going to take some time since we don't know your mother's first name. If only we had that, that would make a huge difference. I'm not saying it's impossible, just that it's going to take some time to go through things."

"That's all I have," I said, feeling my shoulders slump.

"Don't worry about paying me. You pay me when I find your mother." This was another thing I liked about Deborah. She didn't sound scammy. If she didn't find my birth mother, I didn't pay her. She had incentive yet her price was reasonable. I signed on with her that night. I had to keep moving forward on this. More waiting around wasn't for me.

Deborah would keep me updated on her end of my search. She could access Tennessee records and knew the land, the culture, and the people. I felt encouraged, strengthened, and renewed with hope again.

I put away my binders and maps and decided to concentrate on my family and the upcoming holidays. I'd fill my life with the family I had and had created, holding them tight to reassure them that I was their mother. That we would always be family. There wasn't anything more I could do but wait and hope.

Chapter Fourteen

IT FELT STRANGE SITTING IN MY PARENTS' LIVING ROOM that Christmas in 2003, wincing as I sipped on my father's annual Scotch whiskey eggnog. I was observing more than participating, giving Heather and Travis center stage, since the family relationship now revolved around the grandchildren, which was just fine with me. At the ages of sixteen and fourteen, the kids were old enough to grasp some of the things I was going through and knew not to say certain things to their grandparents. We had boundaries. And the less the spotlight shone on Michael and me, the better off we all were.

As I nestled into my favorite spot on the overstuffed yellow-and-white floral couch, tucking my bare feet underneath my legs, I couldn't help but wonder what my parents might think if they knew I had begun searching for my biological family. *Did they know what I now knew from my NID? Did they know my parents were from Tennessee and Alabama and the reason my birth mother relinquished me? Did they know the same story about her that I knew—that she followed my father to California and that they might have been married?*

Feeling the warmth and the relaxing effect of the spirited eggnog, I couldn't help but feel a bit smug about my secret endeavor. I was proud for attempting this search. It was all mine, and something good I was doing for myself. I knew my parents would never have approved, and if they ever knew, I'd be punished in some drastic way. My searching for blood connection would be considered a betrayal. After all, as many adoptees testify, adoptive parents often expect us to be grateful for all they'd done for us, for all their sacrifices. I certainly felt that was true in our family. They'd made my life better and lifted me out of whatever dire circumstances I was supposedly born into. I should be thankful.

And I was thankful. But I doubted that my parents could ever understand how I could love them and also love others, especially people I didn't know. Two different things that seem contradictory on the surface can be simultaneously true. As hard as I tried, I wasn't able to fit my quest and feelings into a nice, tightly fitted box. The situation was too big and too complicated.

I looked over at my teenaged children, laughing with their grandparents. My mother, dressed in black pants and a red silk shirt, enhanced by pearls around her neck, looked as smart as ever. Her perfectly coiffed ash blonde hair and minimal makeup mixed beautifully with her signature red lipstick; it was inspiring to see a woman in her eighties looking so stylish. My dad was more relaxed, wearing slippers and an L.L.Bean flannel shirt, smiling robustly at the kids with a twinkle in his blue eyes.

It was clear that my parents had been wrong to worry about losing their relationship with their only grandchildren years ago. They'd worried that when Heather and Travis recognized they weren't blood-related to my parents, they'd love Michael's parents more, but Heather and Travis adored my parents. Love has no limits in our family, regardless of what my mother and father thought.

I still longed to tell them about my search, but I was afraid of their reaction. Whatever happened on the journey to finding my biological family had to be kept secret. Even with all our struggles, I couldn't bear to lose them. After all, I had already lost my first parents. Family can be complicated, and ours certainly was no exception. Michael, Heather, and Travis knew what might be at stake if we didn't keep my search a secret. I convinced all of us that what my parents didn't know wouldn't hurt them.

That Christmas Day, I finished the eggnog and joined in the fun with my parents, Michael, and the kids. Dave and Joanne, and their two daughters, Caroline and Catherine, were stopping by later that afternoon for appetizers and a gift exchange. I had to keep my searching a secret from Joanne too. She wouldn't understand and I suspected she'd be on my mother's side, not mine, if it came down to taking sides. She was protective of my mother, always acting like I was the enemy or something. Joanne was under my mother's spell; she surely was the daughter my mother always wanted, and I could never top her in my mother's eyes. *Why should I even try to be close to her anymore?* It could only backfire on me—I was sure they talked about me behind my back, wondering what foolish thing I was doing or complaining about how irresponsible I was with this or that.

New Year's Day 2004 came and went. I was hopeful Phyllis could finally send my birth mother another letter. I didn't want to come off as pushy, so I forced myself to wait until the second week of January to email Phyllis, asking when she planned to send the second letter.

Once again the phone rang when I was fixing dinner. Recognizing Phyllis's number, I answered.

"Hi, Phyllis. I saw your number pop up on my phone. How are you?"

"I'm good, thanks. Busy as usual. I received your email this morning about sending a second letter. I thought I'd call you instead of writing. I'm sorry, Diane, but we still can't send another letter just yet. It's just too soon."

My heart dropped. "Really? I'm curious as to why it's too soon."

"Isn't your birthday coming up this month?"

"Yes, next week. Why?"

"Well, we don't want to upset your mother around your birth date because that could be a trigger for her, causing difficulty. The thing is, we just don't know what's going on in her life." She continued, "We don't want to provoke her or upset her, so, I'm sorry, we're just going to have to wait a little bit longer."

I couldn't believe what I was hearing. My heart pounded like Native drums announcing war. I hung up the phone, sounding short with Phyllis, but I didn't care. I was angry. I had no control in this situation. Intellectually, I understood what Phyllis was saying, but emotionally, it was hard to wait. It felt endless. The whole search seemed to be drifting toward a black hole somewhere in outer space.

Nothing was happening on Deborah's end either. She had hit a wall. With no first name or birth date to go on, it seemed she was doomed to failure.

I now had no choice but to wait for whenever Phyllis felt the time was right. It was all up to her. She held the keys to the puzzle to which I only had a few loose pieces.

Three weeks after my birthday, on February 9, Phyllis shot me an email saying she'd mailed the second letter. Maybe this time I'd be lucky and my mother would answer, but I didn't hold out much hope this round. I'd been here before.

It was early Friday evening, about six o'clock on February 13, when the house phone rang. Why was Phyllis calling so late? I picked up the phone and walked into the living room to have some privacy.

"Hello, Phyllis," I said, answering the call, while wiping wet hands on a dish towel.

"Hi, Diane," Phyllis said, her tone whimsical. "Do you have a minute? Are you busy?"

"I'm fine. I can talk. What's up?"

"Well, I have some news for you."

"You do?" My heart skipped a beat.

"I do. I just got off the phone with Frances. She received your second letter and called me right away."

"Oh my goodness. Wait. Are you saying my mother called? Who's Frances? Is that her name?"

"Oh, you didn't know your mother's name? I thought you knew it. Her name is Frances, and I just got off the phone with her."

"Oh geez. I can't believe this! She called?"

"She finally called. We talked for the past hour. She's a nice woman, Diane."

"I can't believe this. She finally called. Wow." I sat down on the couch, feeling numb. I couldn't think straight. *She's alive.*

"She said she received the first letter in October but wasn't sure what to do about it. When she received the second letter, she said she became concerned that someone might have a medical issue. Between you and me, I think she just needed time to build up courage to call and the second letter prompted her to do it."

"Oh, so she did receive the first letter. That's interesting." I thought how she chose not to call the first time around and felt a twinge of disappointment. "So, how does she sound? What happened?"

"Well, she's soft-spoken and was nervous at first. She still has her Tennessee accent. Here's some news, Diane—she never went back to Tennessee after you were born. She lives in California."

"What? Where?" I was shocked. She was here, living in California. *All this time. All my life.*

"Yes. She lives where she's always lived." I could tell that Phyllis wasn't going to give me any more clues than that.

"That's something she never went back home and stayed here. Is she married? Was she surprised to hear from me?" I had so many questions.

Phyllis sighed deeply, then said, "She sounds like she's had a hard life. It hasn't been easy for her. She was married for many years, but she's now divorced. And yes, she was surprised to hear from you, but she was really glad too. I read her your letter, and she became very emotional while I read it to her."

"Oh, she did?" I took that as a sign that she cared, at least a little anyway.

"She sounded very excited to know you had children. She said your daughter is her only granddaughter."

"Oh, really?"

"Yes. She said she has five grandsons, six including your son, and then your daughter is her seventh grandchild, her only granddaughter. She raised four children, one son and three daughters, with her husband, and then she reunited with your older sister. So that means you have five half-siblings."

I have more siblings. This is incredible to hear but too much for my mind to take in now. I'll have to think about all this later.

Another deep sigh from Phyllis. "Your mother said she was sorry but she didn't think she could handle a family reunion. I guess your older sister made contact with her years ago and met the children she'd raised. She said her children had a difficult time accepting her, and it was hard on your mother. Everything is better now between everyone but she doesn't think she could go through something like that again. But she wants to communicate with you, see pictures of you and your children. She's willing to answer any questions you might have, but as far as reuniting with her and her children, that seems to be a no—for now, at least."

She doesn't want to meet me.

My heart dropped. It fell through the floor, into the hard earth and beyond, until it reached the darkness of another world, a black hole. Hope for the reunion I'd always imagined disappeared.

"Oh," was all that came out of my mouth.

"I know this sounds disappointing, but you have to remember, this is just the first call. She's scared. You never know what can happen over time. You both need time to get to know one another. The good thing is that she's willing to get to know you."

I didn't expect my birth mother to not want to meet me.

"Yes," I answered slowly, sounding like an automaton. "At least there's that. What do I do? What happens next? Did you give her my phone number? Did she give you hers? When can I talk to her?"

"Don't worry. I've got all her information for contact. So, per our contract, you can start by writing her a short letter. Let's say two pages, telling her a little more about yourself. You can send pictures, but no more than five. We don't want to overwhelm her. When she receives your letter, we'll wait for her to respond, and when she does, I'll forward it to you and you can write her another one. We'll do this, like let's say, one letter a month for about six months or so, and then we'll see how things are. If you both seem willing and if everything seems okay between you, you can move forward with direct contact."

"Wait. What? I can't just write her myself or call her? I can only send her one letter a month? I don't understand."

"That's how our contract works. We don't want to overwhelm the found party. Relationships that have been lost or strained over decades take time to heal; it takes people a while to accept and readjust to each other. It'll go by more quickly than you think."

"I guess I don't remember seeing that in writing before. So I can write her a letter and send some pictures of my family, then send them to you to mail to her?" I was trying to wrap my mind around how all this could work while managing the bitter disappointment of having to wait even longer. *I feel I'm being treated like a child, not being allowed to contact her myself to hear her voice and get to know her. My mother.*

"Yes. I'll mail your letter to her as soon as I receive it. I know she'll be thrilled to hear from you and to see photos of you and your family. She really is happy you reached out and found her, Diane. I think, given time, things will be very good between the two of you."

Haven't I waited long enough?

After Phyllis and I hung up, I sat on the couch stewing. It seemed crazy. I couldn't believe she was preventing me from talking to my mother and hearing her voice. It was cruel to make me wait months longer. And I wondered, *Did my birth mother want this continued secrecy too?*

I sat down at the computer and wrote an email to my support group telling them what had just occurred. Kathi wanted to call me.

"Hi, Kathi. It's pretty upsetting." I rubbed the back of my neck, which seemed to be stiffening by the minute.

"Sadly, I'm not surprised. This is the Salvation Army. They do good work finding people but then they're cautious about reunions. I think it's hurtful to the adoptee and to the birth mother who wants contact with her child, but you have no say in this. Phyllis is not going to budge; she goes by the book. That's why I was hoping we could find your mother independent of their help."

"Tell me everything she told you about your mother and maybe with some new clues we can find her ourselves. We'll start working on it tonight. And don't give up hope of reuniting with your mother. I agree with Phyllis on this much: your mother is scared. You need to meet her, and don't lose hope of meeting siblings and cousins later on. But first things first. At least she's open to connecting with you, and right now, we need to make that happen as soon as we can."

Her words helped to put everything into perspective and gave me a taste of hope that we could do something about all this. I felt better, although I hated being at the mercy of Phyllis's control and her assessment of the relationship with my mother. It didn't seem right or fair, to either me or my mother, to be forced to wait so long to speak or meet, though intellectually I understood why Frances would proceed with caution.

Frances—that's her name. Frances.

Two hours later, Kathi and Dawn had found a Frances Grace Campbell living in San Francisco. She was divorced, and had given birth to a son and three daughters in the Bay Area, with their mother's maiden name of Douglas.

The key to confirming that this was my mother was discovering where Frances Grace Campbell had been born. This was where my searcher, Deborah, came into play. She had the task of finding out if this particular Frances Douglas Campbell had been born in Tennessee. With help from other searchers she knew in Tennessee, Deborah said she'd have an answer the very next day.

Michael, Heather, and Travis were surprised, like me, that my mother had finally made contact. We sat as a family that evening in our spa, trying to relax, yet take in the moment under the winter sky, looking up at the stars wondering how this journey would go, and feeling grateful to be closer to the truth.

At about ten that night, my support group emailed, telling me they thought they had found my mother's sister, a woman by the name of Vivian Tagaloa. She had eight children, most of whom were also born in the Bay Area. Her maiden name was Douglas but her married surname suggested she had married someone Polynesian.

"Ha!" I laughed out loud, thinking of the cousin we tried to locate through the California Birth Index, the one who had been born a couple of months before me—we would've never considered her a blood relative because of her surname. I never gave serious thought to investigate Nalani Kaimana Tagaloa, but here she was.

It was all too much to process this evening's news. I felt overwhelmed with so many different feelings and I needed time to sort through it all. I was riding a roller coaster of emotions.

The odds were in my favor, though. We knew her address and her phone number. I could make contact on my own. I didn't need Phyllis anymore. Tomorrow, Deborah would let us all know whether this was my mother or not. If it was, a long-locked door would open, finally revealing a new path.

Sleep was impossible that night. I tried calming myself with chamomile tea and a hot shower, but nothing worked. I was too excited. Eventually, after midnight, I fell asleep visualizing how it might be to meet my mother in person.

Chapter Fifteen

DEBORAH CALLED THE NEXT MORNING ON MY CELL PHONE. I was at the day spa where I worked part-time on Saturdays as a receptionist. I will never forget the two words she said that told me we had found my birth mother: "Tennessee social."

I called Deborah several hours later when I got home. It had been difficult to concentrate at work that morning. I think I told everyone who came in what had happened overnight and that morning. I was flying high. Everything in the world seemed wonderful that day.

That afternoon, Deborah encouraged me, as did Kathi and Dawn, to move forward without Phyllis at the helm of my reunion. She offered to call my mother the next morning.

"I can chat with her, Tennessean to Tennessean," Deborah said. "I've done this many times before with other clients and I'm confident I can soothe any fear your mother might have. I know how she grew up. I know her people. I think it'll be better if I test the waters and call her, explaining why we want to move forward without Phyllis and the involvement with the Salvation Army, rather than you cold-calling her. Just my opinion, Diane. What do you think?"

"I think that sounds like a good idea. It'll probably be good to see how she responds and find out how she feels about this from her end. As much as I'm nervous about it and afraid I might not get to hear her voice, I trust you and have faith it will all go well and that she'll understand, and maybe even agree that it's too hard to wait another six months to speak with each other. Thank you, Deborah."

"Yeah, the good thing in our favor is that we know she wants contact with you. That's a great sign."

"Yes." I nodded my head and thought how fortunate I was that Frances was open to knowing me.

Sounding animated, Deborah added, "I think we should have a plan this week. After I call your mother tomorrow morning—and I'm thinking positive she'll be receptive—I'm going to text you two words—'send flowers'—and then you'll know she's open to hearing from you directly."

I laughed a little, and said, "I love it. You think I should send her flowers?"

"If it goes like I think it will, I most definitely think you should. Order and send them Monday. Then, mail her that letter with those five photographs you were going to send to Phyllis. I'll tell her you'll be sending her a letter with family photos, and after she gets them, she can call you directly. How does that sound?"

"Oh wow." I raised both arms over my head and took a deep breath. "Is this really happening?"

"I think it is, Diane. Get ready."

After we hung up, I grabbed a fleece blanket and wrapped myself with its softness and warmth. I sat outside on the patio, in the stillness of the winter afternoon, listening to the wind whistle through the pine trees on our back hill. The crisp air felt good on my cheeks while I reflected on how fast things were happening. *It was only yesterday that Phyllis and Frances made contact. And now I know where she lives, where she has always lived, all my life.*

I had only one worry about tomorrow—that my mother, Frances, might not react well to Deborah calling her. The fear unfolded inside me, fear that I might never get the opportunity to hear her voice. But I couldn't go where these thoughts wanted to take me. Instead, I made the decision to trust Deborah, and the process, and that this journey was unfolding just as it was supposed to.

I called my good friend and neighbor Lynne, who lived across the street. Throughout my search journey, we had spent many a night in her backyard spa drinking wine and talking about the what-ifs along the road.

"Heat up the spa, Lynne. No wine tonight—instead, I'm bringing champagne. We found my mother."

The next morning Deborah texted, "send flowers."

I looked over at Michael, Heather, and Travis. We were watching some show on TV when I heard the chime on my phone signaling a message.

"Deborah just texted 'send flowers.'"

All three of them jumped on me at once, giving hugs with joy. Wide smiles of happiness. It felt surreal.

Deborah said the phone call went well. My mother, Frances, answered her phone right away, recognizing a Tennessee area code. I got a chuckle out of that. Initially, Deborah said, she was surprised to know we had found her and was caught off guard by that, but settled into the conversation easily and ended up really opening up to Deborah, talking for over an hour.

"Your older sister, who was also relinquished, works in the Bay Area. She's been in reunion with your mother and siblings for nearly fifteen years. I guess they're pretty close now."

My four half-siblings my mother raised with her husband of

nearly twenty years all lived in or around the surrounding Bay Area as well. I had a few first cousins still living there, and some in Alaska, Hawaii, and American Samoa.

Yes, my aunt Vivian had married a Samoan man. She'd had nine children, eight with her husband, and one, her ninth child, with another Samoan man after her divorce. That baby had been relinquished at birth, and like my older sister, had found and met the family years before me. Unfortunately, my aunt Vivian had passed away in 1972.

Deborah added to her story, in her charming, southern voice, "I liked your mother, but she's had a tough life. She's also a strong woman, Diane. I think you both will be just fine. Just remember to take it slow. It might take your mother a while, but I think in time she'll come around to wanting to meet you and introducing you to her family."

I was thrilled. And amazed to think we'd be talking to each other soon, that I'd be able to hear my mother's voice, maybe by the end of the week. I was so overflowing with excitement and gratitude that it was hard to concentrate on anything else that day.

That evening, I sat at the dining table and composed a short letter to my mother. I still didn't know how to address the letter even now that I knew her name. *Do I call her "Mother"?* That seemed uncomfortable; even though she was my mother, she also wasn't. And calling her Frances didn't seem quite right either. I decided to address the letter formally—"Dear Mother." I needed to ask her what she preferred when we spoke.

Meanwhile, I wasn't sure what *I* wanted to do. I was comfortable writing "mother" to Frances, but not saying it verbally. I already had a mother and felt that calling Frances "mother" in person was a betrayal of my mom. Even though both were my mothers, my adoptive mom was the one who deserved the title all these years. For now, I put the question aside.

I had purchased a specific black pen and cream-colored linen stationery to write Frances. Michael printed out five photographs: me as a baby, a photo from when I was four years old, my senior high school portrait, and me on my wedding day, along with one of Michael, Heather, Travis, and me. The photos seemed just right to pique her curiosity for more.

After dropping Heather and Travis off at school Monday morning, I mailed the letter. It was a big moment watching the letter drop down into the mailbox to begin its journey to my biological mother's home. This time, I signed it "Diane." She'd have to know me by my amended name now, which made me wonder what she'd think of that. In her mind all these years, she knew me as Loretta.

I also ordered pink tulips to be delivered that afternoon. We were on our way. The plan was in the works. I only had to wait for her call. Deborah was more than confident she'd call so I just went with it. No worries. I enjoyed the high I was on, anticipating my mother's voice.

On Wednesday evening, February 18, I heard the phone ring and I recognized the number. It was seven o'clock sharp. She must have waited to call after the dinner hour was over. I took the phone into the dark living room. Michael was in the shower and both kids were doing homework in their rooms. I was alone for this moment.

"Hello," I answered tentatively, taking a deep breath. I wanted to be mindful, to be present, hearing her voice for the first time. I wondered if hearing her would bring a deep-seated, familiar memory to my consciousness from when I was a newborn in her arms.

"Hello, is this Diane?"

Oh my gosh. This is her.

Her voice was sweet, soft, and slow. She had a definite Southern drawl.

"Yes, this is Diane." My heart began pounding louder and louder.

"Oh, hi, Diane. This is Frances, your birth mother."

Amazingly, she sounded calm and comfortable while my nerves and heart were singing.

"Thank you for the beautiful flowers. I love tulips," Frances exclaimed, sounding excited. "I got your letter today with the lovely pictures of you and your family. Your children are beautiful. I cried seeing the pictures of you as a baby and little girl, especially the one of you at four years old. You look so much like your father in that photo."

My father, the invisible parent. I hadn't ever considered that I might look like him. I always thought I'd favor my mother. I loved hearing that she cried seeing my pictures when I was little. That tugged at my heart.

"I'm so glad you liked the flowers and my letter." I was tongue-tied, pacing back and forth in the living room, unable to sit down.

"Diane, I hope you know I have always loved you and wondered about you all your life. I never wanted to relinquish you, but under the circumstances, I wasn't able to keep you. It broke my heart. I had no job, and I wasn't married. In those days, you couldn't keep a baby like you can today. My best hope for you was letting you be adopted by a family that could provide for you, something I wasn't able to do. I hope you're not angry with me. I did the best I could for you under the circumstances. I hope you understand."

I sat down on the couch and took a deep breath to take in everything she just said. Her confession went beyond my expectations and placed a healing salve upon my wounded heart. Her words were just what I needed.

We spoke for an hour. I was so nervous, but every minute became easier as I slowly floated back down to earth from the clouds. It wasn't too long or too short. I didn't ask too many questions. Questions could come later. I was trying to take these moments with her slowly and not scare her off. It's strange to think of scaring your mother off. I couldn't imagine not wanting to know a child I had given up for adoption. I followed her lead that night and kept things light. It was awkward not having a template for how to interact in a situation like this. *My mother is a total stranger to me.*

When we said goodbye, she told me, "I love you, Diane."

I was surprised by her immediate, open display of affection. I was so used to my parents, who rarely told me they loved me. They wrote it in cards, but I wasn't used to hearing these words out loud from a parent figure.

I answered back, "I love you too."

I slept like a baby that night, with a deep sense of relief. After a lifetime of wondering and over a year of searching, I had heard my mother's voice—again. I knew her name and how she felt about me. Something I'd yearned for all my life.

Frances promised to send me a photo of herself the next day. I couldn't wait to see what she looked like.

Three days later, the card arrived. Seeing her handwriting for the first time, I gently placed my forefinger over her writing and traced her lettering. How similar our handwriting was. More proof we were related.

Gingerly, I opened the envelope and pulled out a bright, multicolored floral card. Inside, she had written a short but sweet note saying how happy she was that I had searched for her and she looked forward to getting to know me and my family. I loved her kind words, but the piéce de résistance was the photograph. I stood still in the kitchen, mesmerized, staring at her image for what seemed like ages. *This is amazing. I think I may look similar to her but I'm not sure.*

Just then, the phone rang. It was my friend and neighbor Mary.

"Mary, you won't believe this but I just picked up the mail and got a letter from Frances. It has her picture."

"Well, bring it over! I want to see."

Ten minutes later, I was sitting at Mary's kitchen table. I let her open the envelope.

She gasped and said, "Oh, Diane! It's your mother!"

I nodded my head, then took a sip of Mary's always perfect latte. "Yup. I know. There's definitely some resemblance going on, don't you think? I can't believe I'm seeing her."

"There's definitely some resemblance between you." Mary looked at me with tears in her brown eyes. *I love that Mary knows how much this search means to me.*

Then Mary added, "But I'd like to know what the heck is going on around her." She giggled and we both started laughing.

It was a good question.

"Diane, do you think this is her apartment?" Mary asked.

"I don't know. But she looks like she's getting ready to go to a Christmas party, doesn't she?"

"Oh yeah. That's it. Look, there's a wrapped Christmas present by her feet."

We looked at each other and laughed again.

Then we pored over every detail, all of the knickknacks surrounding her. There were vases, books, wrapping paper, lotion bottles, feathers, and all sorts of jewelry on a high-top dresser. There was a *Mona Lisa* painting hanging crookedly on the wall above the dresser. There was so much going on. I got a kick out of the fact that this was the one photo she decided to send me.

She wasn't the little, Southern grandmother I had envisioned, dressed in a flowered-print, cotton shirt dress with black flats and pearls with white hair combed into a simple bob. She was also not the fantasy mother I dreamed about, who wore Ann Taylor suits and carried a leather envelope purse.

Frances did look good. She had written that this photo had been taken a couple of years earlier when she was seventy years old. You could tell she had been quite attractive in her younger years. She stood in the doorway with one hand on her hip and a pretty smile on her face. She looked tall, statuesque even, with a full, hourglass figure. She had on black slacks and a red silk-like blouse, with medium black heels. We noticed she had painted her nails bright red, and wore makeup topped off with red lipstick. Her dark red hair was cut pixie short and adorned by large, gold hoop earrings. *This is my mother.*

"She's not what I expected," I said to Mary. I took another sip of coffee and shook my head.

Mary got up from the pine table to refresh our mugs and said, "You know that fantasy you had of your birth mother walking in a hotel lobby wearing Ann Taylor? Well, that's your mom, Diane. Your fantasy mother is your mom, not Frances."

She was right. My adoptive mother would wear Ann Taylor.

As far back as I could remember, I'd wondered if I might be related to people who resembled me, whether I saw them at a grocery store, the mall, a doctor's office, on television, or at an airport. I didn't have to wonder anymore. I had answers now. Here was my mother, who reflected, like a mirror, our shared history and roots. Years of yearning and wondering, shame and confusion—over. This moment, with the phone call, the photograph, and the letter, was healing. It was a new beginning.

Chapter Sixteen

I WOKE UP TO THE SUN RISING OVER THE OAKLAND HILLS. The down comforter had enveloped me like a cocoon during the night. Surprisingly, I had slept hard, like a rock. I looked past the glass sliding door onto the balcony that beckoned me to arise, for today was the day. It was Saturday, April 24, 2004, the day I would finally meet my first mother, Frances.

Opening the slider allowed a gust of cool ocean air into the room. Seagulls, hovering on a wind current above me, squawked loudly. I stood stretching on the balcony of the Hyatt Regency San Francisco, looking at the view. Rooftops in assorted colors and shapes looked like a giant's stepping stones, paving the way to the renowned Fisherman's Wharf and the sparkling bay beyond. The sky was clear and the city was beginning to hum. It was destined to be a beautiful day.

I called for room service, requesting eggs Benedict and a pot of coffee. Looking over at the clock, I was pleased to have three hours to get ready before Frances arrived at eleven. Plenty of time to prepare and not feel rushed.

I had prepared for this trip for weeks, planning every detail in my mind. We had decided to meet at the hotel where I'd be staying because Frances didn't drive and it would be easier for her to meet me there. I wanted it to be special, so I reserved a club-level room with a bay view and balcony.

Frances and I had spoken on the phone more than a half dozen times over the past two months, slowing getting to know each other a bit more before our reunion. It made me happy she was feeling more comfortable. We no longer needed Phyllis to intervene in our relationship. I wrote Phyllis after Deborah gave the green light to move ahead with Frances. I let her know that through my online support group and private searcher I had been able to locate and make contact with Frances and that both of us were happy and comfortable getting to know each other now. Phyllis said she understood, and Frances and I moved forward.

Once we settled on a date to meet, I started reading as much as I could about adoptee reunions: what to do and what not to do, what to expect and what not to expect. I felt as prepared as I could for this day but it was still hard not to feel nervous.

An hour later, while I was finishing up breakfast, Frances called.

"Hello, Diane, I'm so sorry." She was breathless and sounded nervous. Her voice was shaky.

"Hi, Frances," I said, concerned she might tell me she was going to cancel. I held my breath and closed my eyes hoping that wouldn't happen.

"I'm so sorry but I'm having trouble getting ready this morning." She sounded as if she'd been crying.

"Are you feeling okay?" I winced. *Please don't cancel on me.*

"Oh, yes. I think I'm just nervous." She paused.

"I understand. I'm pretty nervous, too, but I'm sure we'll be okay once we see each other."

"Yes. I think you may be right. I think I need more time to get ready. Can we meet a little later, say at twelve o'clock?"

"Sure. We can push it back another hour. That'll be just fine," I answered, feeling relieved and able to breathe again.

"Thank you, Diane. I just need some more time."

"That's okay. Did you still want to meet in the lobby?"

"Oh, yes. I should probably tell you I'll be coming on the BART [Bay Area Rapid Transit]. There's an entrance from the BART that goes directly into the hotel lobby so maybe we could meet near there?"

"Perfect. I'll see you soon."

"Thank you. Love you." I wasn't sure I'd ever get used to hearing her say those words to me.

Frances. That's what she wanted me to call her. She told me that when I write to her, I could put "Mom" in parentheses after her name. She said that's what my older sister Stephanie had done for years, and it seemed to work well.

"I know you have a mother already. Even though I'm your mother, too, your mother raised you and I know that's what you call her, so just call me Frances."

So, that's what I called her: Frances. My first mother was now my second.

I pictured Frances at home preparing to meet me—again. I imagined the last time she had seen me was as a newborn. A lifetime away for both of us. Memories that had lain dormant for decades might be resurfacing as she reflected on that moment.

I was a reminder of a past she had been forced to forget, but now had to remember. Here I was, back in her life. My mere presence probably caused her subconscious to pull up memories of my father, her grief, her shame, and her loss. I guessed these were bubbling to the surface as she got dressed, getting ready to meet me.

I felt for her. Today, I wanted her to see that I was happy, that I had lived a good life. I wanted to relieve the hurt and shame she had buried long ago. I wanted her to feel better. Maybe I wanted to feel better too. Perhaps I was trying to convince us both that my being adopted had turned out okay, after all, that it had been bearable for both of us. Even though we both had experienced trauma from our separation, we had survived, and hey, here we were—together again against all odds. We had endured. The celebration would, of course, be tinged with sadness as well. It was sad for both of us, because we had spent our lifetimes apart from each other, and no matter how well this meeting went, we couldn't fix the past. Nobody could.

It was time. I looked around the room. The bed was made, and the room picked up. The eucalyptus-lavender candle I had brought sat on the nightstand, ready to be lit. The CD player waited atop the hotel dresser, ready for me to push PLAY. Soon Andrea Bocelli's *Romanza* album would fill the air, together with the candle's warm scent, hopefully calming our nerves and helping our senses hold this moment.

A small, navy blue photo album wrapped with silver ribbon lay on the small table awaiting Frances. I'd made the album for her, filling it with photographs from my childhood. I thought that Frances might have had fantasies about my life, just as I had about hers. Since she never saw me again after I was two weeks old, she might want to see what I looked like as a four-month-old, a six-month-old, a toddler, and even as an older child and teenager. She seemed just as curious about my adoptive parents as I was about my siblings, so I also included a few snapshots of my adoptive parents and my brother John. I also had some photos of Michael, Heather, and Travis, as well as a poem I had written about her when I was sixteen.

I took one last look at the photograph Frances had sent me

two months earlier. Just one more look to be sure who it was I'd be looking for downstairs. I was fairly confident I'd recognize my mother right away. I wanted to believe that.

It was time to go. I placed Frances's photograph on the nightstand, grabbed my room card, and took one last look around, and at myself in the mirror. I saw my children in my reflection and wondered—after meeting my mother in person, would I now see her in my reflection as well?

I slowly closed the door, knowing that the next time I stepped over the threshold to this room, my mother would be beside me.

Chapter Seventeen

IN THE LOBBY OF THE HOTEL, I DECIDED TO SIT IN A burgundy Queen Anne chair with wings like arms that hugged me as I waited to greet my mother. My spot was perfect. It was about twenty-five feet from the BART escalator. I'd have the advantage of seeing her before she'd see me. My heart skipped a beat just thinking about that moment. You couldn't tell from my outward, seemingly calm reserve that, inside, my cells were screaming with anticipation.

The lobby of the San Francisco Hyatt Regency was huge with a view of all the floors. On the main floor of the lobby was a restaurant, bar, and lounge complete with a dance floor. Someone was playing the piano near the bar, its notes echoing through the air. There were so many people here. I wondered how it could be so busy, but then, it was spring in San Francisco.

I took a few deep breaths to relax while I wondered if anyone would notice my mother and me embracing when we met. I hoped Frances wouldn't scream or make a spectacle. I didn't want that, but I did want an embrace. I wished we could've met somewhere more private than this bustling hotel lobby.

More than thirty minutes passed and Frances had not arrived. My stomach was beginning to knot up.

I was fidgety, crossing and uncrossing my legs as if movement would make time pass faster. I couldn't sit still and decided to walk to the escalator. I looked down the steep moving steps, and amid a crowd of people coming up, I saw a woman standing on the landing with her back to me hovering over a trash can. She was sorting through several bags. I seemed to recognize her body and how she moved as she shuffled through her bags. She seemed familiar.

Then I registered her short red hair. *Oh my God. That's her.* Gasping, realizing this really was her, and how close she was, I backed away. I didn't want to meet her as soon as she got off the escalator. I hurried back to where I'd been sitting and sat down on the soft cushion. My heart was racing and I felt annoyed with myself for walking over to the escalator knowing that now I'd have the memory of seeing my mother for the first time hovering over a trash can.

I was supposed to see her first as she was now, walking toward me, a tall, shapely woman with short, spiky red hair, carrying a bouquet of baby-pink roses and two large cloth tote bags. She wore an orange rayon blouse over a red tank top. Long, sparkly orange beads hung loosely around her neck and gold hoop earrings dangled and danced with her body as she walked. A well-worn brown leather satchel hung across her chest. Her pants were black as were her sturdy shoes.

She's so bright. Bright, tall, and a bit disheveled. So this is the woman who brought me into this world and with whom I share half my genetic code and history.

Frances.

As I stood up, the lobby and people around me disappeared. It was now only Frances and me. Time stood still as she dropped her bags on the carpet in front of me in a rush, somehow keeping the flowers in her grip. Like a mother bear, or a mother who hadn't seen her child in far too long, she pressed her lips against mine, kissed me hard, and taking me into her arms, held me tight. I was under her spell, wrapped up beside her body as I was the last time she held me, when she was my everything.

Frances let go and took a step back to look at me, still holding the bouquet.

"It's so good to see you, Diane," Frances said, breathlessly.

"Oh, it's so good to see you too!" I smiled, looking into her green eyes, trying to catch a glimpse of her soul, our connection, or maybe, from somewhere deep inside myself, a memory.

"Oh!" Frances said excitedly. "You look just like your father." She seemed surprised.

I was also. *My father—I hadn't been thinking about him, just her.* "I do?"

"Yes, you do," as she nodded her head, smiling. I could see tears gathering in her eyes, and I noticed her hands were shaking.

"Why don't we go up to my room? We can relax, have some coffee and some privacy?"

Frances nodded in agreement and smiled sweetly. "Oh, these are for you." She handed me the pink roses, which smelled heavenly. I thanked her and picked one of her bags off the floor to carry. I wondered what she brought. I held the bag and roses in one hand as she held my other. Our hands nested perfectly.

The glass elevators of the Hyatt looked like rocket jets lifting us to the sky as it silently carried us to the club level and my room. Frances and I stood in the corner of the crowded elevator, holding hands. Standing so close, I had a chance to quickly study her.

Her hair was a different color than mine, but the texture seemed the same. Her skin was beautiful—she hardly had any lines or wrinkles, and she was very fair, much fairer than I. She smelled of Ivory soap. Her makeup was old school—turquoise eye shadow and red lipstick, probably favorites from years gone by. She was still attractive for her seventy-two years, and you could tell that when she was young, she had been quite pretty. Frances caught me staring at her. She smiled and squeezed my hand. Our day had begun.

Once in the hotel room, Frances found her spot at the small table. I was busy setting the scene for us: lighting the candle, opening the slider for fresh air, placing the roses in water in the ice bucket, and hitting the PLAY button for Andrea Bocelli. I called room service for a platter of fresh fruit, cheese and crackers, and coffee service for two.

"Oh, is this for me?" Frances asked, holding up the photo album.

"Yes, it is! I made that for you. I thought you'd like to see a bit of my life that you missed."

I hoped I wasn't too presumptuous and that it wouldn't be hard for her.

"This is lovely, Diane." Frances paged through the photos, a smile on her face. She pointed to one in particular and said, "You look like your father here. You seem to favor him more than me."

"Oh, really?" I brushed my hair from my face, wondering why she saw more of him in me than herself.

She was looking intently at a photo with my parents holding me as a toddler. "Your adoptive parents were both very attractive, especially your mother. I like seeing pictures of them, seeing the people that raised my baby." She looked up. There was a sadness surrounding her as she claimed me. Her baby. "I'll look at these photos at home. Thank you very much," she said as she retied the silver ribbon and placed the album by her handbag. Maybe it was too much for her to take in all at once.

I sat across from her and smiled. *Here we are.* Andrea Bocelli belted out beautiful music in the background while the lavender scent began to waft in the soft breeze moving through the room. Frances was no longer a figment of my imagination. She was real.

"Do you have that paperwork from the social services?" she asked, looking around the room.

"Do you mean my NID?"

"Yes, that's it. Did you bring a copy of that with you? I'd like to read it."

"I did. I even made you a copy that you can keep." I smiled as I handed her a manila envelope.

Frances began reading and right away announced, "Oh no. This isn't right." She began to look upset and said, "This didn't happen that way."

I was curious about what she was reading and what I could see happening to her. "What's up?"

"This isn't true. I didn't meet your father two weeks after relinquishing Delores."

"Who's Delores?" There was so much I didn't know. Was I ready to find out more?

"Your older sister. That was her given name." Frances's red lips were pursed together hard.

So Delores was my older sister's birth name. Interesting. Frances had named her too.

"Frances, this is what was given to me by my social worker, from notes when you interviewed with social services when you were twenty-three years old."

"Well, they're wrong. They didn't get much right." She had an indignant expression on her face.

"I guess it's good you're reading this, then. You can tell me what's right."

"I don't want to read this whole thing right now. I can already tell most of it is not true." Frances gruffly placed her copy back in the envelope, then into one of her bags on the floor.

I didn't know what to make of her reaction and felt bewildered by her outspoken behavior.

Frances was looking around the room. "This is a really nice hotel room." I sensed tension in the air and felt awkward now. Something had shifted after she read the NID.

Just then, there was a knock at the door, announcing room service had arrived. *Thank goodness.* A diversion of food and coffee can always help break the ice.

"How do you take your coffee? I take mine black—do you?"

"Oh no. I have cream in mine." Here was a difference between us. I drank black coffee like my mother Madge. I smiled to myself thinking I probably did quite a few things like my mother Madge as I fixed both of us plates filled with cheese, crackers, and fruit, then sat down again at the table.

I gratefully took a sip of coffee followed by a deep breath before I said, "Can I ask you a question?"

"What is it you want to know?" Frances asked abruptly. Her face looked annoyed.

"Well, if you're comfortable with it . . ." I lingered with my words. I wasn't sure what kind of mood she was in. "I'd like to know a few things about . . . my father."

Frances had a mouth full of cheese and crackers. She took her time finishing her bite, then slowly took a sip of coffee before answering, "I don't remember much about him. It's been a long time, but I can tell you that you were conceived in Nashville." She gazed into the distance.

But a few minutes ago, she sure seemed to remember what he looked like.

"I guess I'm asking for anything that you do remember about him. I'd love to know his name."

I had waited to ask her about my father in person rather than on our phone conversations. It seemed better to ask when I could see her expression when she talked about him.

"His name was Robert."

Robert. Robert Stewart. Finally, a name for this ghost man that hovered in the background.

"Your father was the love of my life," Frances continued. "He was a very handsome man. We had a lot of fun together. I remember he drove a fancy, brand-new convertible."

I was probably conceived in that car.

I sat, listening intently. This may be the only time she talked about him and I wanted to remember everything she said, everything she remembered.

"We were engaged to be married." *They were engaged!*

"I was so in love with him." Her slow, southern cadence was apparent now as she went back in time. "One afternoon, when I was shopping for my wedding trousseau, the FBI came looking for him at my grandmother's house where I lived at the time. She knew Robert. She answered the door and told the FBI she didn't know where he was. Well, I did, and once he heard the FBI was looking for him, he decided he had to leave town. He left for California and I never saw him again." She looked away, down toward her handbag. I wasn't sure I believed her.

"What? He just left?" I was stunned as I learned these things. This was not the Disney version of my fantasy.

"Yes. He broke my heart. I was devastated." Frances lowered her eyes and moved the fruit around on her plate before deciding on a strawberry to bite into.

Yellow flags were flying. *Frances had to have seen him in California. Wasn't he the reason she moved to the Bay Area? Didn't my NID say he knew about me and wanted to be listed as my father on my birth certificate?*

Later, Kathi and Dawn would tell me not to believe what Frances said today but believe the notes in my NID. They'd say she'd had time—decades—to change her thoughts and story, to push her memories so far back she could no longer remember certain things that were too difficult or triggering from her past.

I answered her, "That must've been hard not knowing what happened to him, then finding out you're pregnant."

"Yes, it was. It was very hard." Frances looked down at the floor again.

"I'm so sorry you had to go through such a difficult time like that." I put my hand on top of hers for a few brief seconds.

I knew it was difficult for women during that era. Unwed mothers were subject to societal shaming. Even if they wanted to keep their babies, and most did, they were forced to give them up for adoption. You couldn't be a single, unwed mother like you could today. I can't imagine how difficult that must have been for millions of women. You would almost have to disassociate yourself from your situation and your child in order to handle the trauma.

"So why do you think the FBI was looking for him? That's kind of scary."

"I don't know. I don't think he murdered anybody or anything like that."

"Well, that's good to hear," I said with a smile. Frances didn't return the smile. She wasn't looking happy, so I decided not to push her further on this. "Do you remember where in Alabama my father was from?"

"No. I'm afraid I don't. I think he came from one of the larger cities but I'm not sure. It was so long ago. I just don't remember." She took a mirror out of her well-worn handbag and checked herself, which I found interesting. She had detached and didn't seem interested in helping me anymore.

"Do you remember his birthday?" *I knew this was a long shot, but I wanted to ask. I mean, I remember my old boyfriends' birthdays; she might remember his.*

"No, I don't."

"Did he have any siblings? Did you ever meet his family?"

"I'm sorry. I don't know if he had any siblings. I don't remember meeting his family."

"I know it was a long time ago. It's sure nice to know his name."

"You have his eyes, and you seem to have your father's personality."

I laughed and said, "Well, I hope he was a nice guy. What did you like most about him? I guess if he drove a convertible, he must've been fun-loving in some way?"

"Oh yes, he was very nice. We had a good time together."

I could sense she wasn't going to give me anything more. No stories about him or about them. I questioned how well she knew him. She remembered only a few snippets of the man she said she once loved. If she remembered anything else, she wasn't telling me.

"Oh, I brought pictures for you! So you could see everyone." Frances leaned over and brought up a crumpled shoebox from one of her bags. The box was nearly overflowing with photos. She plopped it on the table. I guess we were done talking about Robert.

Frances pulled out a studio portrait of herself surrounded by her four children—Colin, Julia, Allison, and Colleen—when they were preteens and teenagers. I was excited to finally see them. The first thing I noticed was that we didn't resemble each other, and my heart dropped. I couldn't understand why they looked *so* different from me. My sisters had long, thick, dark brown hair, a medium complexion with either green or dark brown eyes. They were beautiful children but they didn't look like me.

"I don't think I resemble any of them," I blurted out to Frances, my head shaking with wonder. It was disappointing.

"Well, that's because their father was Indigenous. He was from the Tlingit tribe in Alaska."

"He was an Alaskan native?" I was shocked. *So that's why we didn't resemble each other. My siblings favored their Indigenous genes rather than their Celtic and Nordic ones.*

I was familiar with the Tlingit people in the Pacific Northwest. The Tlingits and the Haida were southeast, coastal Indigenous tribes in Alaska and in British Columbia, Canada. I had read books about them that my father gave to me as a young girl. It was a fascination I'd had since I was a child. In the fourth grade, I had waved my hand frantically, asking to do my state report on Alaska, my first choice. And, as of this writing, I've lived with five Alaskan malamutes over the course of nearly forty years. I couldn't believe my half-siblings were Alaskan natives. The synchronicity gave me chills.

I wasn't as surprised when Frances showed me pictures of my first cousins. I already knew from Deborah that my aunt had married a Samoan man and, like my siblings, my cousins favored their father's genes. There was one, however, who stood out among them, with reddish-blond hair, green eyes, and freckles, favoring the Douglas clan. All my female cousins had beautiful, long, dark hair down to their waist. There was no way my fine hair would ever grow that long or look as good if it did.

I saw pictures of my second cousins who played college football, strong-looking young Samoan men with their hair down to their waist, worn in braids. Samoan tattoos, *Tatau*, were proudly displayed on their chests and arms. Nobody would have guessed we were related, but we were. I loved the diversity in our family, but I wished I had a peer who resembled me in some way.

The only people I resembled, besides my mother, were my grandparents, whom I never expected to see pictures of. It was a lovely surprise. Frances told me my grandfather retired as a tillerman firefighter for the Nashville fire department, and my grandmother retired as a telephone operator with Southern Bell. They had been divorced a long time but had remained friends, even after my grandmother remarried one of my grandfather's best friends. My divorced grandparents even flew together from Nashville to visit their daughter and grandchildren.

Frances had lots of stories to tell with each photo, and most were sad. Her ex-husband had died from alcoholism and had been homeless. She told me he had started drinking alcohol at age seven to keep warm on the Alaskan waters when he'd go out on fishing trips with his father and uncles. He could never beat the drinking, which was why she ended up divorcing him. She couldn't take the emotional and physical abuse anymore when he drank. She left him, becoming a single mother with four teenagers to raise and very little money to do it with.

My aunt Vivian Tagaloa had died from Guillain-Barre syndrome when she was only thirty-seven. She was divorced from her husband, the father of eight of her nine children. After their divorce, all eight children were split up. A broken family—some were adopted in American Samoa, some adopted or fostered in California. All but the youngest spent their early childhood far away, in American Samoa. Frances said that after everything they'd been through, it was remarkable that all eight siblings reconnected as adults and united as a family once again.

My aunt's ninth child, Iolana was born out of wedlock and adopted in the Bay Area. Her father was also Samoan. She was now in her midthirties. Iolana, who goes by Lana, had searched and reconnected with Frances and the family years ago, just like Stephanie had. Frances said she enjoyed Lana, but that she had married a man from Ireland and had moved there to be near his family several years ago, and that they had lost contact.

There were many hard stories that day, which weren't easy to hear. I felt the pain of them. I wasn't expecting such sadness. I remembered what Deborah had said, that Frances had had a hard life. And so it was with her children too.

I could feel a headache coming on.

Frances never learned to drive and depended on public transportation. She raised her children in the Mission District, known as the Mission, one of the oldest neighborhoods in San Francisco. The Mission was historically known as the center of San Francisco's Mexican American community. It had its fair share of drug activity and gangs. It was a very different upbringing than the one I'd had.

One of my beautiful sisters, Allison, ended up on the streets for twenty years as a heroin addict. I couldn't help but wonder how my life might've been if I had been raised in the high-crime, dense, urban area my siblings were raised in.

There were, however, some good stories. My uncle, who was still alive, was a television news editor in Nashville, who worked with Oprah in her early days. My great-grandfather had been a police officer with the Metropolitan Nashville Police Department, and he, like his firefighter son (my grandfather), had been a security officer in retirement at the Tennessee capital in Nashville.

My roots ran deep in Nashville, and I came from good stock. It seemed my mother and aunt got into problems when they left their hometown. *What would my mother's life have been like had she returned to Nashville after I'd been born?* She might've had an easier life. But that was only a thought that passed, not reality.

My head began spinning after several hours hearing these sad stories.

"You know you can take some of these photos home with you and make copies, if you'd like," Frances offered, as I was hiding in the bathroom downing Tylenol. My head was pounding.

"Really?" I looked at myself in the mirror. I didn't see Frances. I only saw myself.

"Yes." She grabbed another pile of pictures and pushed them toward me as I sat down. On the top photo, I recognized a cousin in his backyard. There was a woman sitting beside him. She looked around my age, with shoulder-length, light blonde hair. She had a sporty look to her. I noticed we dressed similarly: sport watch, Ray-Bans, a sage V-neck T-shirt, and navy capris topped off with flip-flops. She was smiling and looked comfortable next to my cousin.

"Who's this?" I asked, pointing to the blonde woman in the picture. There was something about her that piqued my curiosity.

"Oh, that's Stephanie."

That photo changed everything for me.

Chapter Eighteen

I LOVED LOOKING AT THE PHOTOS FRANCES HAD OF MY sister Stephanie. I saw an attractive woman who looked happy and confident.

"Oh wow," I said, as I clasped my hands together. "She looks great. Do you have any more pictures of her?"

"I think there's a group of them here." Frances shuffled through her photos and placed several more in front of me. My eyes widened as I stared at Stephanie in the photo with Frances and my sisters Julia, Allison, and Colleen.

I thought Stephanie and I resembled each other. She stood out from my other sisters with her blonde hair. They were all tall, all attractive. It was a happy photo of all of them standing together with our mother.

I remember Phyllis telling me Frances did not want to go through another reunion experience because of how it went with Stephanie. Frances didn't want her children to know she had a second baby out of wedlock. One was enough. From the photo of Stephanie, Frances, and my sisters, it looked like everything had worked out well between them. They looked relaxed together, which gave me hope that maybe someday I'd be able to meet them.

"Does she live in San Francisco?" I asked, looking over at Frances. This was exciting. *Maybe I'd be able to meet at least her.*

"No, she lives north of the city."

"Do we share the same father?" I asked earnestly and cautiously, looking at Frances with wide eyes as I took a sip of coffee.

"Oh no, you don't have the same father. You're half-sisters," Frances answered matter-of-factly.

"Is she married? Does she have children?"

"No."

"Oh," I answered. A twinge of disappointment charged through me knowing Stephanie and I wouldn't share this in common, but I had close friends who weren't married and didn't have children. It didn't really matter; we could still have things in common with each other.

"She looks great for being fifty—it's amazing to see her. I think I see a resemblance between Stephanie and my daughter." I smiled at Frances while sifting through more photos to try to find more pictures of my older sister.

A few minutes later, I heard muffled crying. I looked up to see Frances push herself away from the table and hang her head. She was sobbing. Her body shook and heaved uncontrollably with each deep sob. Then, she began moaning. I didn't know what to do. I didn't know what was happening. I just sat there wondering why she was crying, so hard, so suddenly.

"Frances," I said softly, reaching my hand across the table. "Are you okay?"

She mumbled something I couldn't understand and kept crying, getting louder by the minute. She sounded as though she were in pain. I didn't know what to think. I was dumbfounded by her outburst of tears.

"Did I offend you in any way? Did I say something to hurt you?"

She shook her head no.

I stood up and put my arm around her shoulders. "Frances." I felt helpless, awkward. I didn't know her and had no idea how to help. She literally was a stranger to me.

She mumbled something.

"I don't understand what you're saying."

She tried again through her sobbing. I went into the bathroom to get her some tissues. *What the heck is happening? Why is she crying like this?*

"I'm sorry. I don't understand." I kept repeating this to her, standing beside her, but she was incomprehensible and uncontrollable. I began to think maybe there was something wrong with her that I didn't know about.

Then she practically yelled, "Stephanie's my third, not my first."

It didn't make sense. She repeated her words, a bit softer. "Stephanie's my third, not my first."

I just looked at her, confused. She sat up and said more clearly through her tears, "Stephanie is my third daughter I gave away. I gave away three daughters, not two. Stephanie is my third baby, not my first. Delores is my first daughter, and I don't know where she is."

My mouth dropped open as I looked down at her. Her green eyes, now red and swollen, with mascara streaking her smooth, white cheeks, reminded me of a sad clown. Andrea Bocelli was singing "Per Amore" and the lavender candle flickered happily, but I felt sick to my stomach.

She gave away three babies. How could she have done that? What was wrong with her? Didn't she learn her lesson after relinquishing two? Three? I wanted to throw up.

Frances was calming down. She had her mirror out and was wiping her face and blowing her nose. I couldn't say anything to her yet. I went into the bathroom to gather myself, however I could. I was shaken by all these hours of talking, all the sad stories, then the photographs, and now this.

Just like that, I had another sister. Stephanie was actually my younger sister, not my older one. *Where is Delores?* I felt disgusted and had little compassion for Frances in that moment. I felt a little guilty that I was so judgmental, but those were my honest feelings. *Who does this? You'd think she would've been more careful. Who can give away one baby, let alone three? The three of us were close together in age. Who was this person, my mother? Had she been a prostitute? Only prostitutes or drug addicts relinquish multiple babies. Was she stupid or just naive?*

I looked at myself in the mirror, glad I didn't see Frances looking back. Placing both hands on the counter, perhaps to ground me in this moment, I realized I still had the rest of the afternoon with her. I lowered my head and shook it, wishing Michael were with me or a friend. Several friends had offered their company and support, as did Michael, but I thought everything would be fine. Wonderful. But now . . . this was too much.

Frances had lied to me. She lied to Phyllis and Deborah, too, and now she had tried to get away with pawning Stephanie off as my older sister. Why she broke down and told me the truth, I had no idea, but my gut feeling that yellow flags were flying around was correct. *I can't trust her.*

Walking back into the room, I saw that Frances had composed herself and was dusting her face with powder. She looked up and said, so calmly, so matter-of-factly, "I'm sorry, Diane. Delores Ann is your older sister, not Stephanie."

I sat down at the table and asked, "How many years apart are Stephanie and I?"

"Two years."

I couldn't believe it. She had relinquished three babies

within four years. Geez. *How did she do it? How did she survive this trauma? Were we easy to give away?*

"Now, Diane," Frances said, sounding firm in her southern drawl. "Nobody knows any of this, that I gave away three daughters."

She looked at me, hard, catching my eye. "There were only two people who knew I had relinquished three daughters—my mother and sister—but they're both gone now, so you're the only person on this earth who knows, and I want to keep it that way. I don't want you to ever tell anyone about this. You have to promise me to keep this a secret."

Frances stared at me, then continued, "I know you want to meet my family and all, but I can't do that again. I'm sorry. I'm happy to have a relationship with you, but I won't introduce you to my family. You have to promise me that you won't ever get in touch with any of my children and tell anyone about Delores. I can't have my family knowing I gave away three babies. I'm sorry that Stephanie connected with me first. I know that's not fair to you, but that's just the way it has to be. You can take these photos home like I told you, but that's all I can give you. Can you do this for me? Can you promise you won't ever contact anyone or tell anyone?"

I sat there, speechless.

Another secret. This time, it was between my birth mother and me. A secret to protect her from herself. I wanted to cry, but I had to give her an answer. I didn't know what to say. I felt stuck in a morass of secrets and shame and the past—hers, not mine. I was stunned by her request and her forthright manipulation. She seemed tough, and I felt heartbroken. My dreams of that day were completely shattered by now.

"Okay," I answered, meekly, my heart not in line with my words. I felt there was no choice but to agree.

"Good. Thank you, Diane," Frances said with a half-smile. She put her purse away and took a sip of cold coffee, looking over at me, triumphantly.

An hour later, at nearly four o'clock, we were seated in the hotel restaurant. I'd ordered a bottle of merlot and looked forward to drinking a good portion of it. But I felt as though I was treading water with Frances, which made it hard to unwind. Frances was talkative and seemed fine, joyous even. It was as if she had lifted her burdens off her shoulders and placed them on mine. I now felt like I carried the weight from her sad stories and the secrets she had carried for decades.

After our early dinner that dragged on far too long, with Frances doing most of the talking about her not being old and still enjoying dancing, I told Frances I was exhausted and needed to head back to my room to go to bed early before getting together the next day. She understood and said she needed to get back home and rest herself. The next day we had plans to spend the afternoon in Sausalito together, which now was the last thing I wanted to do. What I really wanted to do was just go home.

Eating lunch at a seaside restaurant the next day with my mother in Sausalito should have been wonderful. I had expected it to be—back when I had illusions, or rather delusions, and was holding onto a fantasy of who Frances was supposed to be.

I'd had hardly slept the night before thinking about everything. I felt like I hadn't had enough time to reflect on it all. And, today, observing Frances, I did not like her. I wondered if I even wanted a relationship with her, yet not having one seemed distressing.

I couldn't help thinking how she had tried to con me about Stephanie, plus the fact that I was now the middle daughter of three she had relinquished. Telling me that she wouldn't allow me to meet the rest of my family and that I had to promise to never tell anyone about myself or Delores seemed transactional and cruel; all of this made me sad.

I had already lost my roots, my history, and my family. Here she was, when family was within reach, taking it away, along with any hope that I'd ever know the other people I was related to. *I am so close.* If she had only said she needed more time to tell her children, I'd feel better and would understand, but she didn't. She didn't seem to care. It was more like she was ashamed of me, caring more about herself and how she would look if her children knew she had relinquished another baby. It was hard for me to think about being around her, and it was hard to be told I needed to be a secret, kept from those I wanted to love.

In the late afternoon, we returned to my hotel from Sausalito. I asked Frances up for a cup of hot tea but I didn't offer dinner. I took my shoes off, propping my feet up on the bed from the stuffed chair I was sitting in. I had opened the sliding door, allowing the ocean breeze coming off the bay into the room. It felt good. I could breathe more freely. It was almost over.

I had asked a lot of questions about Stephanie at lunch. Even though Frances had forbidden it, I wanted to find her. She was my sister. We were close in age and resembled each other. We had both been adopted and both had searched for our biological family. Surely, we had a lot in common.

It was nearing six o'clock as Frances stood in the corridor, just outside my hotel room as we said our goodbyes.

"Thank you for the wonderful weekend," Frances said,

smiling sweetly, as she put on a heavy brown jacket for her jaunt back home.

"Oh yes," I answered, politely. "It was great. We finally met and reconnected. Thank you again for letting me take some of your photos home. I promise I won't take long making copies."

Frances bent down and kissed me on the lips, then said, "I love you, Diane."

I was taken aback. She was definitely more outwardly affectionate than my mother Madge. I don't think my adoptive mother ever kissed me on the lips, and she rarely, if ever, told me she loved me out loud. Frances was an enigma. I was even more confused.

"I love you too," I answered, feeling a little sheepish. But I did love her, in some way. I wondered if I would ever let my children meet her. *I'm not sure about her, who she is and who she had been. Can I even tell Michael all of this, or will that be breaking my promise?*

I waved goodbye and watched as Frances walked down the hallway toward the elevator and disappeared, her back to me, just like the first time I saw her.

Chapter Nineteen

THE NEXT DAY, KATHI CONVINCED ME TO DO TWO THINGS before I headed home. The first was to drive by where Frances lived, and the second was to visit the Salvation Army address in Oakland where I was born.

Once in my car, with scribbled directions to Frances's address, I called my friend Mary as I drove down some of San Francisco's steep hills toward the Tenderloin District. I had no idea where or what the Tenderloin was. I was clueless that it was famous for its gritty, violent, high-crime streets where drug deals were made out in the open, during the day. It was not a place for tourists.

I was more shocked with each passing block how much worse it got. At one point, stopped at a red light, I watched as a few seedy-looking people began jaywalking in front of me, yelling obscenities at a down-and-out crowd hovering on a corner. The hard-looking group looked like people of the night. I was two blocks away from where Frances lived. The next block revealed the large Tenderloin police station with several police vans parked out front.

"There isn't a Starbucks down here," I said to Mary with a nervous laugh, trying to lighten my spirits. "There are quite a few scary-looking people walking the streets, though."

Still on the phone with me, Mary asked, "Are your doors locked, Diane?"

"Yes, they are. Okay, I'm on her block now. Oh my gosh, Mary." An all-night porn palace ruled one side of the street. Vietnamese markets and cafés were prevalent in the old, run-down buildings.

"Oh geez," I said into my red cell phone. "I'm here."

"Tell me! What are you seeing?"

I stopped my car and tried to explain, my heart sinking. "Okay. Her building is an old brick building with a large, black iron security gate. It's not pretty. It's not a nice neighborhood. It's scary. This isn't a good area at all. I had no idea. I think it's one of the worst blocks down here. I want to cry. I can't believe she lives in such a place."

"I'm so sorry, Diane. Please be careful."

"Mary, there are no trees here."

"It's not what you thought, is it?"

"No, this whole weekend has not been what I thought. So much for my naive vision of Frances living in a quaint, tree-lined Victorian neighborhood." I laughed a little, as I felt tears welling up. Reality was hard sometimes. "I see a street block full of homeless people lying on the sidewalk ahead of me. I gotta go, Mary. I have to get out of here and find my way to the Oakland Bridge. I'll call you later. Thanks for being with me this morning."

Tears slowly flowed down my cheeks. I was stunned to see that my birth mother lived in such a horribly sad neighborhood. I didn't understand. *Is this what the Tenderloin is?* It seemed it was one sad thing after another when it came to finding out who my birth mother was. I felt compassion for her and wondered what else I didn't know about the truth of her life.

When I arrived at the Salvation Army on Garden Street in Oakland, I was in a funk. The address wasn't in the beautiful hill area of Oakland where picturesque, charming California Craftsman bungalows nestled amid pine trees and old oaks that overlooked the bay. I was downtown, in a rough, older section of the city. Of course I was.

The Salvation Army was at the end of a cul-de-sac. Small, old wooden homes that needed paint lined the street on one side; their only redeeming feature was the front porches framed by beautiful, full-grown maples, pines, and Chinese elms that stood as sentinels over time.

Across the street were several buildings and a large grassy park with steep cement steps. I know now that those steps were once the entrance to Booth Memorial Hospital where I had been born, before it collapsed in the 1989 Loma Prieta earthquake.

I got out of my car and walked around the premises. The only remnants of the hospital were the trees and the large cement steps. *If only these Chinese elms could talk . . .*

Years later, I would read a memoir titled *The Third Floor*, written by Judi Loren Grace, a young woman who spent time here and gave birth to a son she was forced to relinquish in 1962. She shared photos of the hospital, a large, three-story, architecturally elegant stone building, yet creepy-looking, like something out of a horror film.

I remembered the story Frances told me over the weekend, that when the young women gave birth, they had cake and balloons for the mother and baby. Frances said she loved it. Maybe she had never had a birthday party before, but when she told me this story, I thought celebrating the separation of mother and baby with balloons and cake sounded sick. A happy birthday party for the baby who would grow up, more than likely, with trauma and certainly loss. *A party for the mother losing her child for life. Who thought of such a twisted celebration?*

Ostracized from society for getting pregnant and not being married, the women were sent here to live out their pregnancy away from family and friends and to give birth alone. They didn't have a choice whether to keep their baby or not. These women were called "the girls who went away," which is the title of a well-documented, historical book on the Baby Scoop Era: *The Girls Who Went Away: The Hidden History of Women Who Surrendered Children for Adoption in the Decades Before Roe v. Wade*, by Ann Fessler.

Driving home to Southern California that afternoon, I wept the entire five hours, thought long and hard about everything that had happened over the weekend, and decided that as much as I wanted a relationship with my birth mother, I wanted one with my sister just as much.

When I got home, I told Michael about my weekend. He couldn't believe it. I still couldn't either. I felt hurt and angry toward Frances with how she tried to deceive me and how she was determined to keep me from knowing anyone in the family. I understood about the children she raised and my cousins, but I didn't understand why I had to be kept a secret from my sister.

After a long, hot shower and more thinking, I sat down at the computer and contacted my online support group asking them to help me find Stephanie.

On the drive home, I thought about my NID and how it told me about my older sister. *If mine had that information, wouldn't Stephanie's?* Over the weekend, Frances had shared that Stephanie had an NID too. That clinched it for me. I was sure that Stephanie's NID told her about both Delores and me, and if my hunch was right, she had never mentioned Delores or me to her siblings or cousins all these years. She could keep a secret.

I also thought that since Stephanie had been in reunion with the family for so long, she might help me make sense of Frances and the sadness and confusion that followed meeting her.

It didn't take my group long to find Stephanie. I had remembered the correct information about her, and now I had her phone number. I decided to call her that evening.

I watched the clock like a hawk, waiting for seven o'clock, and in the privacy of my bedroom, I dialed her number.

"Hello," a pleasant-sounding woman's voice answered the phone on the third ring.

"Is this Stephanie Hughes?" My heart was pounding.

"Yes ..."

"You don't know me, but my name is Diane. I just spent the weekend with someone you know in San Francisco, someone we're both related to—Frances Campbell."

"Oh, really?"

"Well, you might know nothing about me." I paused for a few seconds. "I'm your sister. I'm Loretta, now known as Diane."

There was silence on the other end of the phone. The only sound I heard was my heart racing, driven by worried thoughts that she might not be willing to talk with me and hang up.

"Oh wow, that's great!" Stephanie cried out enthusiastically.

"Yes, we're sisters." I heaved a deep sigh of relief.

"How did you find me?" Her voice sounded calming and her cadence was similar to Frances's.

I told her how I was adopted and how I had searched for family, like her, finding Frances just a few months before and that we had met in person for the first time over the weekend. "I didn't know you existed until Saturday afternoon. I basically listened to clues from Frances, came home, and asked for help finding you from my adoptee search support group."

"Well, I'm really glad you found me! So, you're my sister?" She repeated her words, probably to process what was happening out of the blue. *I know those surreal feelings.* "Are you a full- or half-sister?" she asked.

"Frances says we're half-sisters. We're close in age, though— only two years apart."

"Very cool."

We spoke for three hours that night, the first of many conversations to come. I learned how she found Frances so many years before the internet—by hiring a private attorney working for Adoptees Liberty Movement Association (ALMA), who went before a judge and pleaded her case. She said she was lucky to have had an experienced attorney and a compassionate judge who released her original birth certificate and identifying information, which was rare. With her birth mother's name in hand, she was able to find her that year.

Stephanie said she met our siblings and some cousins not long after meeting Frances.

"Wow, you've known them all a really long time." It made me feel a little sad that I would not be privileged to know my family like my sister did.

I wasn't surprised when Stephanie said, "I've known about you for a long time. I just had no idea where you were or how to go about finding you. I didn't know your birth name or your adopted name."

I knew it. Stephanie had to have known about me from her NID. I was now sure she knew about Delores too.

"Oh, really? How did you know about me? I don't think Frances would've told you," I asked, with a soft laugh.

Stephanie laughed. "No, she didn't tell me about you."

"I'm assuming you knew about me from your NID?"

"Yes, that's where I found out about you, but, of course, there was no identifying information given."

"I'm not surprised I was mentioned in your NID. Frances

seemed to have divulged a lot more information when she was younger than she does now. Was anyone else listed on your paperwork?" I asked.

"You mean like another sister?"

"Yes." I held my breath. Surely Delores was listed there too.

"I know about another sister if that's what you mean," Stephanie said hesitantly. *Bingo.*

"I knew you knew!" I cried out. "Her information is on my paperwork, too, so I figured if she was on mine, we'd both be on yours."

"Yup. I've known about her for years too."

"Well, that's why I felt justified finding you. Frances doesn't want me to know you. She told me she doesn't want me knowing anyone in the family."

"I'm sorry to hear that. You can't always take what she says to heart, though. I've learned that over the years. She changes her mind about things."

"That's another reason why I wanted to reach out to you, especially knowing you've had a long relationship with all of them."

Stephanie was a big help answering questions about Frances. Stephanie laughed when I told her I thought Frances might have been a prostitute or drug addict.

"Oh no. I can pretty much guarantee she wasn't either of those. I think her biggest problem was that she was naive and got herself into trouble too many times. She's not a big drinker and she never took drugs. She's pretty conventional."

I felt relieved. I told Stephanie how Frances tried to pass her off as our older sister, Delores.

"I guess she didn't think anyone would find out she relinquished three daughters. But, oh my God, to think she was pretending I was Delores." I imagined Stephanie shaking her head in bewilderment.

It was hard to come to terms with the fact that my mother had been forced to give up three babies. That the unwed mothers were told to forget their experiences, to move on with their lives; they'd have other children. It was heartbreaking.

What was Frances's childhood like? Was it a happy one? Years later, I'd learn she and her sister were split up from their brother when their parents divorced, with their brother living with their father, and Frances and Vivian living with their grandmother. Meanwhile, their mother moved in with her new husband. *That doesn't sound like a stable and good family life.*

I thought about the three daughters Frances had raised and the three she'd lost. There were three of each, three to redeem the first three she lost, with a son providing the division between us. *I wonder if that coincidence ever occurred to her.*

It was easy, beyond any expectations I had, to talk with my sister. By then, I needed some good news, a positive connection with blood relatives, and I got it. All the hard work of searching and hoping had finally paid off. We agreed to keep in touch regularly through email and phone calls, to send each other photos of ourselves and of our lives so far. I fell asleep that night feeling full and overjoyed.

Next, I needed to tell Frances that I'd found Stephanie. That wouldn't be easy, but it was the right thing to do. Stephanie had revealed she'd asked Frances about me when she first met her, but Frances didn't know where I was and didn't want to search for me. She gave Stephanie the strong impression she didn't want Stephanie searching either.

Stephanie warned me, "I'm concerned how Frances will react to learning that you found me. She might be upset, but even if she is for a while, I think she'll eventually come around. She doesn't seem to stay angry long."

I was hoping for a positive outcome when I answered Frances's call a week later. I'd written her, thinking it would be the easiest way to tell her I had found Stephanie. I told her how much it meant to find her because we shared so much in common. I hoped she would understand. I didn't apologize. Stephanie and I had a right to know each other.

"You betrayed me," Frances exclaimed fiercely when I picked up the phone.

"I'm sorry. I didn't mean to betray you in any way. I just wanted to find my sister and give us a chance to know each other."

"How would you like it if I called your parents and told them what you're doing behind their backs?"

Ouch. That stung, and scared me. *Would she really do that? Is she threatening me?* "No, I wouldn't like that and I'd be very upset. I understand what you're saying but I haven't contacted your children or anyone else, only Stephanie." *Did she not read my letter?* "I felt confident doing this because I was sure that Stephanie knew about me from her NID, and I was right. She did. She's known about Delores and me for years and has never revealed it to anyone. And I thought that if she searched for her birth family, like me, she was interested in knowing family. I thought she and I would have a lot in common with both of us being adoptees. And, if she could keep that secret about Delores and me all these years, then I figured she could be trusted to keep one more, just as you asked."

Silence.

Frances's tone changed. "She knows about Delores?"

"Yes. Delores and I are both mentioned in her NID, her

paperwork, just as I thought they would be. She has known about us all along, before she found you. And, Frances, you really don't have to worry about her revealing this because she never has in fourteen years. Stephanie understands. She gets it. So do I."

"I didn't know she knew about both of you."

"She does. So, see what I mean? She's never said anything to anyone, so you can rest assured she's not going to say anything now. Why would she? She doesn't want to hurt you and neither do I. I didn't tell her anything she didn't already know."

"Okay." Frances let out a deep sigh before she added, "I guess that makes me feel better knowing she's known all along and has never said anything."

In that moment, I began to feel differently toward Frances. Her approach to conflict was like night and day compared to my adoptive mother's. Frances listened and seemed ready to learn more. We had climbed over a hurdle together and we both came out the other side better for it. Stephanie had been right—Frances didn't stay angry long.

As I contemplated my new family members over the next few days, I recognized that I'd taken a huge risk. I felt fortunate that Stephanie was so welcoming and that Frances was able to understand why I chose to contact my own sister. I believed everything would be okay between the three of us.

Over the next several months, I continued in good contact with Frances and Stephanie, making plans for Stephanie and me to finally meet in person in August. We also planned to have lunch together with our mother. I felt blessed by the powers that be. I had them both in my life, and all was well.

Chapter Twenty

MY CONVERTIBLE VOLKSWAGEN BEETLE WAS PACKED, ready for the seven-hour drive to Stephanie's. Pink, purple, and gold bloomed in the cloudless sky as if painted in watercolors as the sun rose over the mountains while I drove north. Feeling high with excitement, mindful, and loving the cool morning air that surrounded me with the black canvas top down, sipping on coffee, I freely and loudly sang along with Joni Mitchell to one of my favorite albums, *Hejira*.

Later that afternoon, Stephanie and I would finally meet in person for the first time.

I opened my hotel room door and saw Stephanie standing on the threshold, holding a bottle of champagne, to celebrate us. She was tall, taller than Heather. Her blonde hair hung loose past her shoulders. She wore a Mexican-style white blouse with a spring green skirt, a coral-colored necklace, spring green dangling earrings, and white sandals.

We immediately hugged and kissed each other on our cheeks, and I commented how much she resembled my daughter. I felt like I was looking at Heather in the future. There was a strong family resemblance between them. My hotel room had a small table for two, next to a large window that overlooked a lush garden with overgrown trees. It was here that we sat down, nervous and happy, to enjoy our champagne before dinner. It didn't take us long to feel comfortable with each other considering it's an odd place to find yourself in, meeting a sibling at forty-eight years old for the first time. I felt as though I were on a date. It was exciting and dreamlike—surreal.

Stephanie had made reservations at a lovely outdoor venue next to a small lake in town. We got a good buzz on from our wine with dinner and talked up a storm. We had so much to catch up on. The evening couldn't have been more perfect.

The next day, Stephanie drove us into the city to meet Frances for lunch on Geary Street. Sitting across the table from both my sister and mother was another surreal moment for me that weekend. I'm not sure there are even words to describe the feelings I had. It was hard to believe this had really happened to me, that I was actually sitting, having lunch with my biological mother and sister.

It amused me that we ordered the same meal and desserts. I was so surprised. And delighted. Frances and Stephanie found it humorous how much the similarities excited me. I wanted to know everything about them: their favorite colors, food, TV shows, movies, music, books.

"So, Stephanie, what's your favorite color?"

"Hmmm. Probably green."

"Oh my gosh, that's my favorite color too!"

It turned out we both loved the outdoors as well as hiking, swimming, the beach, camping, and travel. I was ecstatic finding out how much we had in common.

For the next two years, Frances, Stephanie, and I had our own private family gatherings. Frances talked freely about the children she raised. I felt like I knew them all well, as it seemed I knew every detail of their lives. Frances's oldest two children, Colin and Julia, never married or had children. Her third child, Allison, had sons who had been raised by her husband's family, as she struggled with drug addiction. Thankfully, she was clean now and doing well. Frances's youngest daughter, Colleen, had been married a long time. She and her husband had moved out of the city, buying a home in the suburbs where they raised three sons.

I spoke to Frances on the phone regularly, and every so often would timidly hint that I still wanted to meet her children. "Oh yes, one day I'll introduce you," she'd say, "but I'm just not ready to do that yet, but soon." Her words kept me hoping for a long time.

There was never any talk of meeting my cousins, even though Frances was in touch with most of them. I'd heard all about their lives, too, but gave up thinking I would ever meet them. I began to lose hope of ever meeting my siblings, either, as the months and years went by. Frances was never ready to tell them about me and I feared she never would be.

By now, we had been in reunion for more than two-and-a-half years. It became emotionally challenging over time to hear about these family members while not being "allowed" to know them. I knew this was my own selfish desire and I understood Frances's position and respected it, although I had my grievances. I thought, *One day they'll find out about me, and then what?*

I imagined meeting them at her funeral or memorial. Then they'd find out we shared the same mother, that we were half-siblings, but she wouldn't be there to talk and tell them the story.

Her story, herself. None of us were children anymore, we were all well into adulthood, and I thought we shouldn't be treated like we were ten. If only Frances would take that leap and give us all a chance to get to know each other.

I could vent to Stephanie about my worries, and she empathized. She thought I should meet them and was frustrated Frances kept holding them back. She also thought that once the siblings knew about me, Frances would be fine.

I wasn't so sure. If I made a move, I'd be "betraying" her again, acting against her wishes. I gave much thought about this dilemma for over a year, discussing the pros and cons with my family, friends, and support group. Everyone I spoke with encouraged me to reach out to my siblings even if Frances didn't want it. This seemed like it would be another betrayal. *Didn't I promise her years ago?* I had, but I was starting to wonder why. *Why am I going along with what Frances wants for so long when it just feels wrong?*

Stephanie suggested meeting my brother first, so when the weekend arrived in September 2006, when I was finally introducing Michael, Heather, and Travis to Frances, I decided to stop by the small coffee shop where my brother Colin was co-owner, on our way into the city. I'd play it by ear, see how busy it was, and if the vibe seemed right, I'd introduce myself.

Michael weaved our car on the coast highway through pines and cliffs from Santa Cruz to Pacifica, then headed toward South San Francisco near my brother's coffee shop. Michael was leaving it up to me whether we'd stop or not.

I still had time to change my mind. I wasn't sure about this, but Stephanie had encouraged me so I felt buoyed by her enthusiasm and familiarity with my brother.

"I think I'll give it a go," I said to Michael.

"Are you sure?" Michael asked.

"I'm not sure if this is right. I just know I'd like to see him in person, then I'll take it from there."

We parked near a sea-weathered building in the middle of a shipyard meant for boat repairs and marine mechanics—far off the beaten path. Knots of nerves gripped my stomach. The four of us would stand out among the tattooed fishermen who looked like they were from a bygone era.

We carefully opened the glass door and claimed a table in the far corner. I looked over and saw a tall man with his back to us rinsing dishes in the sink behind a large, old-fashioned counter. Above him was a handwritten menu blackboard. The turquoise walls seemed bright as the sunshine streaming through the large window.

When the young man turned around, I knew this was my brother Colin. He was around six foot four or five, slender, and had our mother's green eyes. My heart accelerated with excitement. I looked over at Michael and the kids, and, smiling, I nodded my head that this was him.

He smiled over at us and asked, "Can I help you?" *How perfect those words are—if he only knew.*

I went up to the counter and placed our orders: coffee for me and fruit smoothies for Michael and the kids.

"Okay," he said. "I'll have your orders up in a few minutes." It was strange to see him in person, especially as I knew so much about him and his life.

I didn't know what to do. We were the only ones in the shop so I asked myself if this were a sign to go ahead. I was too afraid to say anything in that moment, so I sat back down with my family.

"Mom," Heather whispered. "Say something. Do it now before anyone else comes in."

"Yeah, Mom. Now's the time. Just do it," added Travis.

I remembered how Stephanie loved Colin and thought he'd be the easiest one to reach out to. I walked over to the counter. "Are you Colin Campbell?"

"Yeah, I am." He smiled again, which encouraged me.

"Do you know Stephanie Hughes?" I could feel my stomach churning.

"Oh yeah, I know her really well. Do you know her too?"

Here's my opening . . . "Yeah, I do. As a matter of fact, we're on our way to visit her this weekend." I turned around and openhandedly pointed to my family sitting at the table in the corner. They shyly smiled and waved back.

"Oh, you are?" Colin was adding fruit to the smoothies. He looked over and smiled back. "That'll be nice. Well, tell her I said hi."

I guess he's not seeing any resemblance in me to Stephanie or to himself in any way.

"We're also going to be seeing your mother too."

He stopped midway through pouring juice into the blender. He looked over at me, tilting his head to the side, his green eyes squinting. I could see he was now wondering who we were, that something wasn't right here. "My mother?"

I took a deep breath. *Here goes. I've opened Pandora's box.*

"Yes, your mother." I smiled and nodded my head. *No stopping now, Diane.* "We're having dinner tonight with your mother at Fisherman's Wharf." I paused. "And tomorrow morning, we're picking her up to spend the day at Stephanie's." *Now you've really opened the box. You've let the lid fly open.*

"Why would you be seeing and picking up my mother?"

"I know this must be really weird for you to be hearing this from a stranger. My name is Diane and I've known your mother for almost three years now." *What the hell am I doing?*

Colin blinked a few times. "How do you know my mother?"

"Well, this is really awkward telling you this in person, cold-like, out of the blue and all, and I know it'll be hard for you. Before I say anything, I want you to know I had no idea how to do this any other way. Stephanie encouraged me to reach out to you first, so here I am. I'm your sister. I'm a half-sister, like Stephanie, an adoptee who searched for my biological family and found your mother, who is my mother too. I found her in 2004."

"Oh wow." Colin shook his head.

Now you've done it. You can never take it back. It's out. You are no longer a secret. "My husband is here along with my two children." I gestured toward the three of them sitting wide-eyed in the corner. "They're meeting your mother, their grandmother, for the first time tonight. I'm so sorry to have to tell you in this way, Colin."

"I don't even know what to say. You came in here, where I work, to tell me this?"

"Yeah, I did. I know. It's not so good, and it's weird. I actually wasn't sure if I'd say anything, but since we're alone, I felt it was a sign to go ahead. I know it's such an awkward moment. It's hard to see you in person and not say something."

Colin took a step back along with a deep breath, then smiled. "Well, hello there. So, you're my sister, huh? How long have you known Stephanie?"

"I met Stephanie soon after I met your mother. I've known her for quite a while now and I've always wanted to know you and your sisters."

"Of course, as you can expect, I'm in shock to hear this, but I'm happy to meet you. That's your family over there?" Colin looked over and my family waved and smiled. He smiled warmly and waved back. Then Colin quickly turned on the blender, then poured our drinks.

"Colin, I'm really happy to meet you. Your mother talks so highly of you and your sisters. I feel like I already know all of you. I've been waiting for her to introduce me. She'd said she would, but it's hard for her."

"I need to call my mom to find out what's going on. So, you're really her daughter, huh?"

"Yes, I am."

Colin shook his head again, looking at me intently now, seeing the traits I shared with his mother.

Just then, an older man walked in and greeted Colin by name before he sat down at the counter. We were no longer alone.

"There's something I need to ask of you," I said, and winced. "If you wouldn't mind waiting until Monday to call your mom, that would be so helpful. She's looking forward to meeting her grandchildren and spending the day with us tomorrow. But on Monday, you can call her and tell her I was here and tell your sisters about me too. I'd love to hear from them. I've waited a long time for this. It would mean a lot to me and my family if you could just wait a day to call your mother."

"Okay." He shrugged his shoulders.

"Thank you. I so appreciate that." I put both my hands up to my chest and crossed them.

"I can do that. I'll wait to call her and my sisters until Monday. I'll give you that time." Colin smiled as he wiped the counter and handed the new customer silverware and a glass of water.

"That's so kind of you. I know this must be shocking to hear. It was hard for me to do this, telling you like I did, so awkwardly."

My family had gotten up from the table and were standing beside me.

"I know you're working. I don't want to keep you. I hope we can talk again soon."

"Well, I guess thanks for stopping by and telling me. It's probably about time. Tell Stephanie hello and that I'll be calling her soon. I can at least give you all a hug goodbye."

We hugged each other, and as we drove off toward our hotel, I had mixed feelings about how things went. I didn't know him and was afraid he'd call Frances—because why wouldn't he? *Who the heck am I to him? A nobody. A stranger who walked into his life saying she's related to him. I asked a lot of him.* Michael and the kids tried to reassure me it went okay and to be happy I finally met him, but I wasn't so sure I had handled it in the best manner. I wished I didn't have to go behind Frances's back to meet my siblings.

Michael, Heather, Travis, and I met Frances in the same wonderful Italian restaurant on Fisherman's Wharf, where I had met my friend Karen several years before for dinner on the eve of meeting my biological mother for the first time. The restaurant held a good memory and now another one was being made.

Frances seemed shy. She didn't ask many questions but she smiled a lot, listening and nodding her head to Heather and Travis as they talked about school and sports, and their lives up until now. I think she enjoyed meeting her grandchildren, who were now sixteen and eighteen years old.

The next day we picked up Frances in front of her apartment in the Tenderloin. She seemed relaxed about me picking her up this time. I'd forewarned Michael and the kids about the neighborhood and the gritty, upsetting scenes they might see. Even so, it was hard to be prepared for such a sad and sordid environment.

Stephanie lived in a charming cottage on a private ranch surrounded by vineyards and horses, north of San Francisco. Large, mature oaks and black cottonwoods were home to various birds and provided shade from the late summer sun. The six of us gathered round her rustic firepit and savored the barbecue dinner that she and Michael had prepared, followed by traditional s'mores for dessert. It was an easy, fun day. A family day. I loved it. My only concern was Colin; in the back of my mind I wondered if he had called Frances and left her a message on her home answering machine.

I hoped that by tomorrow Frances would be just as involved with my family as I was with hers and it would be hard for her to let go of us. *I guess I'm being a little manipulative with her emotions, but wasn't she with mine over the past two-and-a-half years? I mean, how long do I have to wait until I get to meet my siblings?* She dangled their lives in front of me with promises, taunting me, and then, at the last minute, she pulled the curtain down every time, extinguishing any hope I had. It was getting harder and harder. I was tired of being a secret.

The next day, while Michael was driving us home, my cell phone rang. I could see from the area code the call was from the Bay Area. I answered it.

"Can I speak to Diane Wheaton?" It was a woman's voice.

"This is Diane." My chest tightened up a bit.

"Hi, Diane, this is your sister Colleen. I just found out about you from Colin, and I'm thrilled to know about you."

I closed my eyes and let my head fall back into my seat. Colleen was my youngest sister. I was so grateful that my brother had respected my request. I was almost in tears from relief.

Colleen and I spoke for about twenty minutes with Colleen

asking questions about how I found her mother, where I lived, and how the weekend went. We talked easily together and she promised to call me later that week. Another sibling! She sounded excited and warmly welcomed me into the family, just the opposite of how Frances had almost convinced me it would be. Maybe everything would be all right.

Three days later, Frances called. Stephanie warned me that she'd heard from our siblings, who were seeking confirmation that I was legitimately their half-sister. Stephanie also told me they were meeting with Frances in person over this, holding a family meeting. My hands began sweating as I answered her call.

"I don't know who you think you are stepping into my life and ruining it!" Frances yelled through the phone. "I have a mind to call your parents. How could you do this to me? I told you I wasn't ready for you to meet them yet!"

I let her yell. *I understand her reasoning and I'm sorry she has to go through this hardship with her children. And I didn't respect her wishes. Even though I considered pros and cons for over a year and had gotten all kinds of advice, was it really okay? Was it the right decision? Maybe not, but on the other hand, did Frances have the right to keep us from each other?*

I apologized. I told her that I was sorry I hurt her and that it was a very difficult decision, one I agonized over for a year or more, hoping she'd make good on her promise to tell her children about me.

"I didn't want my children to know I gave up two other babies," Frances cried out.

"I didn't tell them about Delores." I bit my lower lip.

"You didn't?" Frances's voice got quieter.

"No. There was no need for me to tell them about Delores."

"Oh, you didn't? Well, damn it, I said something because I assumed you told them about her too."

"No, I didn't do that."

So, the big secret was finally out. All four of her children now knew about Delores, Stephanie, and me. Frances had admitted to relinquishing three babies. Everything was laid out on the table. Transparent. (Except that Stephanie and I still knew nothing about our mysterious birth fathers; Frances held those cards close.)

I'd heard from Stephanie that my siblings were having a hard time accepting that their mother had given away three babies before they were born. I felt for them. It was still hard for me to accept, and I hadn't been raised by her. I could only imagine how disappointed and hurt they all must have felt. I hoped they felt empathy toward her too.

I hoped in time that their hurt would heal and that someday we could get to know each other, but I doubted this would ever happen. I might have ruined the chance for any kind of a relationship. They were angry with her for never telling them her secret, and adding me into their lives might bring up too many emotions to deal with. I had understood the risks, but I'd gone ahead anyway. I just wanted to love them and hoped that love would heal all of us over time.

I was relieved that Frances didn't want to end our relationship, but she made no effort to hide how upset she was. I was grateful she loved me and didn't want to cut me off, when in her eyes, I might've deserved it. It never ceased to amaze me how different she was from the mother who raised me.

But now, if any of my siblings wanted a relationship, I was available. As it turned out, my two youngest sisters, Allison and Colleen, were eager to know me from the beginning. They held none of the grudges Colin and Julia seemed to hold against me for pushing the envelope.

Several weeks later, after things had calmed down, I made a decision that, no matter what, I would never seek out my cousins or my uncle and his family. I was done. I didn't want to risk losing my mother or my siblings. From then on, I would leave any type of meeting with my cousins or my uncle up to the powers that be.

Part Three

———

"There are no secrets that time does not reveal."

—Jean-Baptiste Racine

"Love is the bridge between you and everything."

—Rumi

Chapter Twenty-One

THERE'S A BEFORE-AND-AFTER TIMELINE I LIVE WITH now. It splits everything in two: my life before April 11, 2007, and my life after.

On that early morning in April, I was following Heather in my car to drop hers off for scheduled maintenance. My phone rang. I saw it was my parents' number and answered it.

"Diane?" My father's voice sounded shaky.

"Hi, Dad, what's up?"

"It's your mother. I need you to come here as soon as you can."

"What do you mean? Did something happen to Mom?" My stomach tightened.

"Your mother's on her way to the hospital. She collapsed during the night. I don't know what's wrong with her, but I need someone to check on your mother for me and for someone to take care of me. Joanne is on her way to the hospital."

Joanne. He called her first, of course he did. In fairness, Dave and Joanne lived only ten minutes from my parents, so it made sense he'd call her first, but still, it bugged me. She was the preferred child.

"I'll be there as soon as I can. I'm driving with Heather to drop her car off at the dealership, and then we'll come. We'll get to your house in an hour or so."

"Okay." He sounded worried, and probably so did I.

When Heather and I walked into my parents' home, we found my dad sitting quietly in his recliner in the family room, his weathered face wearing a weary look of concern. My dad's thick, full head of hair, now white as cotton, looked crumpled, as if he hadn't brushed it in days. The worried look in his eyes made me wonder if he was frightened this may be the moment he would lose the love of his life.

My father, at eighty-seven, wasn't as mobile as he used to be. He didn't drive anymore and could hardly make it down the hall to the bathroom using a walker. With each passing month he seemed to be getting more fragile, no longer the strong man he once was.

"What took you so long?" he asked while repositioning himself in his chair.

"I know. I'm sorry. There's always so much traffic," I said, putting my purse down on the kitchen counter. I looked around and, as usual, the house was in order despite the early morning chaos.

Heather leaned over and kissed her grandfather on his forehead. He grabbed her hands in his and smiled up at her.

"Have you heard from Joanne yet?" I sat down in my usual chair, the ladder-back in the corner.

My dad looked over at me. "Joanne called just before you walked in. She said they're trying to find a room at the hospital. I guess she's stable but still unconscious. They're going to start running tests."

"Oh, Dad. I'm so sorry," I said, shaking my head in disbelief. "So what happened this morning?"

"I waited for your mother to come in and make coffee like she always does, but she never came in, so I checked on her and found her lying on the floor next to her bed. I don't know how long she had been lying there. I talked to her but she wasn't answering me, and when I felt her, she was cold, so I called 911. I didn't know what else to do."

"That was a good call. So the paramedics came and then what happened?"

"They came and couldn't wake her. They said she was alive and breathing but was unconscious, so they took her to the hospital. I called Joanne to meet her there because I couldn't go and then I called you."

"Oh, Dad," I said, continuing to shake my head as I walked into the kitchen. "Have you had any coffee yet, Dad? Or anything to eat?"

He shook his head. "I'm not hungry."

"I'm going to make a pot of coffee and make you some toast. You need to eat. After that, Heather and I will relieve Joanne at the hospital and check on Mom."

Heather and I walked into the emergency room and saw Joanne standing guard in the hallway next to my mother, who was sleeping on a gurney. She looked as white as the sheets wrapped around her.

We gave Joanne a hug and I said, "Thank you for being with my mom, Joanne. I really appreciate it."

She smiled and said, "Of course, Diane. I'd do anything for your mother." *This is probably very true.*

I looked down at my mother and caressed her left arm. I

took her cool hand in mine. She didn't respond to my touch.

Whispering in her ear, I said, "Hey, Mom, it's me, Diane. I'm here and so is Heather. You're in the hospital. They're going to take good care of you and we'll be right here. I'm staying with Dad, so just rest. You're going to be okay."

I had never seen my mom unconscious. I looked across the bed at Heather who was holding her grandmother's hand with tears in her eyes. Seeing my mom like this wasn't easy for either of us.

We found out that my mom had congestive heart failure and water in her lungs. She ended up being in and out of the hospital for five months with various illnesses and procedures. She'd come back home, we'd hire a temporary caregiver, and a week later, she'd be back in the hospital for one reason or another.

Finally, she was well enough to enter the hospital's rehabilitation center for six weeks before coming home for good.

I lived with my father for five long, intense months. I discovered he lived and slept in his blue recliner in the family room. Apparently, this was his new bedroom. Before living with him, I had no idea he no longer slept in bed beside my mother. I took over what my mother used to do—clean the house, pay bills, shop for groceries, do the laundry, and run errands. I watered her beloved yard and gardens—all kinds of flowers and trees planted decades ago. Fortunately, my parents had a housecleaner who came monthly and gardeners who came every week, so I didn't carry the full burden. I enjoyed watering by hand like my mother did and keeping my father company in the evenings.

It wasn't easy, but I look back fondly on this time with my father. Even when he slammed his cane hard against the family room wall from his recliner, yelling out my name toward the upstairs den where I was either reading or watching television, I knew one day I'd miss even that, and I do.

My father slept most of the day. In the evening, after dinner, I'd sit in my mother's matching blue tweed recliner and watch television with him. I turned him on to *American Idol*. He loved the music on that show. He seemed to have difficulty understanding conversations like the news and other shows, but he didn't have a problem understanding music.

I visited my mother twice a day, first thing in the morning and again in the late afternoon before dinner. After visiting her, I often treated myself with morning walks along the cliffs below their home, on the Ocean Trails Reserve path. Being at the ocean's door was soothing and meditative. I was home.

Sometimes, I called my sister Stephanie after walking and we'd catch up on Frances and the family, and I'd tell her about my parents and missing my kids. Other times, I drove down to the trail parking lot to call Frances. I couldn't risk talking to my sister or Frances with my father around. Frances and Stephanie understood what was going on and that I had to put my life on hold. It felt good to know I had their support, just like I had from Michael and his extended family.

Frances mentioned several times she wished she could have met my parents to thank them for raising her baby. I knew, of course, that could never happen, but I wished it could have.

Twice a month I drove the short distance around the hill into the maritime seaport of San Pedro, for a break. I parked on one of the main downtown streets near a small café and quaint bookstore. With coffee in hand, I entered the enchanting bookstore with overstuffed chairs, the smell of incense, and melodious instrumental music. The smell of fresh paper and bindings intoxicated me.

It was the perfect place for feeling far away from everything, and it became my sanctuary those five months. Each trip, I stocked up with books to indulge my joy of reading. In the quiet afternoons in my favorite spot in my parents' home—the living room—I'd plop down on the yellow-and-white floral down couch to read, which usually led to a nap.

During the summer months, I also developed a routine that helped me through this difficult time. After dinner and before sitting with my father, I would go outside on the back patio to put out a bowl of fruit and fresh water for a mama raccoon and her seven energetic and curious babies. I'd then go back inside the house and sit on the dining room floor, leaning against the wall, far enough away from the sliding door so they couldn't see me, and enjoy a glass of wine while enjoying a private viewing of the cautious mother and hungry babies munching away on the free fruit and water. I looked forward to this simple joy on those warm, summer evenings alone.

On the weekends, Michael, Heather, and Travis came down to visit when they could, but it was getting more difficult. Travis was now seventeen, a senior in high school, and had a summer job. He was also busy with the Los Angeles County Fire Explorers. Meanwhile, Heather was working part-time as an aesthetician and going to college full-time, so her time was limited. Michael worked near my parents' home, so he'd often pop over at lunchtime during the week. I always looked forward to seeing my family. I missed them, along my friends. We all tried to make the best of it while my mother recovered.

If she recovered. In the beginning, when I was told my mother might *not* recover, I realized my father would need care around the clock. That meant I had to quit the job I loved and had worked hard for—teaching. The year before, I graduated and passed state boards to be an aesthetician and had worked in several high-end day spas. My British instructor thought I'd enjoy being a teacher, so she took me under her wing and brought me on board at the school I'd attended, to train me as a state board instructor. I loved the job, loved the people I worked with and the students. It was hard to leave.

I suppose I could've hired help for my parents, but I felt the weight of responsibility to care for them myself. There was also a silver lining—it gave me an opportunity to know my father better. Our relationship had been good lately, but having my father ask for my help made me feel needed, something I hadn't always felt.

By then, it had been three years since I'd found and met Frances, and through that time, my parents and I hadn't had any issues—we had all got along well. I knew they were getting older and perhaps a bit softer emotionally, not quite as volatile as in the past, but it made me wonder, too, if something had shifted in my own psyche. Maybe finding my biological mother and sister and learning more about my birth family had a deeper impact than I realized. Maybe, subconsciously, I didn't feel as needy toward my parents; maybe it was easier for me to let go of their sometimes thoughtless and hurtful comments. I didn't know for sure why we seemed to get along better after I found Frances and Stephanie, but I thought it interesting that I felt more confident and at ease with myself and my adoptive parents than I had in a very long time.

During the months I lived with my father, I started noticing little things he did and said that concerned me. He was becoming forgetful and had bouts of unreasonable anger. He had a difficult time with change, like having caregivers come into the home or trying something new to eat. He refused to see any of his physicians.

One evening when visiting my mother in the hospital, I called my father as I always did, to let him know I was on my way home, to his house. But when I walked into the family room, I noticed an ashen color on my father's face with an expression that could be painted panic-stricken.

"Dad, what's wrong?" I wondered if he had heard some horrific news in the past ten minutes since speaking to him.

"What are you doing here? You just called and said you were on your way home."

"Yeah, and here I am. What's the matter, Dad?" I asked, confused, putting my purse and keys down on the kitchen counter.

"I thought you were on your way home, to your house."

My brows furrowed. "Why would I be doing that?"

"Because your mother died so you were going to go home now."

I felt sorry for his confusion and gave him a hug in his chair. "Oh, Dad, nooooo. Mom is just fine. I just left her. She's doing great. I was telling you, like I do every night, that I was coming home—to you."

"Ooohhh." My father let out a deep sigh. "I thought Mom passed and you were now going home."

"Oh my gosh, Dad, why would I, if anything ever happened to Mom, why would I leave you alone here?" I shook my head and smiled, trying to relieve him of the fear I saw in his face.

"So, she's okay?"

"Yes, Mom is just fine. All is well."

He smiled and shook his head as if he couldn't believe he had misunderstood something so simple that happened every day.

This was the first sign my father was mentally failing. *What is ahead of us?*

Another time, my dad asked me to follow up at one of his banks about a letter he had recently mailed to them. Speaking to the bank manager on behalf of my father, he gave me a grim look as he passed me my father's handwritten letter, and said in a kind, soft-spoken, voice, "I'm so sorry, but I think your father has lost his mind."

I looked at the manager wondering what he meant by this. I opened the letter and couldn't believe what I saw. It was scribbled words, letters put together in ways that made no sense. It was gibberish.

"I'm so sorry," the manager said as he looked down. Tears came to my eyes.

After that incident, I realized that something was wrong with my father, which I attributed to the beginnings of dementia. It was hard to understand. *How did my father manage to send that letter out?* I made myself a mental note that I needed to start paying more attention to his speech and behaviors and to give him more grace when he acted unreasonable.

Before my mother could come home, I attended occupational therapy trainings provided by the hospital for family members who were caregiving so I could learn how to help her around the house and get her in and out of a car safely. I also needed to find trained medical care—twenty-four-hour care. My father and I interviewed lots of people, finally settling on two women, Ruby and Sheri, certified nurse assistants who would share the duties by working three days on and three days off. They came with great recommendations from the hospital's social services.

I got busy preparing a room for them, making it as pleasant

as possible. My dad wasn't happy about strangers living with them but he wanted my mom home, so reluctantly, he accepted his fate.

The day finally arrived when my mom came home. I helped Ruby become acquainted with where things were and I dedicated a labeled notebook to instructions for the household. I didn't have to worry too much because my mom was home and could tell Ruby where things were and how she liked things done. It was her house, and my mom was feeling good, happy to be home again. I wasn't needed as much so I decided to head home that evening.

I packed the things I had brought into my childhood bedroom and said goodbye to my mom, who was getting ready for bed with help from Ruby. I walked over to my dad, who was sitting in his recliner, and jokingly said, "Well, here I go, Dad. It's been fun. Fortunately or unfortunately for you, you get to see me again in two more days."

He looked up, not smiling at my silly words but looking troubled, with tears in his blue eyes. I didn't know what to think when he said, "I know you have to go, but I can't help but feel that you are abandoning me."

My heart sank. I had come to love my father even more while taking care of him, and his expression of sadness tugged at my heart. I'd never imagined I could feel this way.

"I'm not leaving you, Dad. Mom's home now, and you've got really good help. I'll be back before you know it—in just two days! Plus, I'm as close as a phone call away." I bent down and hugged him, kissing him on his warm cheek. He grabbed one of my arms and held on tight with his thinning hands.

I walked out the oak double front door at a slow pace. After five months living with my father, our relationship had grown into the best it had ever been. Our time together had been a gift.

I left that night feeling compassion for my father and happiness that I was going home and that my mother was better. I already missed them both. Perhaps from now on, we'd be closer. I hummed with happiness as I imagined this.

One month later, my mom was thriving and my dad was accepting the changes that came with her being home again. I came down to their house weekly, spending a night or two, so I could do grocery shopping, errands, watering, and taking my mother to medical appointments. Our caregivers were great. We were fortunate that everyone got on well. I think my mom enjoyed their company.

One evening, during the last week in September, I was sitting with my father watching television.

All of a sudden, he turned his head and, looking over at me, said in a serious tone, "Before we go any further in all this, there's something you need to read."

He pulled a manila envelope from where he kept his current papers and mail. *Are these my adoption papers? The ones I haven't seen since finding them at nineteen? Is he giving them to me?*

"Okay," I answered tentatively and slowly opened up the silver clasp on the back of the envelope, pulling out a thick stack of papers stapled together. It wasn't my adoption papers. It was my parents' last will and trust.

"What's this?" *Why does he want me to read this? Is there something wrong, or does he just want me to be aware of their wishes?*

"I want you to read through it. We can talk about it when you're done." My father's face had a stern look that reminded me of years ago.

"Okay," I answered. My heart started to pound. *This is weird.*

Sitting next to him, in my mother's recliner, I started reading the legalese. I read several paragraphs over and over. It wasn't long before I comprehended what was going on here—my parents were cutting me out of their will. My mouth fell open. I couldn't look at my father. I didn't want him to see me. I felt vulnerable and uncomfortable sitting next to him.

I kept my head down and continued reading. *Oh my God. I can't believe they did this.* They had made a generation-skipping trust. The trust went directly to my children. Everything went to them including the sale of the house, all of it managed by Dave as trustee, with Joanne as backup. Not me. I wouldn't oversee my own children's inheritance. I winced as their hurtful knife went through my heart.

I couldn't believe what I'd read so far, and I wasn't finished yet. There was something else. The last thing they requested was that their personal items were to be split between Joanne and me. Fifty-fifty. I couldn't believe this. *Do they hate me but feel obligated to give me something?* I felt used, but most of all, betrayed.

A pang of hurt and bewilderment ignited inside me. This was beyond anything I could've ever imagined my parents doing. *Fifty-fifty with Joanne? How could they? How can they think I'd be okay with this?* I guess they didn't care whether I was okay with it or not. *How hurtful to do this to your only living child. To me, their daughter. I can't imagine doing this to Heather, but then, this whole scenario with Joanne has been hurtful for years. She truly is the daughter my parents wish they had.*

As hard as I tried, I couldn't stop the tears from welling up. My chin and lower lip began to quiver. I didn't want my father to see how he had hurt me. I didn't want to appear weak.

"Wow," I said, standing up, my legs buckling as I tried to get a grip on my emotions. I found myself speechless.

"That's your copy," my father said, pointing at me with his bony finger and staring.

"Okay. That's good because I'm going to need some time to process this." I looked back at him, my eyes and face hard like a rock, trying to keep my tears at bay.

"Well," he answered, shuffling himself and putting both arms firmly on the arms of his chair. "I think you should know your mother and I made that will and trust a long time ago when we weren't happy with you. We've never changed it because, well, I'm sorry, that's just how we felt. But I think you needed to know about this before you continue on with us."

Continue on? Does he mean my caring for them? Being there for them? Does he not really care anymore now that they have full-time help?

I looked toward the large window in the kitchen-dining area, at the darkness outside that seemed to reflect the darkness I felt from my father.

"Okay." I nodded my head as I looked around, but not over at him. I pursed my lips and silently walked out of the room, walking upstairs to pack up my clothes. I couldn't bear to stay another night.

Chapter Twenty-Two

FEELING CONFUSED, FOOLED, AND UNLOVED, I AGREED WITH
my father on one thing: he was right—I did need to know about
their will and trust before I continued taking care of them, if I
did decide to continue, which I wasn't sure I'd be able to do.

I tried to talk myself out of falling down a dark hole into the
land of doubt and depression. But what was left to hold on to?
They cut me out of their will. It was no trouble at all to topple
downward into a dark blue abyss.

In Mary's sunny kitchen one afternoon, staring into my
caramel-colored latte, lost in thought, I watched the steam spiral
toward the ceiling before vaporizing into the air, like how I was
feeling about my relationship with my parents.

"You know, Mary," I said abruptly, turning around in my
chair to face her while she fixed dinner. "I remember years ago,
my dad asked me if I was okay with Dave as their executor. I
felt kind of awkward about it, but I didn't have a choice in the
matter. They were going to do what they wanted to do."

Mary spun around with a cooking spoon in hand and waved
it into the air. "You're right about that, Diane. They always do
what they want to do."

"My dad said Dave would only accept being their executor if
I knew about it and was okay with it."

"That was decent of Dave." Mary nodded her head while pushing back hair from her eyes before putting the casserole in the oven.

"Yes, it was," I agreed. "Dave and Joanne are basically good people. I don't think my parents would have ever asked me—they only did because Dave asked them to."

I had called Ruby, my mother's caregiver, the day after I left my parents' house, and told her I was going to take a break and asked her to call me if there was an emergency. I was fortunate there were no appointments scheduled, which gave me time to try and figure out what I was going to do. As far as I knew, my mother and Ruby knew nothing of what had transpired between my father and me.

I considered calling it quits with my parents. Every person I spoke to, especially my childhood friends, encouraged me to end my relationship with my parents. They all said in one way or another, "Enough is enough."

It was easy for them to say—the situation *was* awful and it seemed obvious that cutting myself off from my parents would be the healthiest thing to do—but it wasn't so easy to *do*. They were my parents, and they were becoming more and more fragile. I was so conflicted: mad that they had nearly erased my existence with their generation-skipping trust; grateful they were being generous with my children.

That first night home, I read and reread the documents and began to stitch together the timeline. I noticed the year they made their decision was the same year, 1992, that I had told Heather I was adopted. That was fifteen years ago, when they'd stopped talking to me for nearly a year, until my father called to tell me I needed to apologize or they would take me out of their will and end our relationship. Well, now I knew that when he had called the following year, they had already made their decision and written me out. And when my father called to ask me about Dave becoming their executor, he was lying. *Why all these betrayals? What had I done?*

I tried to understand why. I knew they felt betrayed by my telling Heather the truth, but their response seemed cruel. Plus, the fact that in all these years they'd never made any changes to the trust confused me. Apparently, they'd been so afraid Heather and Travis would love Michael's parents more that they became vengeful. Clearly, they had never given me any grace or forgiveness. It was hard to fathom such a hard, unforgiving attitude.

Is this how they still feel about me? My dad said it is. How can they still feel this way? They'd enjoyed a loving relationship with Heather and Travis, one that I thought was actually closer than with Michael's parents. *But why get caught up in all this competitiveness?*

More than anything, and much more than the money, I can't get over why I have to share my parents' personal belongings with Joanne, whom I now feel has been elevated to my own status as daughter. This hurt me deeply. I didn't feel special as a daughter. I felt like I was someone they felt obligated to mention.

The pain brought back memories of the triad relationship between my mother, Joanne, and me. One in particular was hard to get over.

I was twenty-six years old and had a job I loved as an administrative assistant in human relations at the same aerospace corporation my father worked at. I lived in my own apartment across the street from the beach. I took sailing lessons once a week in Marina del Rey, and crewed Wednesday nights in a local regatta. Other nights after work, I rode my beloved bike along the Strand, a bike path on the beach, for exercise and me-time. Life was good.

My mother's birthday was coming up, and I could finally afford to do something nice for her, something special. I called my father at work.

"Hi, Dad, do you think Mom would like to see *Dreamgirls* at the Shubert Theatre for her birthday?" *Dreamgirls* was a popular Broadway production that earned thirteen Tony nominations and won six. Both my parents enjoyed plays and musicals. I had grown up going with them to all sorts of productions, so I thought this would be a fun thing for my mom and me to do together.

"Yes," he said, sounding enthusiastic. "I think she'd like that."

So, I bought two tickets and invited my mother in a pre-birthday card. I wrote out my plan: I would take her to lunch in Century City, and afterward, we'd go to the Shubert Theatre to see *Dreamgirls* for her birthday. She said yes and seemed happy. We didn't do things often outside of my weekly Sunday night dinners at their home, so I looked forward to the day.

A few days before our date, my father called me at work.

"I'm sorry but your mother hasn't been feeling well the past few days. She doesn't think she'll be able to make it Saturday and asked me to call you to tell you it might be best to find someone else to go with you to the play."

I couldn't believe it. Well, I could. I was hurt. I didn't believe my father. My mother wasn't sick—she just didn't want to go with me or be with me. I ended up asking one of Ellen's sisters to go with me, as Ellen was out of the country, sailing in the South Pacific.

The worst part was finding out from my brother a week later that my mother was just fine that day. John said, "Mom and Joanne went to lunch together to celebrate her birthday, and then did some shopping that afternoon."

It hurt hearing this, but I was glad to know the truth. I was beginning to digest the fact that Joanne really was the daughter my mother seemed to love the most.

So it's no surprise it took me a few nights to call Joanne about the trust. I wanted to know if she and Dave knew what was in it. I dialed her home phone and Joanne answered right away.

"Hi, Joanne, it's Diane."

"Oh, hi, Diane." She sounded friendly, even happy to hear from me. "Is everything all right with your parents?"

"Oh yeah, they're fine. Say, do you have a few minutes to talk?" I was standing in the quiet of the dimly lit family room. I rubbed my forehead as I slowly sat down on the edge of the couch.

"Sure," she answered.

"Okay, good." I paused and took a deep breath. I disliked confrontation, but I had to know what they knew. "Well, last week my dad gave me a copy of their will and trust. He asked me to read it. I was quite surprised by what was in it." My voice began to shake.

"Surprised? What do you mean?" Joanne asked. *Does she really not know what is in the trust?*

"There were a few surprises," I said. "The first was that they made a generational skipping trust, skipping me and giving everything, split evenly, to Heather and Travis. The second surprise was that I'm supposed to split their personal belongings with you, fifty-fifty."

Silence. Then, Joanne answered, "Oh, really?"

"Yup." I could feel my chest getting hot and my heartbeat accelerating. I didn't want to get emotional with Joanne, but it was all too much, and before I knew it, tears were flowing down my hot cheeks. I closed my eyes and took another deep breath. I was weeping but I didn't care anymore. "Joanne, I know you and my parents are close, but this is very hurtful for me, what they've done. I don't understand it. It's not about the money, either—it's the point of it, what they mean by this. I'm their daughter. I'm actually their only surviving child, but it seems I hold no special place in their hearts. I could never do this to either of my children so I don't understand how my parents could have done this to me. I get it about Dave being their executor. I'm not upset about that. It's all the rest of it."

"So, splitting their personal items between us is upsetting to you?"

"Really, Joanne? Yes. Yes, it is. I'm their daughter. You're not." I tried to say this as nice as I could. "I'm sorry. I can certainly understand some special items they'd want you to have—that's fair—but it's *everything* split between us."

I had lost it, lost control of my emotions and probably any reasonable thought process. I couldn't stop the flow of tears or my shaky voice, and I couldn't believe Joanne didn't get it. It was as if she felt entitled to my parents' things as much as I was.

Am I going crazy? Joanne was literally a neighbor girl who had kept in contact with my parents since childhood. Sure, over the years, she and Dave became close to them. I guess I never realized the depth of their relationship and how much they were involved with each other until now.

"I'm sorry, Diane," Joanne said quietly, calmly.

My tears had finally stopped, and, wiping my eyes, I asked, "So did you know?"

"Know what?"

"What was in the trust?"

"No. I didn't know." Joanne sounded defensive. "Dave and I only knew he would be the executor because they didn't want you to have that burden. I didn't know any other details. I don't think Dave did either, and if he did, he never said anything to me."

I laughed to myself hearing my parents didn't want me to be their executor because they didn't want to burden me. I didn't believe this. I didn't know what to believe anymore. "So, you don't have a copy?"

"No," Joanne answered curtly, then added, "Diane, honestly, I didn't know any of this until right now. I'm sorry you feel this way about me and that this has happened to you. I want you to know that you can have anything you want of your parents' things when the time comes. I won't stand in your way."

"Well, of course I'd share things with you. I know you love my parents. It's just that I'm hurt by their request because this is obviously how they feel about me. It's not about things or money. It's about my parents loving me. I don't mean to offend you, but I needed to know if you knew about the trust. These are my parents, Joanne. I hope you can understand my feelings."

I'm not sure she did understand, but I was glad I spoke with her. I felt better knowing she wasn't hiding this knowledge all these years. I had no choice but to take her word. We bid each other a cool goodbye.

The next thing that needed to be done was to figure out whether, or how, to continue my relationship with my parents. I didn't know if my mother knew I'd read the trust. This might've been my father's doing. For days, I considered all sides, wrestling with the pros and cons and how I might feel if I never saw them again. I thought about Heather and Travis and how sad they'd feel never seeing their grandparents again.

I tried to see my parents' perspective over the previous years so I might understand why they felt they needed to willfully cause me pain after they died. I knew they had their own demons, as did I.

What bothered me most was my conclusion—I still wanted to see them. It sounded sick or emotionally weak to me, but that was how I felt.

What is wrong with me? How could my friends say they could call it quits so easily when I felt responsible for my parents, loyal even, and loving toward them despite how damaging it might be for me to continue our relationship? I knew I struggled with abandonment issues, and this situation was certainly a big trigger. *Maybe I have Stockholm syndrome? A trauma bond?* I felt crazy because who in their right mind would go back and take care of people who'd treated them so horribly?

I called and got an early morning appointment with my former therapist, Dr. Goldman. I think he squeezed me in. I drove down to his new offices in the South Bay a few days later. He had come a long way from a one-man office to owning his own building with a large practice that carried his name. I wasn't surprised by his success.

I waited quietly in the Zen-like reception area, surrounded by calming hues of sage, cream, and gray with living plants and trees, until the young receptionist called my name. I hadn't seen Dr. Goldman for fifteen years. When he saw me, he stood up, smiling, looking the same, only now with a full beard and graying temples. He walked over to me, this tall, gentle bear of a man, and gave me a hug. I sat down in a familiar, oversized, well-worn leather chair, just like in the old days.

It was as easy to talk with him as the day we first met. I explained to Dr. Goldman my current situation and my crazy idea of wanting to continue overseeing my parents' care. I told him that I had done a lot of thinking, processing all sides, and that even though I was terribly hurt by my parents, I also felt grateful for what they would be doing for my children and their future, which, honestly, would ease things for Michael and me as well.

"My biggest problem isn't the money," I continued. "It's accepting having to share things with Joanne, that I feel they think the same of her as they do me—almost like another daughter. I'll need a lot more time getting over that, if I ever can."

"That's understandable, Diane," Dr. Goldman assured me.

"After so much consideration, so much thinking, I've come to the conclusion that I could live with myself better after they're gone if I continue overseeing their care. I know it may sound strange to most people, but I feel like it's the right thing to do. I'm following my heart. Even though they've hurt me deeply, I still love them and feel responsible for their care at this point in their lives. This is where I'm conflicted. Do I sound crazy?"

"No, Diane, you don't sound crazy," Dr. Goldman said. "It sounds like you've taken your time and given this situation a lot of thought. Your decision doesn't sound hasty. If this is how you feel, despite what's happened, and you want to do this because you're grateful to some degree and feel responsible for them as their only child, then that is your answer. You know what you're stepping back into. If it ever gets to be too much emotionally, you can always step away. You have control over your situation. You can always hire people to take care of them if you ever change your mind. You don't owe them anything, but what you're saying is you want to honor your parents with love and respect, and there is nothing wrong with that, even if they don't deserve it. You need to remember to honor and take care of yourself too."

Driving home after seeing Dr. Goldman, I felt lighter. Better. I did have control. I could do this. I saw my parents more clearly, in a different light now. Perhaps I finally saw them as they were, as they had always been, as hurting, insecure, fearful people. In our family, adoption had not been our friend. It was our deepest struggle, one we all wrestled with.

Adoption is trauma. Fifteen years before, I had unintentionally hurt my parents by telling my daughter my truth, and now I was being punished for it. Their fear brought up their anxiety, which caused them to perceive my honesty as betrayal. That became their breaking point. In their eyes, I had crossed the line. They might have wished they could erase me from their lives. It seemed as though they'd tried.

They wanted to pretend adoption never happened to them, to sweep it under the rug. Adoption, they believed, was something you should never talk about. It was shameful. It was shameful they couldn't have children. It was shameful John and I were born out of wedlock. They'd said to both of us growing up, "Don't ever tell anyone you're adopted. It changes things."

Why should I be ashamed? Should I have been ashamed of myself? No. I have nothing to hide and nothing to be ashamed of.

I could have asked and paid the caregivers to take care of the house and drive my parents to their medical appointments, but I didn't. I could have hired a finance manager, but I didn't. I chose to take care of them. I'm sure my decision to go back sounded insane to some of my friends and family. Sometimes, it sounded that way to me.

I made the decision that I would love them as best I could even with all this and be there for them, as I had these past six months. I'd make sure they had the best care because that's what love does. I did it because I wanted to honor the good times we'd had, the privileged life they had given me, and the love I felt from them as a little girl. I was grateful they would gift my children when they could have easily given it all to charity or, worse and certainly more hurtful, to Joanne and her family.

I didn't want to feel resentful of my own children. It would have been easy to feel that if I had allowed negativity and bitterness to fester. I had to rise above the hurt and see the silver lining. Moving forward in gratitude and love toward my parents would be how I could learn to cope and not reap bitterness. It wasn't that I didn't hurt anymore; I did. And, while I still didn't understand why they didn't change the trust in all these years, I told myself that was their decision, their journey, their legacy. It wasn't mine. I needed to set a good example for my children. The right thing for me was to take care of my parents, to love them in spite of themselves. We were all imperfect. Love was the healer. Feeling grateful was the catapult.

So, the next day, I called Ruby and told her I'd be down the following week to take my mother to her doctor's appointment.

Chapter Twenty-Three

RETURNING TO MY PARENTS' HOME THE FOLLOWING WEEK, it was as if nothing happened. That was just as well, because I didn't want to get into a discussion about the trust. I didn't want to make myself feel worse just when I was doing better, moving forward, and allowing emotional distance between us.

The strange thing was that both of my parents seemed genuinely happy to see me. I even wondered if my dad had forgotten what had transpired two weeks before. I guess I shouldn't have been surprised; this song and dance between us was nothing new.

I took my mother to her medical appointment. She was in good spirits seeing me again, and I think she even said she missed me. And, just like before, I took care of her and relished the time we had together. Over the next few weeks, I was encouraged that I seemed capable of doing this, and it felt right. Sometimes I still wondered if I was crazy for going back and caring for my parents. But then I would remember why I was there, and I'd suck it up and put on my emotional armor so I couldn't get hurt by them anymore.

My youngest biological sister, Colleen, called later that week and invited my family and me to come up for a family reunion at her home later that month.

"It's time," Colleen said. "We've all waited long enough to meet each other."

It had been a little over one year since we first talked on the phone. Colleen invited my brother Colin and two of my other sisters, Julia and Allison, along with Frances and Stephanie.

At the end of October 2007, Mike, Heather, Travis, and I met Colleen, her husband Adrian, and two of their three sons for dinner on the patio at their favorite barbecue restaurant.

I didn't experience the same buildup of nerves as there had been with Stephanie. I had been talking to Colleen on the phone for over a year by now, and for over three years, I'd been hearing about her life from Frances. I already felt I knew her well, yet seeing her for the first time was just as wonderful as meeting Stephanie. It was just different. It was great to have our families with us too.

"It's so good to finally meet you," I said to Colleen, after we embraced. I stepped back to get a better look at my youngest sister. Colleen was as tall as Stephanie with soft, hazel eyes and long, golden brown hair pulled up into a casual bun. She favored her father's Indigenous side, but I saw glimpses of our mother in her. She was very pretty.

"It's so good to finally meet you too, Diane," Colleen answered with tears in her eyes, which made mine tear up as well. *Finally, I'm meeting you . . .*

Adrian, my new brother-in-law, was gregarious and friendly. Colleen was fun. They all were. We stayed late on the patio laughing and getting to know each other. I think we were the last to leave the restaurant. The evening went by fast, and I was amazed how easy it was between all of us. It didn't feel like the first time we'd been together.

Falling asleep that night, I mused how the next day I might be meeting my other siblings and thought maybe I'd have my

Antwone Fisher moment. When I was first coming out of the fog, I watched a film entitled *Antwone Fisher*, a true story of a young adoptee finding his biological family. In one of the last scenes, he meets his extended family in a beautiful, dreamlike setting, like a Thanksgiving dinner, where all his family members welcome him into their lives. That scene in the film gets me every time. I can so relate to that feeling of loss and to finally feel and have that moment of connection with family welcoming you with open arms back into the fold.

Driving to Adrian and Colleen's home the next morning, I took in where she lived, noticing everything I could about her life, her grocery store, the local dry cleaners, the restaurants. This was where she'd been living for years—undetected, unknown, another secret. Maple trees on both sides of the street welcomed us to her neighborhood.

We parked our car out front of their two-story, ranch-style home. Adrian and Colleen greeted us with warm hugs and kisses on our cheeks, with Adrian crowing, "Diane, *mi casa, su casa!*"

"Thanks, Adrian," I answered, smiling widely. I really liked him. And Colleen. *This will be a good day.*

My nephews were in the kitchen, cutting up tomatoes and chopping chiles for the salsa. The backyard was lovely—it was designed for family get-togethers with a built-in barbecue and pool. They had gone all out for this day, which touched me, offering plenty of food to snack on plus an array of lunch choices: hamburgers, BBQ chicken, grilled brats, with several salads and salsas, as well as beer and soft drinks stacked in the cooler, and a lineup of red and white wines.

Heather and Travis were enjoying themselves. The boys, first cousins, gathered in the family room and bonded over video games, while Heather stood beside me, laughing and joining in the conversation with her new aunt and uncle.

Stephanie was the next to arrive, and I noticed the ease with which my two sisters greeted each other and the similarities between them. A wisp of sadness came over me thinking how long Stephanie had known everyone, how she had been able to meet our grandmother on her visits from Nashville. Stephanie was fortunate that she'd never been a secret to the family and that Frances had welcomed her with open arms, eager to have her meet her children—because giving up one baby was acceptable.

An hour later, Frances arrived with my sister Allison and her boyfriend.

Allison happily surprised me, but then I didn't know how she'd be after her long struggle with heroin. She was as tall as my other sisters and my daughter with long, dark hair falling to the middle of her slender back. She wore tight jeans, knee-high black leather boots with a short, black leather jacket over a patterned indigo tank. She had our mother's green eyes, and she was gorgeous—exotic. She could've been an actress or model.

Allison walked toward me, her arms opening like wings, and graced me with a long embrace as if she hadn't seen me in years. I found myself tearing up at her warm welcome.

For an hour Allison and I sat holding hands while talking. Allison was lovely, and she emanated warmth toward me. I hoped she felt the same coming to her from me. I would never have known she struggled as an addict. She was a strong woman to have been able to overcome such a tough addiction. I admired her.

At one point during the day, I was sitting in the kitchen-dining area, savoring my glass of red wine and observing all three of my sisters talking together while restocking appetizers. Colleen noticed me staring at them. I had been thinking how interesting it was that I could love my sisters so easily, while hardly knowing them. They seemed to feel the same way. It seemed like an immediate bond between us. We were family and it felt magnificent in that moment.

Colleen asked, "Are you getting overwhelmed, Diane?" She smiled. Stephanie and Allison turned to look at me. All three smiled together.

I laughed, feeling wonderfully happy being there with them and, from the wine, nodded my head yes, and exclaimed, "You're all so tall!"

We laughed.

"We have our mother to thank for that, don't we, Mom?" Colleen yelled toward Frances who was sitting in the adjoining family room watching her grandsons.

"I don't think I'm overwhelmed. I'm feeling very happy, a bit buzzed, reflecting on everything, all in a good way. I'm feeling celebratory," I said, smiling. "It's so surreal seeing the three of you together, knowing you're my sisters. It's just amazing."

"It's real, Diane! You're our sister and we love you," Colleen announced. She came over and hugged me. Colleen was always warm and welcoming.

About an hour after Frances had arrived, Colleen got a text from Julia saying that she and Colin wouldn't be able to make it.

"Don't take it personally, Diane," Colleen said. "They hardly ever come to family stuff. It's rare to see them. I wish they had come today, but I'm not surprised."

I was disappointed not to see Colin again and meet Julia, but I took Colleen's advice and didn't take their absence to heart. I had heard from all my sisters that Julia had issues about being jilted, once again, from her position as the oldest daughter. First, there was Stephanie walking into her life, and then me, and with me came our oldest but still missing sister, Delores.

I'm sure it was difficult to fathom that your mother relinquished three babies before you were born. I got it—it was hard for me. It could rock your world. I think it really affected Julia, which made it impossible for her to meet me, even though I was as much a victim in this situation as she was.

I will be the first to admit I hadn't handled my first meeting with Colin very well. I could only hope, in time, he could forgive and understand my mistake. Neither Stephanie nor I knew any other way at the time. What was done was done. I wrote him later, offering my apology, but I never heard from him. I wrote Julia, too, telling her that I wasn't going to push myself on her, but if she ever wanted to meet me, I would be there. I respected their need for distance and was aware that not everyone was happy with who I was and what I represented.

Allison, on the other hand, had loved the letter I sent her. Holding my hand, she confided, "I was moved when you wrote and told me how you were interested in Alaska since you were a little girl and that we were always connected in some way to each other by synchronicity, by something bigger, something metaphysical, by something we don't understand."

Synchronicity is a magical phenomenon. The concept was first introduced by the Swiss psychiatrist and psychoanalyst Carl Jung, who said that synchronicity described "circumstances that appear meaningfully related yet lack a causal connection." In other words, there is no logical explanation.

But when I found out that my siblings were native Alaskans (Tlingit), my lifelong interest in Alaska and Native American culture made sense; it seemed to be coming from a deeper connection. I didn't understand it, but I found it moving and intensely profound. I think Allison did too. I've read that this phenomenon is common in adoptees and in adoptee circles. I've often heard the term "adoptee synchronicity." And this was it—what I had experienced.

My reunion at Colleen's home was a dream come true; it had become my first Antwone Fisher moment. My children and I were surrounded by people who were related to us, from my side, who were there for us, who wanted to know and love us because we were family. It was unconditional. I felt full, as if I could float past the maple trees as we drove away that evening and home the following day.

Two weeks later, back home, I received a call from Ruby and Sheri. Ruby did the talking.

"Diane, Sheri and I think you need to make an appointment with a home health physician to come see your father. We're spending more time taking care of him these days than your mother. He's getting difficult to take care of. He might need some medication to help calm him down."

"Oh, really?" I was surprised to hear Ruby say this, then remembered the strange letter to the bank manager last summer.

A week later I was at my parents' home, meeting a hospice physician who was evaluating my father because he refused to go to a doctor's office. The following week, the physician called my mother and me. "I'm so sorry to tell you, but your husband and your father probably has Alzheimer's. That's my diagnosis of what's been going on with him."

Alzheimer's. What the heck? My father has Alzheimer's.

"The best-case scenario for your father while he's living at home is to have him under hospice care."

I couldn't believe it. He didn't seem *that* bad, but then Ruby and Sheri said they had to physically struggle with him on several occasions. He was still strong, although getting more frail. He was also headstrong and afraid these days. I thought back to the bank letter and all those little signs of misunderstanding, unreasonableness, and paranoia over the simplest things this past summer when I was living with him.

"Your father probably has had Alzheimer's for a while. People can get quite creative hiding the fact that they are losing their minds. I'm so sorry, but under hospice care, he can get the help and medication he'll need," the physician continued.

Ruby reassured me, "We can now get some good meds to help with his anxiety. We'll take good care of him, Diane."

Only one month later, my father began experiencing hallucinations. I began staying overnight two nights a week to spend more time with my parents and to help Ruby and Sheri. Alzheimer's is a sad disease. They call it "the long goodbye," and it really is. I witnessed my father having a hallucination, seeing a room full of people, strangers standing in line for coffee in the family room and kitchen.

He would ask me, nervous and worried over something simple, "What are all these people doing here? How can I ever get a cup of coffee?"

"Don't worry, Dad. I have connections," I'd say, while patting his arm, trying to relieve his concern. Smiling, I'd bring him a cup of coffee, which calmed him for the moment.

It was hard to watch him leave us. He had to be put on a stronger medication for his hallucinations because he began to get violent, even with me. He tried to take a swing at me one day because he was scared. He had several of these outbursts with Ruby and Sheri too. We couldn't lose either of them—they were so good at what they did and so kind with my parents and me.

Several weeks before Christmas, Ruby said my father needed to begin to transition to a hospital bed. He wasn't able to walk well anymore, even with his walker, and it would be easier for them to care for him in a hospital bed.

"He'll be more comfortable too, Diane," Ruby went on to

say. "He'll be able to stretch out and rest better rather than sitting and sleeping in his recliner."

Of course, my father fought this change, but with help from my mother, Ruby convinced him to try it. Fortunately, Ruby and Sheri had years of experience. We decided the best spot for my father was to be in the hub of the home, in the family room–kitchen area. So, Michael and Travis moved the larger couch into my father's den, making room for his hospital bed. He surprised himself by liking being able to stretch out just as Ruby had said. It must've felt so good.

Ruby and Sheri used a lift sling to move him from his bed to his recliner or wheelchair, so he wasn't always stuck in bed. We could move him around in his wheelchair, take him outside in the yard, and even help him sit up next to my mother in his recliner so he could watch TV with her.

Christmas this year was such a dichotomy. I felt content and happy for having my birth family in my life—my sisters and my mother. I knew them so much better now, and things were going well between us. I felt that the path ahead would be nothing but good as we got to know each other better. It certainly had been that way with Frances and Stephanie.

On the other hand, there were my elderly parents and all that we had gone through this past year. I was still feeling confident in my decision to take care of them, especially with my father's diagnosis. My mother was better every day, though I had a twinge of suspicion she might have dementia too. But, geez, my parents were now in their late eighties. They were as good as they would ever be, and I felt like grief had come early, settling in my heart.

Finding and forming a relationship with my blood family was one of my greatest accomplishments, after marrying Michael and having my children. This had been a tough year, but it also had been one of love. I had cultivated a deeper relationship with my parents, who also gave me one of my greatest heartbreaks, but I survived it, and landed on a higher mountain made from forgiveness and an ability to see the silver lining. I had learned to climb a bit higher, be a bit stronger, and have more confidence in my decisions, by listening to my heart and instincts. As the new year approached, I moved cautiously into the unknown days ahead.

Chapter Twenty-Four

IT HAD BEEN A TRADITION FOR THE LAST TEN YEARS OR SO that on my birthday my parents would sing "Happy Birthday" over the phone. I always got a kick out of it and appreciated that they could be sweet and sentimental. Our relationship was clearly complex. This year, 2008, my father had a tougher time conjuring up the words to the song. I think I appreciated the attempt even more, since he was slowly losing his ability to speak and find his words, just like he was losing, or had lost, his ability to read, write, and recognize numbers.

Life had settled into a routine once again at home with Heather and Travis. It was Travis's senior year in high school, and I wanted to be home more. Ruby and Sheri were doing a wonderful job caring for my parents. Depending on the week and my mother's medical appointments, I only needed to spend one night a week away from home.

My father was adjusting to living in a hospital bed. Some days were better than others. It helped immensely having his bed in the family room where he could enjoy being in the hub of the home and near my mother.

Over the next few months, he began to have even more delusions and hallucinations, but now he was seeing frightening things that made him thrash around and try to crawl out of bed. During these episodes, he wanted to punch anyone who came near him. I had to call the hospice physician and ask for help. We needed new medication to calm him down even more and to stop the hallucinations. The new medications helped. Finally, my father could relax and not have the anxiety and fear that his hallucinations triggered. Such is the terrible disease of Alzheimer's.

I was the last one to take him outside in his wheelchair to hear the birds and feel the warmth of the sun that spring. He was slipping away from us, every day, every week, ever so slowly. It wasn't long afterward that he began calling me "Judy." He was always happy to see me, his aging eyes lighting up in recognition, but he wasn't seeing me anymore; he was seeing his youngest sister, Judy, who had passed away years before. I would joke to my mom, Ruby, and Sheri, perhaps covering grief on my part, saying, "I hope he liked her!" We'd laugh and then we'd all sigh . . . it was hard to see him going away.

In May that year, I took a week off to visit my biological family up north. It was Stephanie's fiftieth birthday so I joined her for a few days in Calistoga, a small town in Napa Valley known for hot springs, mud baths, and wineries. By day, we lingered in the mineral hot springs pool, and by night we enjoyed candlelit, organic dinners under the stars with a good bottle of wine. I always had a good time with Stephanie, and at this point in our relationship, four years in, I was feeling sisterly.

After celebrating with Stephanie, I stayed overnight in San Francisco to see Frances, but first, I met Colleen for lunch.

I was still getting to know her, and this would be our first time alone where we could sit and talk in person. The restaurant she chose had a panoramic view of San Francisco Bay, framed by pine trees and maples, their leaves glistening in the sun.

We had barely ordered margaritas before Colleen asked, "What made you decide to search?" and "What was your life like growing up?" We had never talked about my search journey before or what my life was like growing up. I liked that she was just as interested in knowing me better as I was about her. I still had some missing pieces about her life I wanted to put together, so I hoped today would be a good day to ask her a few more questions.

After telling Colleen a bit about my childhood, it was my turn to ask. "So, how was your childhood? How was Frances as a mother?"

Colleen put her fork down and looked at me with no expression before removing a lock of hair from her hazel eyes. "Well, comparing my life to yours growing up? We might as well have been raised on different planets. I think we come from two different worlds."

I took a big gulp of my margarita, almost choking, and looked up at her. "What do you mean?"

"Well, both of my parents worked throughout my childhood. Mom didn't cook; our father did—when he was home and wasn't drinking—but we never had sit-down dinners with sterling silver candlesticks."

"Well, to be honest, Colleen, neither did anyone else I knew." I tried to laugh off the embarrassment I felt for my parents' formality. I might have shared too much with her.

She continued, "I never had any new toys. I never had new clothes. Everything was always secondhand. I never even had a bike. My parents never owned a car, and they never owned a house. I never had a yard to play in. When we went grocery shopping, we took a bus. And we never went on a family vacation." Her face looked hard, like stone.

"Oh, Colleen, that must've been tough."

"No, I don't think you understand." She looked at me, not smiling.

Is she angry? I wasn't sure where this conversation was going.

Colleen added, "But I understand that it was probably hard for you growing up without your biological family, not knowing anyone or seeing anyone who resembled you or was like you. That would be hard, but it was also hard to grow up poor, without much of anything. Like I said, we come from two different worlds."

I sat back in my chair and looked out the large picture window at the sailboats on the shimmering bay, and for a few minutes, I felt foolish. *I should have known better than to tell her how I grew up.* Even though I didn't go into great detail, it was enough for Colleen to know how different our lives had been. I knew my siblings didn't have the opportunities I grew up with. I was just answering her questions truthfully. My life was and is what it is.

Heck, we were all victims of fate, of our circumstances, of our mother's decisions. I'm not sure Colleen understood the full cost of growing up without knowledge of one's beginnings and history. We both had suffered in our own ways. I felt for Colleen. I could only imagine how it must have felt to grow up wanting things and having to work really hard for what she and Adrian now had. Perhaps in her eyes, I had pranced into her life, after living a golden and carefree life on easy street. I could see how that might have caused her to feel resentful in some way. I guess I didn't explain well enough how devastating the wondering and loneliness had been. Sometimes it was too much, too intimate, to tell someone my deepest feelings and angst.

At any rate, I don't think she got me that day.

"I'm really sorry, Colleen," I offered. It was the only thing I could think of saying.

Colleen nodded her head. "Don't be sorry, Diane," Colleen answered matter-of-factly. "It's not your fault. It's not anyone's fault."

I left that afternoon feeling sorrowful and somewhat guilty for being adopted by a couple who had given me opportunities. My story wasn't unique—adoptions by financially secure, older, infertile couples were quite common at the time. Both Stephanie and I had the benefit of being raised in this way, but that didn't mean it had been our choice. If you had asked us as infants, we would have chosen our mother. Any baby would.

Even though my life had been relatively easy and financially secure with opportunities for experiences and travel that my biological siblings never had, it didn't make up for the lifelong feelings of loss and lack of confidence. I wish Colleen could have understood this.

On my way to pick up Frances, I wondered again what my life would have been like had I grown up in the Mission District. It was a far cry from the fun-loving Southern California beach life I'd enjoyed. My siblings were more familiar with street gangs that became their identity and parks that were their backyard. It was a harder life for sure, though not necessarily horrible, and I know some grew up determined and fighting to live a better life, like Adrian and Colleen.

What if my mother and father had married and I had grown up in Nashville? What if?

I could ruminate on the "what-ifs" for hours. My life would have certainly been different, but different doesn't make it better or worse. It's just different. Different planets. Different worlds. It was what it was. Neither of us had control over how our lives began.

And now, here I was, in yet another world, carefully driving through the Tenderloin, looking around, wondering how Frances could live here and how her kids could be okay with it. But I think I understood a bit more now—they might not see it as awful and scary as I did.

Frances was waiting for me. She waved and smiled when I pulled up at the curb outside her gated Section 8 apartment. My heart felt heavy, but it felt good to see her again too.

We drove to San Francisco General Hospital to visit my sister Allison, who'd been in a horrific motorcycle accident with her boyfriend several weeks before. She was still recovering from the surgeries she had required to save her leg. Her boyfriend hadn't fared as well. He was alive, but unfortunately, he'd lost one of his legs from the knee down. It seemed there was always some sort of sadness, like a dark cloud that hovered over me, when I visited my biological family.

The clicking of our heels on the well-worn tile floor of the hospital sounded like a military cadence as Frances and I made our way to the nurse's station to ask for directions to Allison's room. An older woman, wearing a dark blue sweater over moss-colored scrubs, looked up from her computer with a smile and answered, "You must be her sister Diane?"

I jerked my head back a little, surprised that she knew me by name and that my sister had mentioned me. "Yes, I am."

"She's been waiting for you," she answered, smiling. I loved that Allison had told her nurse about me. I smiled to myself as Frances and I continued our march down the hallway.

Entering Allison's room, I stopped abruptly and gasped because standing in the room was a tall, matronly woman with long, dark hair. At first, I thought it was my elusive older sister Julia, but then Frances hugged and kissed her and said, "Hi, Kailani. It's good to see you."

Kailani. The oldest of my aunt Vivian's children. The matriarch of the Tagaloa tribe. The one my sisters told me I desperately needed to meet because she was the keeper of the family secrets and stories.

After my messed-up meeting with my brother Colin, I made a vow to leave the meeting of my cousins up to the powers that be, and here was my moment. I couldn't believe my good fortune. Something bigger than myself had stepped in, leaving me innocent of any accusations of manipulation, and there wasn't anything Frances could do—she *had* to introduce me.

Allison was the first to break the ice. Smiling, knowingly, she blurted, "Hi, Diane! It's good to see you. Thanks for coming."

Frances nodded her head and acquiesced, waving her hand nonchalantly toward me. "Oh, Kailani, this is Diane; and, Diane, this is Kailani." *Frances knew. What is done is done.*

I smiled at Kailani and put my hand out to shake hers. "Hi, Kailani. It's so nice to meet you."

My heart was pounding. I wanted to tell Kailani that I knew all about her, that we were first cousins and that I was so happy to finally meet her, but this wasn't the right place or time. Frances wasn't confessing me yet. I would have to wait, continuing to be silent and kept a secret.

For the next hour, Kailani must have asked me twenty questions. I could tell by her furrowed brow and puzzled expression that she was trying to figure out who I was and how I, a conventional-looking white woman from Los Angeles, would know Allison. And, how did I know Frances well enough to have picked her up? What was our connection? I'm sure Kailani had a thousand questions running through her mind, and as much as I wanted to answer her honestly, I had to be evasive because Frances was sitting nearby, listening to our conversation.

When Kailani was getting ready to leave, she came over and stood in front of me and asked in her melodic Polynesian accent, "Diane, do you mind if I hug you goodbye?"

"No, not at all. A hug is good, Kailani." I smiled and reciprocated her warm embrace.

She then whispered in my ear, "I feel like I've known you all my life."

I wanted to tell her that, in a strange way, she had. Kailani was three years old when Frances, pregnant with me, had lived with her.

Kailani held me in her arms a few more seconds, then pulled back and looked at me, giving me another once-over. She was trying hard to figure out who I might be.

"It was really nice meeting you, Kailani," I said, wondering when we'd next be able to connect, knowing that door had to be opened by Frances.

Not five minutes after Kailani had left, Frances announced to Allison and me, "Well, I guess the cat is out of the bag. I'm going to have to tell Kailani who you are." Frances offered me a sheepish smile.

It took Frances a month to tell Kailani about me. She promised both of us she'd share our phone numbers with each other, but it wasn't until Thanksgiving that year that my sister Colleen, frustrated with the situation, gave me Kailani's number. The next day, I called Kailani and a new chapter in my reunion began.

From the beginning, Kailani and I got on well. She had a good sense of humor, knew all the family stories, and was more than willing to share. I knew that once Kailani got to know me, she'd be calling her siblings and telling them about me. I looked forward to hearing from my other cousins soon.

It was now Christmas and my father had been bedridden and under hospice care for over a year. He didn't speak much anymore, and on the rare occasions he did, his words sounded garbled. He didn't seem to grasp our conversations anymore either. He still recognized my mother, Ruby, Sheri, and me, though I was still probably Judy to him. I was always amazed that he tried to thank Ruby or Sheri after they fed him. I loved seeing the good side of my father shining through.

The past six months he had become thin and frail from eating nothing but soft or liquid foods and from being permanently bedridden. No longer did my father laugh, make jokes, or carry on with his grandchildren. Those days were gone forever, now to live only as memories.

But that Christmas Day we had a surprise. My father awakened alert that morning, and when we arrived for lunch, he seemed to recognize us, especially Heather and Travis. He smiled and held our hands and tried to talk. We couldn't believe he was with us—we had missed him so much. Ruby was so happy to see him alert that she got him dressed in a warm flannel shirt, sweatpants, and slippers. Michael and Travis helped her with the lift from his bed to his recliner. Once again, he was seated next to my mom, and there he reigned Christmas afternoon. It would end up being the last time he sat in his recliner and the last day that he was present with us, in the moment. That was our best Christmas gift that year.

By the first week of 2009, my father was sleeping around the clock. His breathing had become heavier and deeper since that amazing Christmas Day. He sang no birthday song on my birthday that year. Hospice told us he was beginning to transition and gave my mother and me pamphlets to read, to prepare for the inevitable. My father's journey without us was getting closer.

My mother was getting tired. My father's illness was wearing on her. She seemed accepting of where my father was, where they both were in life. She was also her sweetest self these days. *Is it because she has dementia?* I didn't know, but I was happy we were getting along and I found myself overlooking the trust issue. I had made my decision in 2007 and had stuck to it, trying not to focus on the hurt they had inflicted but rather on the moments I had left with my parents.

I found it interesting that Joanne hadn't been around much since my father had become bedridden. My mother didn't seem to mind, and I heard from Ruby that she sometimes refused her calls. I didn't know why.

By the last week of January, my father wasn't doing well. Hospice was coming around more often and Ruby and Sheri were on high alert. On Wednesday afternoon, before I got ready to leave for home to celebrate Michael's birthday the next day, I decided I needed to talk with my father. Hospice had told us he was getting closer, and I was afraid this might be the last time I saw him. He had been restless all day so I hoped he might be responsive to my voice. No matter what, I needed to say these things to him before I left, just in case.

I stood by his bed, stroked his thin arm, and tried to wake him.

"Dad? Dad, can you hear me?" I picked up his cool, translucent hand and held it. With my other hand, I gripped the cold, hard steel of the bedrail. "Dad?"

To my surprise, he opened his eyes. He looked at me, at first with a blank stare, and then, I swear, he recognized me. Not as Judy as he had most of the past year, but as his daughter. His eyes began to well with tears, which nearly made me choke up. *Be strong. You can do this.* Tears rolled down his soft, white cheek like raindrops. It looked as if he wanted to say something, but he didn't know how anymore.

Taking a deep breath, I reassured him, "It's okay, Dad. I'll take care of Mom, so you don't need to worry about her. We're all going to be okay together. We don't want you to go, but if you need to, you can go now. Everyone will be okay. We all love you very much."

My father's eyes held my own for a few minutes. I knew he was there, and I felt that he knew it was me.

"I love you, Dad." I squeezed his hand and bent over and kissed him on his cool forehead.

I planned to come back Saturday morning, as I was told it would probably be a few more days before he passed. On Friday afternoon, Sheri called to tell me hospice had just left.

"Diane, you need to come down as soon as you can. Your father is dying. I'm sure you'll want to be here."

"I'll pack up and be on my way."

Los Angeles traffic on a Friday afternoon isn't easy. I missed saying another, final goodbye to my father by ten minutes. Sheri said he passed so peacefully, with my mother sitting next to him, that my mother didn't even know he was gone yet.

Sheri wanted me to be the one to tell her. My mother took it better than we all expected. She was stalwart, but that's who she was. I knew she'd miss her lifelong best friend: the twelve-year-old-boy she first met at their local park, her high school sweetheart, and her husband of sixty-four years.

She was surprised that he was gone so quickly and that she hadn't known. Her grief was private, though; we weren't allowed to see. Over the next week, she carried on dutiful and proud, a faithful wife taking care of her beloved, late husband. I drove her to the funeral home and helped her pick out a handsome, carved, dark wood urn. She wanted to keep him home with her.

I think we all felt relieved that my father's suffering was over. We knew he didn't want to live like that, and at the end, he wasn't really living anymore. Now he was released from pain, from the fears and loneliness and the mean tricks his Alzheimer's-stricken mind played on him. I hoped he was with his beloved mother, his siblings, and with John.

My mother placed his urn on the coffee table in his den. She thought that was the perfect spot for him and said, "Just like I did for years, I can walk down the hallway, see him in there, and still say hello."

Chapter Twenty-Five

JUST A FEW WEEKS AFTER MY FATHER WAS GONE, MY parents' house returned to normal routines, sort of. The couch was back in place, where his hospital bed had been. The medical equipment was gone. But it was quieter—the TV volume was lower. And it was surreal to walk into his den and see his urn on the coffee table.

We were concerned about my mother and how she would be, alone after all these years spent with my father, but she graciously accepted her fate. I asked my mother if she wanted me to go through my father's clothes and his books and things, but she wanted everything to stay the way he left it.

Ruby had an idea about a month after my father passed.

"Mrs. Mason, why don't you go have some fun at the Palm's Senior Center? You know, people bring their therapy dogs and cats to be held and cuddled. They serve a great lunch and there are people you could meet who are your same age. Would you like that?"

"Oh, Ruby, I would!" My mom perked up.

I chimed in, "I think that's a great idea, Ruby." I nodded my head toward my mother, who was sitting in her chair in a pink blouse and navy pants. She was wearing makeup and looked grand.

We decided my mother could go once or twice a week, depending how she felt. Ruby and Sheri would drive her, and when I was in town, I would help out too.

She loved it. She liked to stay for the catered lunch, and once on her "pet days," her favorite days, I went with her, staying for lunch and meeting her new friends. This was good; it gave her something to look forward to each week.

My mother surprised me when we were out together running some errands. She asked me to drive her to her bank, where she asked for a signature card and added me to her checking account so it would be easier for me to pay her bills and get access to money if she, or we, needed it in an emergency. My mother didn't want to sign checks anymore; she said she was tired. The fact that she trusted me made me feel good and that I was on the right path taking care of her.

My mother turned eighty-eight in March, two months after my father died. I wanted to make her birthday extra special so she wouldn't feel so lonely with my father gone. I baked a family favorite casserole called a hot salad, and served it with Hawaiian rolls and a green salad. For dessert, I baked the original red velvet cake recipe from the Waldorf Astoria, which was worth the effort.

For her birthday present, I purchased a small, red Brighton handbag that would be easier for her to carry. She loved Brighton purses. Michael, Heather, Travis, and I, along with Ruby, celebrated her birthday on a sunny Saturday afternoon on the back patio.

"I think I had the most lovely last birthday," she said. "It was perfect."

We didn't like her saying it was her last birthday, but we were glad she enjoyed herself. It turned out to be a beautiful day together, even though we all missed my father.

While all these things were going on with my parents, I continued building my relationships with Frances and Stephanie. As time went on, I had to force myself not to tell my mother about them. It made me sad that I was too afraid to tell her, to share with her.

Before my father died, one of the times when Stephanie was visiting, we drove past my parents' home. We parked my car across the street and sat for a few minutes, deliberating whether we should go knock on the door and visit them, telling my parents that Stephanie was my biological sister who had found me. Or, we thought we could pretend she was a friend, so she could at least meet my parents, but that seemed too risky. My parents were astute and I was afraid they would somehow recognize similarities between Stephanie and me, so we decided it was best to do nothing and we drove away.

I wished I could have confided in my mother and told her everything I'd found out about myself. If only she could have known that finding my biological family had nothing to do with my feelings toward her, that finding my biological family didn't make me love her less. On the contrary, I might have come to love and appreciate her and Dad more. I came to the hard conclusion that, at this point, what she didn't know wouldn't hurt her, and I didn't want to hurt her. I also wasn't willing to risk losing the sweet relationship she and I were now enjoying. Life can be so complicated.

Life was also moving on. Travis had now graduated from high school and from the Los Angeles County Fire Explorer program. He was in college majoring in fire science, had a girlfriend, and worked part-time at a local tire store.

Heather was still working part-time as an aesthetician at a day spa, finishing college, majoring in liberal studies and children's literature. In May, she had met a young firefighter named Wes. They were introduced by a mutual friend, and from the get-go, both seemed very interested in each other.

My mom and Ruby were always asking, "What's going on with Heather and her new boyfriend?" Heather's new romance was something joyful for my mother to think and talk about.

That summer, I began to hear from my cousins, one by one, as Kailani told them about me. My cousins lived all over the place, from California to Alaska to American Samoa. Most of them, with the exception of my two youngest cousins, had spent their childhoods in American Samoa running barefoot on the sand and deepening their roots within the island culture.

None of my siblings, and only one or two of my cousins, had ever met my uncle Howard, Frances's brother, the news editor who lived in Nashville. He was an anomaly, along with his son, Luke. Once again, Frances had forbidden me to make contact with her brother and his family; she still wanted to keep me a secret from them and anyone else she knew in Nashville. I wasn't going to challenge her. I had enough going on in my life at the moment and had acquired the fatalistic viewpoint that if it was meant to be, I would meet them one day too.

There was one more cousin out there in the world. I'd heard her name mentioned the first day I had met Frances but hadn't given her any thought, as she was supposedly living in Ireland, a world away, and wasn't part of the Tagaloa tribe. She had been born the ninth child, the last of my aunt Vivian's children, relinquished and adopted, a half-sibling to my aunt's eight Tagaloa children.

This was Iolana, known to the family as Lana. Iolana's father was also Samoan. And now, she was back from Ireland, living in the Bay Area with her husband and young son.

When Lana heard about me from one of her half-siblings, she emailed me, introducing herself and welcoming me into the family. Word was getting around. Some cousins emailed and some phoned me. I was grateful for any and all contact.

I found my cousins eager to meet me and comfortable with my questions about the family. I must give my Tagaloa cousins credit for finding each other as adults. The Samoan culture holds a high value on family. My cousins definitely demonstrated this, including me in their definition of family, which endeared me to them.

We set a date for me and my cousins who lived in California to meet in person, in September. I'd also be meeting Lana, but alone, not with the Tagaloa cousins. I was thrilled to add more layers of family to my life. I was counting the weeks.

My Tagaloa cousins chose the restaurant we'd meet at for lunch in El Sobrante, an East Bay community in the San Francisco Bay Area. The three of them, Kailani and two of her three brothers, Makani and Noah, were sitting at a long table in the middle of the room. I recognized them right away.

But why are they sitting in the middle of the room? I didn't want to draw attention and hoped there wouldn't be overt public displays of affection. I wished we'd had a booth in the corner. More private. More intimate.

Too late. As they saw me walking toward them, all three stood up and shouted, "Diane! You're here!" The restaurant patrons nearby turned to look at me. *I'm doomed.* My new family smothered me with love by bestowing warm, welcoming hugs, plenty of kisses, and bundles of candy leis for me to wear on my neck. This wasn't a bad thing. I just had never experienced such joy from people meeting me. It made me feel loved and accepted.

We spent three hours together, with Kailani doing most of the talking while I listened and asked questions about Frances and the family. Kailani was a great source of family information, much better than Frances.

It was nearly time to meet Lana for dinner. I gave them all hugs goodbye, knowing there was no doubt we would see each other again. They made it clear I would be included in their lives. We were family. I came away feeling overwhelmed by their warm intensity because I wasn't used to such open displays of affection, but it was heartwarming to know they were so happy to have met me.

I drove away filled with love and acceptance. I rolled my sunroof open, turned on Joni Mitchell's *Night Ride Home* CD, and drove across the Richmond Bridge with my windows down, feeling the crisp, cool wind off the bay glide through my hair. *What a day!*

I thought of Lana and what I knew of her life from her emails over the past few months. I knew she had been put into foster care as a newborn and given to her future adoptive mother, who had an affiliation with the hospital where Lana had been born. Her adoptive mother was a huge admirer of anthropologist Margaret Mead and her research on Samoan culture, so when she heard there was a Samoan baby girl born at the hospital she had ties to, one who was ready to be put into foster care, she jumped at the chance to take care of her. She and her husband with two biological sons fostered Lana until they could adopt her.

Lana was not raised in Samoan culture, but her adoptive mother exploited the fact that Lana was a beautiful, half-

Samoan little girl. On weekends, Lana's mother dressed her in Polynesian leis and a grass skirt and made her perform for tourists on the street at the famous Fisherman's Wharf. Lana would later say how she hated being forced to perform for people.

Lana's life as an adoptee wasn't easy. I don't know the exact circumstances, and it was hard for Lana to talk about, but I understand that she had been abused by members of her adoptive family for years. Somehow, Lana was placed into foster care again when she was fourteen or fifteen years old. Abandoned again. She lived in group homes until she was eighteen, when, in her eyes, she emancipated herself from her adoptive family.

When she was twenty-five, through friends, she met a great guy, Niall, from Ireland. They soon fell in love and were married. Lana was forty years old when she and Niall had their first and only child together, a son.

I met Lana for dinner at her favorite Italian restaurant in San Anselmo.

"Hiiii, Diiaanne." Lana dragged out my name as she wrapped me up within a tight hug. She was wearing heeled boots over jeans, a maroon tank top with a short, black leather jacket, and like my other female family members, she stood tall. She was striking and sophisticated. Lana wore her short, dark hair punk style, and her mischievous brown eyes lit up as she greeted me. Her skin was the color of caramel. She had great energy and I noticed that she was a head-turner as we walked toward our dining table.

"Hi, Lana," I said, self-conscious about the "mom jeans" I was wearing. Even though I was five foot seven, I felt like a short, chubby, out-of-touch suburban housewife when I saw Lana's trendy look and the strong confidence she radiated.

Even so, and despite the nearly fourteen-year age difference between us, Lana and I connected easily, talking nonstop over two bottles of merlot until the restaurant closed. She was funny, educated, and sadly, well versed in the world of hard knocks thanks to her childhood.

"Thank goodness I found my husband. He's such a good man, he could have been a priest," Lana told me at dinner. "Niall gets me and is the best father to our son. I feel very lucky to have him in my life."

I was glad to hear she had found someone stable, kind, and understanding after what she had been through.

We talked deeply that evening. We confessed how sometimes we both struggled with Frances, my mother, her aunt. We bonded while laughing about some of our reunion struggles and shared the seriousness about the loss we felt as adoptees. We connected easily, as if we'd known each other for years. It was another magical night similar to the first night I had with Stephanie.

We walked together, arm in arm, toward our cars after dinner under the canopy of fog.

"I love you, Diane," Lana said as we bid each other goodnight.

I felt the same emotion. We had so much in common and, to top it off, like icing on a cake, we were first cousins. It was true I hadn't suffered like Lana had growing up. In contrast, my parents seemed wonderful compared to what she'd experienced. But I knew Lana and I were destined to be close, more like sisters than cousins.

We decided that on my next visit, which had to be soon, I would connect Lana with Stephanie—another reunion.

Chapter Twenty-Six

IN EARLY OCTOBER, JUST DAYS AFTER I RETURNED FROM meeting my cousins, Ruby called.

"Hi, Diane. I think your mother has had a ministroke. Maybe a TIA. I think you need to call her doctor and have her checked out as soon as you can."

Not my mom. Not now.

Later that week, I drove down and took my mother to see her primary care physician, and as with TIAs (transient ischemic attacks), there was no permanent damage. *Thankfully.* Though her doctor told me to be aware that another, larger stroke might occur within the next six weeks. My mother felt fine, we were glad she was okay, and life went on as usual while we were watchful and hopeful there wouldn't be another in her future.

Several weeks later, my mother announced she wanted to make a change on the trust. She couldn't change the entire trust; my father had seen to that. It was complicated, but since my father had passed away, my mother could only change her portion of the trust.

She called Dave. He then set up a phone appointment with her attorney who told her the only thing she could change was when Heather and Travis could receive money from her portion of the trust. She wanted to make the changes because she didn't want her grandchildren waiting years, until Travis turned thirty, to receive her portion as was stated in the original trust.

I arrived at my mother's home after the attorney, his assistant, and Dave. They were all having coffee at the kitchen table with my mother.

Ruby was sitting on the couch in the family room reading a magazine. Her eyes met mine as I entered the room.

"Hi, Diane," Ruby said warmly.

"Oh, hello, sweetheart," my mother added, as she turned her head to see me. "We're waiting for you."

I looked at Ruby and smiled.

"Hi, Mom. Hi, Dave. Hello, Mr. Fletcher, it's nice to meet you."

I leaned across the table to shake hands with the older, white-haired man and his assistant, a young woman who looked to be in her early thirties.

"Thanks for coming, Diane." Dave looked at me sideways with his dark eyes. He wasn't an outwardly expressive guy but he was always decent to me.

The vibe felt awkward. *Why didn't I tell Dave last week to handle this since he was the trustee?* I began to feel embarrassed, imagining the attorney and his assistant wondering what kind of a daughter I must have been to be nearly shut out by my parents' will years ago.

I was glad my mother wanted to make changes to benefit my children, but being there brought up a rush of emotions I had swept away two years ago in order to get on with life. Having to deal with trust issues just brought back the hurt. I wondered all over again why they had set everything up this way in the first place and had never changed it over the years. *Seventeen years ago. All because I told my daughter I was adopted.*

"Just tell me where to sign," my mother said impatiently to the attorney as he sat in my father's chair at the table, shuffling papers while his assistant removed a notary book from her briefcase. I stood in the kitchen behind them, sipping coffee. I held the mug with both hands and took a deep breath, wishing I were somewhere else.

"Madge, this will really help Heather and Travis. This is a good thing," Dave said to my mother, nodding, confirming her signature. He sat close to her to help make sure she was signing in the right spot.

The attorney and his assistant didn't stay long. Dave stayed a bit and talked to my mother in the family room. He and Joanne hadn't been over for a while so my mother wanted to catch up on how they and their daughters were. I went outside and began watering my mother's yard. *I shouldn't have come down here for this. I wasn't needed and didn't have a say in anything. Being here only felt humiliating.* I pulled the hose out and began watering the bushes on the side of the house.

Dave found me and shuffled toward me over the gravel path. "I'm going to go now, Diane. I have to get back to work, but thanks for coming down. I thought you should be here. I want to keep you in the loop when it affects your children."

"Thanks, Dave. I do appreciate that and your helping my mother." I started to roll the hose up while he stood there with his hands in his pockets, looking uncomfortable.

Dave nodded. "I'm glad your mother did this. Even though there are limitations in the trust, it'll make it much easier for Heather and Travis to access their money when the day comes. It'll help them get their life started." He looked across the yard, then back at me. "Well, gotta go. Take care. I'll see you."

I finished wrapping up the hose and stood looking at the yard my mother had designed years ago. Memories came rushing back of cutting the ivy along the sidewalk for hours as a kid and helping cut trees, trim bushes, and plant flowers. Sweet memories. Looking up at the blue sky, the warmth of the autumn sun calmed me before I went back inside to make lunch. I did appreciate my mom making an amendment for my children. Dave was right—it was a good move.

While making sandwiches and getting plates out in the kitchen, my mother, who was sitting in her recliner in the family room, looked over at me and said, "Well, that went well this morning. What did you think, Diane?"

I frowned a little before smiling and answering. "I thought it went well. The attorney was nice. It was quick and easy. Are you happy?"

"It was quick, wasn't it? Yes, I'm glad I could help Heather and Travis out." She put both frail hands on her knees and went on, "Diane, I want to tell you something."

I looked up from placing fruit on our plates. My heart skipped. *What now?* Her serious tone sounded ominous. I didn't think I could handle any hurtful talk or surprises.

"I want to apologize that we ever did this. Your father and I should have never drawn up a trust like this. At the very least, we should have changed it years ago. I don't know why we didn't."

I looked over at her, my face a blank. *What did she just say? Did she just apologize to me?* I was shocked. She sat expressionless. I could feel tears coming up but I pushed them down. I couldn't believe what I'd just heard her say.

"I don't know why we did what we did and now it's too late, but I changed what I could today. I'm sorry I couldn't do more. You and Michael are good parents and the kids have turned out well. They're happy, healthy, and kind people. You and Michael have done a good job raising them. I'm so proud of you."

My mouth dropped open as I continued to fight back tears. *What in the world? My mother doesn't talk this way to me.*

"Oh, Mom." I had a hard time finding words. My chin began to quiver. "Thank you," was all that came out. I was overcome and a little confused.

My mother added with a smile, "I'm glad I could help make things easier for Heather and Travis."

"You did, Mom. You did good today. Thank you." We both smiled.

"What you did today *was* a good thing, Mrs. Mason," Ruby said happily, as she entered the room.

While I finished making lunch, I went mute. I set my mother's plate on the TV tray in front of her while Ruby and I ate at the kitchen table. I was astonished by my mother's words and felt tongue-tied, eating my lunch in silence, trying to process what I could.

I stayed another hour or so. My mother and Ruby wanted to know the latest with Heather and her boyfriend Wes, which was always a joy to share and relieved my contemplative mood. After a while, my mother was looking tired, and I knew she needed to nap. I gathered my purse and jacket, and leaned over to kiss her soft, velvety cheek goodbye. I stood in the doorway and said to my mother, now little and frail but still looking lovely, "Mom. It was a very productive day. You did good. And thank you for doing what you did for the kids today and what you said to me. Very appreciated. I'll talk to you tomorrow. Love you." I blew her a kiss and she blew one back, smiling at me as I left.

On my way home that afternoon, I thought as I drove, listening to the soothing cello music of David Darling, how amazing it was to have heard my mother apologize. I had never heard my mother apologize to me—ever. *Maybe she was finally able to put aside her fears? Maybe I proved to her that I loved her, that I loved them both—otherwise, why would I be there, taking care of them?* This was huge; then I realized that had I not decided to stay and oversee their care, we would never have come to this juncture.

This wasn't about the money. Two years ago, I had been more upset and hurt by having to split my parents' personal belongings with Joanne than anything else. I felt they had put me into a second-class category, giving me as little as they could out of obligation of some sort. What hurt so much was the fact that they didn't seem to value me or even care how this might make me feel. They seemed to value Joanne as much or more, yet I was their daughter. I wondered if this was how they felt about me all along, which made me feel abandoned by the two people I had counted on all my life. More than two years had passed, and I did my best to find a way to have a relationship with them, and the tension and the hurt gradually subsided. Now, my mother at the end of her life was giving me absolution. The trust didn't have a hold over me anymore. Feelings of relief, redemption, and a reframing of the narrative between us began to appear. I was free, and so, perhaps, was my mother.

Around five o'clock on a lazy Saturday afternoon in early November, just one week after the absolution by my mother, Ruby called on my cell phone.

"Diane, I'm here with Sheri. It's your mother. You need to come down here as soon as you can," Ruby said in a hurried voice.

"Why? What's happened?" A twinge of panic rose up in my chest.

"Diane," Ruby said, calmly, "we think your mother is dying. The paramedics are on their way."

"What?" I grasped my chest with the dish towel I had been holding. *How can my mother be dying?* My head was spinning. I couldn't think, and panic was setting in.

"Michael!" I yelled from the kitchen.

He came running. "What? What's up?"

Both Heather and Travis, who had arrived home after work, rushed into the room looking bewildered.

"Diane." Ruby's tone was different now. "Oh, Diane, I'm so sorry. Your mother has just passed." Her voice was breaking.

I bent down low to the ground, still clutching the phone to my ear, and let out a wild, guttural sound I never heard myself make before—"Nooooooo!" Folded over in grief, I kept screaming "no" for a few minutes. Michael and the kids were near me, but they didn't know why I was screaming. *Nooooooo . . .*

"I'm so sorry, Diane. She's gone."

I slowly stood up and tried to grasp that the moment I didn't want had come. I looked over at my little family who looked lost. "Ruby just said my mother died." I felt helpless. Alone.

Heather quickly put her hand up to her mouth and said, "Oh no, Mom. Not Grandmother."

"No, she can't be gone," I said to Ruby. "She was just fine yesterday."

"She was gone in minutes, Diane." Ruby was crying. "It happened so fast."

"Oh my God, I can't believe this." I clutched the kitchen counter, trying to keep myself from falling.

"Diane, the paramedics just arrived. I've got to go. Listen, you need to grab your purse, have Michael drive, bring the kids if they're home, and get down here as soon as you can. Call me on your way. We'll be waiting for you."

On the drive down to Palos Verdes, all I could think about was that I hadn't called my mother that afternoon, that I'd missed talking to her that day. *The one day I didn't call.* I would never hear her voice or talk to her again. I wasn't able to say a final goodbye and tell her how much she meant to me. I physically hurt and my tears were free-falling. Michael, Heather, Travis, and I were silent most of the drive, but every few minutes Heather or Travis would break the silence saying, "I can't believe Grandmother is gone."

Pulling into the driveway that night and seeing a Los Angeles County Sheriff's car parked out front was surreal. *Nothing would ever be the same again.* My mother had left this earth. I got out of the car and walked slowly toward the front door with my family. Heather's arm was around me and Travis walked beside me. Michael opened the door. My mother's neighbors Jack and Sandra were there to greet me and give me hugs. They had tears in their eyes.

"We're so sorry, Diane."

I nodded and walked into the entryway. The family room was on the left. When I glanced in, I saw my mother's lifeless body lying on the floor with a white sheet covering her. I lost it. In front of everyone. In front of the sheriff and the young Sheriff Explorer. I saw Dave and Joanne standing quietly in the back of the living room. *Whatever. I don't care anymore.*

After a few minutes, I gathered myself together and hugged and thanked everyone for being there. Ruby brought me a cup of coffee. We all sat down in the living room. The sheriff was there, waiting for the coroner to arrive.

Ruby, Sheri, and the paramedics thought my mother had a massive stroke. Sheri said, "I had just given your mother dinner.

She was eating and watching TV. I got a call from a friend and when I looked back at your mother, just a few minutes later, she was gone."

Ruby had been on her way to change shifts and arrived a minute or two after Sheri tried to wake my mother. They called 911, then me. My mother was gone by the time the paramedics arrived. Since my mother had a DNR notice on the refrigerator, there were no attempts to resuscitate.

The coroner's team didn't arrive until midnight. I watched them, just as I had eight months earlier, take my parent away. I chose not to view my mother. I wanted to remember her the last time I saw her, just a week ago, sitting in her blue recliner, looking so pretty at eighty-eight years old, waving and blowing a kiss to me, and saying, "Drive safe going home. I love you. See you soon." It was the same day that the attorney and Dave had come over to change the trust.

Sheri said, "The last few nights I found your mother sleeping on the couch in your father's den. She has never done that before."

I didn't know what to make of this. *Was she was seeing him in dreams or having visions? Was he telling her it was time to go? Or was she just missing him? Why did she suddenly make those changes to the trust and apologize to me?*

Sometimes, there are too many questions in life that have no answers. My mother's apology was healing. The trust no longer had a hold over me. My mother and I parted at the end, loving and accepting one another. I wondered if, in some way, finding Frances had helped heal me. I was glad I had listened to my heart and spent these last few years taking care of my parents. We had come a long way since those earlier painful years, and now I had some good memories to tuck away and take with me.

Chapter Twenty-Seven

IT FELT STRANGE THAT JANUARY MORNING, TWO MONTHS after my mother died, to pull into the driveway and walk into the empty, cold house. I made myself a pot of coffee and stood, quietly waiting, looking around at the emptiness of the room while the hot, dark liquid dripped like a heartbeat in the silence.

I couldn't bear to sort through my parents' things over the holidays. The week after my mother died in November, I had gathered their important papers and my mother's jewelry and closed up the house. Except for coming over a few days to water their yard between rainstorms, I stayed away. But now, it was the new year, 2010, and time to begin the task of cleaning out their cherished home of more than forty-five years.

The past two months had been tough. Grieving my mother's death included my father's as well. Losing both of them last year signified the end of a long chapter of two of the most important people in my life. Since I was a little girl, I'd feared living without them. That was one of the reasons I decided to search for Frances. A familiar feeling of sadness and loss hovered over me every day, especially now that I was in their house.

I poured myself a mug of coffee. *Where does one begin?* The two credenzas—one in the living room, the other in the dining room—begged to be first. Deciding what to keep and what to give away seemed simplest here, with these two pieces of furniture that held my mother's sterling silver entertaining pieces, her best dishes and linens.

Even though Joanne was supposed to be given half of my parents' personal belongings, she had graciously acquiesced, saying, "Go ahead and go through your parents' things, Diane. There are certain things I'd like to have of theirs, but please, go through everything first, then let me know what you don't want."

I wasn't sure how to handle the situation between us, so I was glad Joanne let me go through everything in the house by myself. I asked her what she really wanted.

"I'd love to have your parents' living room rug. You know, the blue and white one they bought in Kashmir. I'd love that, if you don't want it? Do you want it?"

"If you want the rug, Joanne, it's yours."

She requested several other things: one of my mother's pearl necklaces and other jewelry, some dish sets and sterling silver serve-ware, along with some Wedgwood pieces and other decor that would remind her of my mother and father. She was considerate, which I appreciated.

Over the next few months, going through my parents' house felt like taking a journey through time, one that ultimately led to a process of self-discovery and reflection. I took my time. I was fortunate to have it and found the entire process therapeutic. It wasn't a chore; it became a labor of love.

I drove down once or twice a week. Sometimes, friends came to help. I happily gave Ruby and her daughter furniture and some clothing, while Ruby's brother received my parents' car.

Wes and Heather met me one afternoon when I was going through my father's den. Wes was interested in my father's military medals, ribbons, and other Navy paraphernalia. Pulling out an old cardboard box from the very back of his closet, I said, "What have we got here? I don't think I've ever seen this box before."

Yellowed newspaper clippings from my father's college basketball days lay next to report cards and old photos of young friends. Underneath it all was a manila envelope.

I gasped.

"Oh my gosh. I can't believe this." I looked over at Heather and Wes, in shock. "It's the same manila folder I found in my mother's dresser when I was nineteen years old."

"What?" Heather cried out. I nodded my head, giving her a weak smile.

"I thought my mom threw these papers out years ago because I could never find them again, but they were here, hidden in the back of the closet probably all this time." *All these years.* I pulled out my adoption decree papers; they were just as I remembered them so many years ago.

"I never looked too deep into my father's closet." I shook my head. That was exactly why the envelope was put here, hidden underneath my father's college memories.

I handed Wes and Heather a copy of the legal document held together by a blueback.

"They either left it for me to find after they were gone, or they forgot about it." I stood with hands on my hips. "And all these years we never talked about it, that I had found my birth name. Kind of sad, really." I was thrilled to have found the documents, and this time, they were mine to keep. "So much has happened since I last saw these papers. Now I know the unnamed woman mentioned. She's not a secret anymore, and neither is Loretta." I smiled, reflecting for a minute how life unfolds sometimes.

I turned around and opened a legal-size envelope.

"What's that, Mom?" Heather was sitting with a wide-eyed expression on the edge of the blue-striped love seat.

"It's a baby-feeding schedule." I let out another gasp as I saw my birth date at the top of the page. "And, geez, I had another name."

"Huh?" Heather cocked her blonde head to one side and looked over at Wes for help, but he just shook his head as he had no idea what I was talking about.

"I was called Sarah in foster care. How about that? It must have been given by social services to hide my identity."

"You just found this out?" Heather asked, with a frown.

"Yup. I never knew this until just now. I never knew I had a different name in foster care. I always assumed they would have called me by my given name of Loretta. I mean, legally, I was Loretta Stewart until I was eighteen months old when my adoption was finalized."

I stood in my father's den, realizing that, at fifty-four years old, I was still discovering secrets.

Every week the house became increasingly sparse, full of echoes. Listening to advice given by a childhood friend, I kept many pieces of furniture and gave my parents' outdoor patio set to my neighbor Lynne, who still has it today. I took several garden pieces, bird baths, and Japanese lanterns, one of which came from Japan when I was a little girl. It's now old and somewhat broken but I love it as it still lives in my own garden at home. I incorporated many of my parents' possessions into our home, which provided some comfort.

Not only did I have many of my parents' things, but I inherited items from my maternal grandparents and great-aunt that my mother had kept after they passed away. My mother's grandparents were from Norway. Between her and my grandparents, there were quite a few family heirlooms.

I loved my grandparents and great-aunt. They were the only extended family I grew up with so I treasured their treasures. But I couldn't help thinking that even though these things meant something to me, they eventually would have no value or meaning to my children or future grandchildren because they weren't their ancestors, nor were they mine. These family heirlooms didn't belong to us.

I kept items that made me happy—my grandmother's desk and chair, my great-aunt's crystal paperweight, photos, and my grandparents' painting of a Pacific Northwest forest that now hangs above our bed.

I packed up sentimental heirlooms consisting of a gold locket with a baby picture of my mother and a braided necklace made from the hair of my mother's grandmother from Norway. Engraved watches, family photos, and diaries were carefully wrapped, as well as a beautiful cream-colored crocheted bed covering my grandmother made. I shipped two large boxes of family heirlooms along with a letter to my cousins in North Dakota whom I hadn't spoken with in four decades.

I received a polite thank-you note from one of my cousins, and I never heard from them again. *The reality is they don't care about me because, really, who am I to them? We aren't blood related. I'm not really their cousin; I am basically a stranger.* I thought how lucky they were to have received such family history and hoped they appreciated it. I would have loved to have had any one of these items from my ancestors to be able to pass down to my family.

It took six months to clean out my parents' home, which gave me plenty of time to think on my past and my relationship with them. In the grieving process, I learned more about myself, my family, and those treasures I took with me for the rest of my life.

In regard to the trust and Joanne, I came to accept that Joanne and my mother had loved each other. Yes, they had a type of mother–daughter relationship. Joanne had known, loved, and admired my mother since she was a little girl. They mutually loved and admired each other, something my mother and I hadn't experienced since my adolescence.

For most of my life, Joanne was "the daughter my mother always wanted." I'd always felt second fiddle—never good enough, never smart enough, never as good of a mother as Joanne was. I couldn't compete with her. Of course, feeling not good enough came from deep within, from my primal grief, my neurological trauma of loss that asked: *Is this why I was given up? Because I wasn't good enough?*

I wondered if I'd pushed my adoptive mother away. Maybe I did, unconsciously; I was understandably a confused and lost child. I think I now understood my mother and her unresolved grief over losing six babies and being unable to conceive. I realized I was adopted to soothe and heal their pain and give them the promise of a family.

They were the winners in this scenario. Adopting me was a blessed event for my parents—their dream come true. I doubt they thought this baby they came to love had suffered trauma of any kind. They appeared to be oblivious to the significance of what had happened to me—I'd spent nearly three months in foster care somewhere, been taken care of by a stranger or two, but it wasn't their fault. They had been told I was a "blank slate." Only time told the truth—that I had my own history and personality. I was who I was and I was different from what they'd imagined. They didn't want differences. They wanted their child to be like them. While this is normal to some degree, they pushed it very far and gave me some real challenges to deal with and a lifelong feeling of abandonment and rejection that kept getting played out with them. This wound was healed in part when I fell in love with Michael and started my own family, but the old history lived inside my body and arose in dreams, fears, and insecurity.

After the death of my adoptive parents, I gained even more understanding of what had transpired in our lives and continued to find ways to process and accept all that had taken place. We'd lived in a quiet, hidden cycle of unconscious pain, with me fighting attachment after the severing of my first bond with my birth mother. No wonder my adoptive mother and I had bonding problems. As Nancy Newton Verrier states in her book *Coming Home to Self*, "It is an anxious attachment completely devoid of the security needed to allow for bonding. This is a fear of abandonment following connection and is perpetuated into adult relationships as a fear of intimacy."

She adds this: "Symbiosis—the mother/baby fusion—is natural at the beginning of an infant's life. That wonderful feeling was severed forever for the adoptee when the first mother disappeared."

I could see now that we tried for decades to find each other.

As I stepped barefoot onto the river rock and gravel paths, watering my mother's garden, memories floated beside me on the sea wind, reminding me of happy moments spent with my parents, how much they had taught me, and how much they had given me. Despite our differences and problems, we continued to try to be a family and show love, no matter how difficult that was. People are complicated, and my parents were no exception; they were as complicated as I was. We three had each endured deep loss. It seemed tragic that we could never talk about important issues between us. My parents were simply not aware that I had suffered trauma—which wasn't their fault. Had they known, I think they would have been better.

Had they thought of my birth mother as a young woman who didn't want to give away her baby, who was coerced by society at the time to relinquish, maybe I would have been listened to better. Maybe I would not have had to hear their put-downs of her, which, of course, I took as put-downs of me because she was my mother. I came from her.

Regrets. I can't hold regrets. Regrets give no solution; they only paralyze. I can't fix what happened decades ago. I have to heal what I can, accept what my life was, what it is now, and move forward. Healing is my own journey through this adoption mire.

And so it was with Dave and Joanne. I could appreciate and accept Dave acting as trustee for my children, and I felt grateful that my parents had thought of my children and given this generous gift. And Joanne, well, I wasn't angry or hurt anymore—I'd had an epiphany. I'd realized that just as I could love Frances and have her in my life without changing my feelings and love for my adoptive mother, well then, so could my mother have Joanne and me, both. I was happy my mother had Joanne in her life.

I looked back and realized that my reunion with my mother and birth family and all I had learned over the past six years—about adoption, my maternal roots, and my history—had helped me heal enough to love my adoptive parents more freely. With a better understanding of them and a newfound ability to recognize their pain in our relationship, I could forgive them for the hurt I felt from some of their actions. I didn't want to feel hurt anymore. I wanted to continue to heal, and when my mother told me she was sorry, I accepted her apology and welcomed the awareness that she'd gained.

In the end, we all loved each other better.

The house was now completely empty. I had the interior updated with new paint on the walls, as well as the kitchen and bathroom cabinets. The yard was trimmed to the point that the house didn't resemble itself anymore, but maybe that was as it should be, since it wasn't going to belong to us much longer. The house was now up for sale.

It took another six months to be sold to the right people. I had even more time to reflect as I came down weekly to water and take in the last remaining scent and energy of my parents, of my childhood home, unlocking old memories and gaining new thoughts on my life and where I now stood.

The day finally came to turn in the keys. Heather had come down the day before with Wes to say goodbye to the house, which, in effect, was a final goodbye to her grandparents. Michael had done his last walk-through the weekend before.

Travis was with me that last day. We took a long goodbye stroll through the yard, starting in the front. I said goodbye and sometimes gently patted a leaf or petal of the evergreen bushes and flowers my mother had planted over the years, taking in the life still left here for others to enjoy. We entered the oak front door, and I remembered all the times I'd come into this house with my childhood friends, high school boyfriends, and my children. I remembered my babies being joyfully welcomed by my parents.

We visited each room in silence, taking one last long look. I had no idea it would be so hard to say goodbye to empty rooms, but the memories rushed past me—my brother in his bedroom, my father lying on the couch in his den reading, and my mother sewing upstairs with her classical music on. And later, Heather and Travis running through the house screaming with delight, playing games with my parents at the kitchen table. It was as if we were time traveling.

Finally, we came to the kitchen and family room, the hub of the home. I placed on the kitchen counter a handwritten letter wishing the new owners well in their new home.

I took the house keys out of my purse, separated them from my key chain, and lay them next to the letter. I took one last long look around before we walked to the entryway where Travis and I both stood still, looking toward the empty living room, the room that held so many happy memories of Christmases past. We gazed at the ocean and Catalina Island greeting us beyond the floor-to-ceiling windows, each of us thinking our own thoughts from our own memories.

"I'm going to miss this house," Travis said, with a quiet sadness in his voice.

"Me, too, sweetheart. Very much. It's hard to say goodbye."

Travis walked out the door to our parked car in the driveway, allowing me to spend the last few moments alone.

I let out a deep sigh. "Goodbye, sweet home. Goodbye, Mom and Dad," I whispered with tears in my eyes as I grabbed the brass doorknob on the heavy oak door, closing it for the last time.

With that, I closed the door to the past, to the hurts that once were painful but now were released, to the secrets that had been hidden but now had been revealed. Finally, I knew the truth of who I was, my roots and ethnicity, my maternal family. All my hard-won research and angst had led to learning the truth and had enabled me to be free—free to love better. I was real now, and I had so many people in my family. I accepted that love can make mistakes and love can also create forgiveness. Feeling a bittersweet satisfaction, I took a deep breath and walked to my car, ready to face the rest of my life.

Wes and Heather were married on a warm summer evening the following year, 2011, surrounded by family and friends in a walnut grove reminiscent of a fairy tale, the sunlight peeking through the leaves like crystals. I loved that Frances and Stephanie were there, and even Dave and Joanne, though that was the last time we'd see each other. Heather's wedding day was beautiful and perfect in every way.

I wished my parents had been able to know Wes—they would have liked him. At twenty-seven years old, he was now an engineer in his fire department, ambitious and destined for more down the road. A good-looking, good guy. Heather was finishing up her degree, planning to work with special needs children. Wes and Heather were two peas in a pod, made for each other. Michael and I were thrilled to have such a great son-in-law and his family be a part of ours. Life, as indeed it does, was moving on . . .

Chapter Twenty-Eight

THINGS BETWEEN STEPHANIE, LANA, AND ME WERE GOOD for several years until Lana's mental health took a turn for the worse in 2013. She had been recently diagnosed with Bipolar I disorder and was having difficulty dealing with everyday life. She was under the care of a therapist and was trying to feel better about her life.

It was certainly understandable that she had emotional trauma. She had struggled to bond with her biological siblings and aunt, struggled with being adopted, struggled with the sadness and depression that comes from deep loss. Eventually, she cut off all her biological family, including Stephanie and me. I was heartbroken. I never expected Lana to let go of me, for we had seemed too close. I missed her so much.

Nine months later, in 2015, Lana came back into my life with apologies for her abrupt leaving. She'd had a tough nine months and was now living at a friend's house, dealing with an impending divorce, and separated from her young son, which was devastating for her.

Six months earlier, she and her husband had a quarrel in which Lana accidentally involved her five-year-old son. Neighbors heard the brawl and called 911. Her husband understood

Lana's issues and never pursued charges, but a district attorney did, which catapulted Lana into the criminal system, the worst place she could be. She had been an at-home mother and not seeing her young son crushed her. She didn't want a divorce either, but her husband felt this was the best decision for their son, best for all of them.

Lana was in my life just a few months before she abruptly went missing again, only to resurface one month later. She called from a mental health hospital she'd been put in after attempting to jump from the Golden Gate Bridge. Police were able to stop her, and she was put in rehabilitation for therapy. Her husband, friends, and I were all very concerned for her.

I stayed in contact with her nearly every day after that call, always worried for her mental health. I encouraged her to keep going, telling her she could overcome this difficulty she found herself in, that there was a way out of this; it would just take time. She was really trying.

After several months, in October, we were able to see each other in person. I had a writing conference to attend in Berkeley, so we made plans that I'd arrive a day earlier to spend it together. Lana was able to get a pass from her transitional housing that day. When she picked me up at the Oakland International Airport, I was glad to see her looking so healthy and happy. She looked so good, she received constant attention from people. In the hotel elevator, one man commented to Lana as he entered, "Wow, you are one gorgeous woman. You certainly can pull your look off well." Walking around downtown Berkeley, having lunch together, I felt as though I were with a celebrity. Tall, exotic looking, with a knack for fashion, wearing boots and her latest crown, her Sinead O'Connor shaven hairstyle, whom she adored—she was certainly striking.

Lana was not only beautiful on the outside, though; she was

beautiful on the inside as well. We had the best day together, laughing and sharing the deep conversations we enjoyed together. Our day flew by too fast. I didn't know that when I hugged and held her tight, kissing her goodbye that evening, it would be the last time I'd see her.

Lana committed suicide ten weeks later on Christmas Day by jumping off the Golden Gate Bridge. She was successful this time.

I had spoken to her the day before, and she had sounded fine. We devised a plan together for how she'd occupy herself on Christmas Day, but I guess she had other plans she never told me about. I found out later she had prepared for this day for weeks, emptying out lockers, closing her post office box, and giving away her last remaining possessions, saving only a few in the trunk of her car.

I was devastated to hear about Lana from Niall, who called me early from Ireland the day after Christmas. Lana had a devoted ex-husband and a six-year-old son. She broke many hearts, leaving us too soon. I'd learned over the years that there are too many adoptee suicides, four times more than among non-adoptees. Sometimes the burden adoptees feel is too overwhelming. Adoption is trauma, and my cousin suffered from how adoption affected her life.

Michael and I drove up to the Bay Area several weeks later to attend Lana's meaningful and intimate memorial and dinner given by her ex-husband who, despite their problems, still loved her and honored her beautifully that day.

The next month, I drove to Santa Barbara and had a Celtic tattoo inscribed on my left ankle by the celebrated Celtic tattoo artist Pat Fish. It's an image from a rubbing of an ancient Scottish stone. The design is in the Indigenous Pict blue to honor the Scottish blood that Lana and I shared and our relationship. I will always miss her. Besides being cousins, we were soul-mates; we were Anam Cara. I hope she has found her peace.

Chapter Twenty-Nine

LATER THAT YEAR, IN THE FALL OF 2016, I FLEW TO NASHVILLE to finally meet another cousin, Luke, and his family. After my uncle, Luke's father, whom I was asked to never reach out to, passed away, my Tagaloa cousin Noah introduced me to Luke and his family. We soon made plans for me to fly out to meet and get a glimpse of the life my mother lived before leaving Nashville, pregnant with me. Luke was kind enough to spend a day driving me by our great-grandmother's home where my father visited while he dated my mother. I saw the designated historic Nashville fire station where my grandfather had worked and the home of my maternal grandmother. The most profound moment was when Luke took me to the grave sites where our grandparents, uncle, and aunt were buried. Kneeling on the warm grass and placing my hands on the earth above them felt incredible and moving. Sadness rose from within, as I knew I was as close to these relatives as I'd ever be, for I was too late. I wondered how my life might have been had I been raised here among family and history. I had such deep roots here.

My cousin's wife and teenage daughter spent the next day sharing the sights from Belle Meade to Franklin to the beautiful

Natchez Trace Parkway with its ancient trees of hickory, white oak, and sugar maples glistening red, purple, gold, and orange in the autumn sun, gifting passersby a canopy of lacy color.

Seeing the hand-built stone walls defining old property lines and the many Civil War memorials along the roads in and around Nashville, my ancestors' home for over two hundred years, gave root to my history.

Upon arriving home, Michael and I received the most wonderful gift. Wes and Heather announced they were expecting twins. We were blessed when two beautiful little girls came into our lives the following May, making Michael and me grandparents for the first time.

Holding my precious little granddaughters in my arms, I began to wonder about my paternal side. I still knew nothing more about my birth father than his name. I'd heard good things about DNA testing, that it could be used by adoptees as an avenue to find missing family. So, I decided to send in my DNA sample to Ancestry to try to find out more about who I was and where I was from. I hoped, by doing this, I could finally know my full ethnicity to share with my children, and now, my granddaughters.

Frances had only said my birth father was Irish. I silently hoped my DNA could also connect me to my father or someone in his family. DNA would be the only way I would be able to find them.

The closest I had come to imagining what my father might have looked like was when I asked Frances several years before if there was any actor she knew who might resemble my father.

"Oh yes," she said. "There's an actor on my soap opera, and every time I see him, I think of your father. His name is Billy Miller."

I had to look him up. I had never heard of Billy Miller. I was glad I asked Frances because now, at least, I'd have an idea of what my father might've looked like. Anything works when you are desperate for answers.

I waited two months for my DNA report from Ancestry to arrive. Finally, at sixty-one years old, I knew my ethnicity from both parents.

Staring at my DNA results, I was captivated. The first thing I noticed was that my people didn't travel far. I was English, Scottish, Norwegian, Welsh, Irish, Swedish, and Danish.

I wish I had known about my Norwegian DNA growing up; I could have held my Girl Scout sign proudly all those years ago.

My generational link showed my paternal ancestors settled in the southern backcountry of the Georgia Mountains and were upstate South Carolina settlers. My maternal side, which I already knew from my genealogy research, had arrived and settled in the Virginia and North Carolina colonies before venturing into Tennessee in the early nineteenth century. My DNA validated my research.

I was stunned how deep my roots were in the South and how long my people had been there. *Generations. Hundreds of years.* Even though I had known for some time about my mother's side, I was still someone who grew up in the West, in the beach culture of Los Angeles's South Bay, a young town by comparison. Now, seeing this historical data, I found it fascinatingly foreign, which intrigued me, just as my birth name, Loretta Annette Stewart, intrigued me years before.

The oddest thing I noticed in my DNA matches was that there were no Stewart surnames. None whatsoever. My two closest matches were second cousins from my paternal side. Both shared the surname of Vaughn. *Vaughn? Where did that come from?*

I was curious and was able to contact both cousins, who were friendly and more than willing to help me find out how we were connected. Neither had ever heard of a Robert Stewart. As one cousin said in his rural North Georgian drawl, "Well, we know you're kin; we just don't know how yet."

Kin. A new word for me. I like it. It sounds like connection. Clan. Blood. Cousin. Family.

One cousin generously mailed a copy of his Vaughn family tree to help me solve the mystery of who my Vaughn relatives might be. It helped to have names, and it was wonderful to see photographs of people I was related to. My other cousin was just as helpful, offering family history and stories, but none of us had any clue as to who or how we were connected.

I then embarked on a two-month quest, obsessively searching for my birth father and his family. I called Frances and asked her, point-blank, if she could have been wrong about Robert Stewart, that perhaps I had been fathered by someone else.

"Oh no, Diane," Frances answered. "Your father was definitely Robert Stewart. That, I remember quite well. There wasn't anyone else who could've been your father."

I was at a loss. I wasn't sure I could believe Frances. And as Kathi and Dawn had taught me years before, I knew I shouldn't trust anyone's word or memory. People forget and people lie, but DNA doesn't. I needed to trust the facts, and the facts were that I was a Vaughn. The only way I could find my mystery father was to continue following the DNA trail before me, so I purchased several large poster boards and started working through the names of my Vaughn cousins' family trees. There were many other cousins on my DNA list, mostly third cousins, who were all connected to both of my Vaughn cousins. *There is something going on here. I am definitely related to all these people.*

I began following DNA groups online and learned what a centimorgan was. A centimorgan is the unit for measuring genetic linkage, which reveals the closeness of the relationship between people and generations. I learned to identify my relationship to my cousins by their centimorgans and added these important measurements, along with their names, to my Vaughn family tree.

Eventually, I worked through three generations, finding that my two Vaughn cousins' lines converged with great-grandparents. I had finally found out how my two Vaughn cousins were related and knew that I was now barking up the right tree, so to speak. But I still had no clues to who my father might be. He was like a ghost.

After months of searching and getting nowhere, I was ready to call it quits. Here I had DNA right in front of me and I wasn't able to get any closer to my father than my second cousins. I had found my paternal side, but nobody I spoke to had ever heard of a Robert Stewart or of a relinquished baby. I could only guess that someone in this family who hadn't yet submitted their DNA had known Frances and wasn't about to confess to any of this.

There was one more place left to look before putting all this searching for roots behind me. GEDmatch is an online DNA data service founded to help genealogists and adoptees search for birth families through different testing companies. I had signed up right after I received my initial DNA results, but there didn't seem to be anything there I needed at the time. I had kind of forgotten about it.

I realized I hadn't looked at my GEDmatch list for at least two months and decided to take one last look before shutting down. After logging in, I noticed my tab had two recent matches waiting for me, highlighted in neon green. Looking closer, I couldn't believe what I saw.

"Michael! Come here! You won't believe what I just found!" I yelled loudly, so he could hear me downstairs.

I stared at the two names in front of me and saw that they had been uploaded just the day before. I couldn't believe my eyes. The first person listed was a man with the surname of Stewart, the second was a woman with a different last name. Their contact information was the same, so I assumed they were related somehow. *Finally, a Stewart!* I couldn't believe my luck.

Looking at their centimorgans, I knew we were closely related. My hands began shaking with excitement as Michael entered the room. "Look, hon! I found my missing link!"

The centimorgans claimed that this was probably an uncle and a first cousin. I was ecstatic.

I was about to go help Heather with the twins, but before I left, I quickly sent a message to the woman listed, telling her we were related and that I wondered how. She had given her email address for contact, which was one of the things GEDmatch was known for, connection. I hoped to hear from her within the next few days, but by the time I got to Heather's house and opened up my laptop to show her the neon names on GEDmatch, she had already answered me.

I was so overcome with emotion; it was hard to respond. I told her I knew we were closely related, and that I was an adoptee with the birth name of Loretta Stewart but was unable to find any Stewarts on my DNA list. I had been told by my birth mother that my father's name was Robert Stewart. Was she familiar with that name?

She immediately responded and said, "Oh yes, I know Robert Stewart. He's my uncle. We must be first cousins. My name is Laurel. My father and I did our DNA together."

Tears came easily. After so long and so many years of wondering, along with the past two months of obsessive searching and hoping, I had found the paternal side of my family. Finally. The date was December 1, 2017. I was euphoric yet stunned by my good fortune just before I was ready to pack it all up.

Laurel and I began to email each other, exchanging information. Her father was my father's older brother. *My uncle.* Laurel told me her father had passed away just the day before from a long illness. She also gave me the sad news that my father was deceased. My heart dropped. I had so hoped he was still alive, but he had been gone a long time already, passing away in 1992, when he was only sixty-two years old. The sorrow of not ever getting to know him or to ever see him or to hear his voice will always remain with me.

Laurel was busy that weekend handling her father's memorial so we promised to talk again the following week.

I called my friend Lynne that evening and told her what had transpired earlier that day. Lynne was as curious as I was, and with a little research, found my uncle's obituary online, so now I could see all my relatives' names. It was amazing. My father came from a large family. He was one of five children, all born and raised in the same town in Alabama. I had aunts, uncles, and cousins.

Later that night, looking again at GEDmatch, I noticed something wasn't right with the centimorgans between my uncle, cousin, and me. *I'm related to this branch of Stewarts for sure, but how am I connected to the Vaughns? Where were the Vaughns in all this?* I was confused.

I checked my centimorgan charts again and realized the numbers of my uncle and cousin weren't high enough to be considered a full uncle and first cousin. *Something was amiss.*

I couldn't sleep so I started researching. At one o'clock in the morning, I was on the 1930 census looking for the Stewart family. I was determined to find out what the mystery was between the Stewarts and the Vaughns.

Finally, I found the Stewarts on the census and began reading. *Wait. What? Oh geez.* The Stewart family had rented a home on the property of a Robert Vaughn. I couldn't believe it. Robert Vaughn was in the same branch as my Vaughn cousins. *Bingo!*

I had found my Vaughn connection! But there was still the question of how I was related to them. There was a Fred Vaughn, Robert Vaughn's son, living on the property as well. After looking everyone up on Ancestry, I concluded that my grandmother had an affair with one of these two Vaughn men. I just had to figure out which one. I hoped it would be Fred, the son of Robert Vaughn, who was close in age to my grandmother.

It took days to confirm that my grandfather was indeed Fred, the son. I felt relieved. Now I could envision a romance between the two of them rather than something worse. It was already scandalous.

Another amazing thing in all of this was that, thanks to one of my Vaughn cousins, I had pictures of Robert, my great-grandfather, and of Fred, my grandfather. Both men were nice-looking in their photos, dressed well, looking like Southern gentlemen. I found out my grandmother had married very young to a much older man. I imagined she might have found the young Fred Vaughn beguiling, perhaps a respite from her hard life raising three small children in hard-hit Alabama during the Great Depression.

I'm not sure her husband, Mr. Stewart, ever knew about the affair between her and Fred Vaughn, but somehow, she must have convinced her husband to name her newborn son Robert, who I believe was named after his biological grandfather Robert Vaughn. A sneaky way to link the family line, but there it was. *The truth found is that my father and I are not Stewarts. We are Vaughns.*

I had to tell Laurel the truth. She had a master's degree in the sciences, so I knew eventually she'd figure out the centimorgans between us. The strange thing was that Laurel grew up knowing my great-grandfather Robert Vaughn. Her father, on occasion, would take her with him to visit Mr. Vaughn on Sunday afternoons when he lived in an assisted living home. *It's amazing how connected our lives can be.*

Knowing the truth about my father's beginnings could help explain why my father was called the "black sheep" of the Stewart family. *Did he feel different from his siblings? Was he treated differently?* He looked different from his siblings. My father looked like the Vaughns: tall, blond, and blue-eyed, whereas the Stewarts were of shorter stature with darker hair. *Did the family know this secret? Did my father?*

The Stewart children, all except for my father, lived stable, middle-class lives. I don't know, and never will know, why my father lived a harder life than his siblings. I've been told my father was a gifted artist and often made his living as one. I was sad and shocked to hear he was in and out of prison for twenty years, serving time for white-collar federal crimes. Apparently, he had taken stolen private airplanes across state lines as well as into Mexico. He was a self-taught pilot and even wrote a book on how to become one. His illegal shenanigans were probably why the FBI came to my grandmother's home looking for him when he was engaged to Frances. *Maybe that fancy convertible my mother spoke of was stolen.*

Years were added to his prison sentences because he had a knack for escaping. I read he escaped nine times. Prison escapes, forgery, identity theft, stealing planes, and piloting them without a license. My father sounded like Frank Abagnale, the American author and convicted felon portrayed by Leo DiCaprio in the film *Catch Me If You Can.* According to the family, they knew of six marriages—that were legal. I had to laugh. *He must have been something.*

My father's siblings have all passed on, but I had the good fortune of knowing his youngest brother for several years before he died. Laurel had cautioned me in the beginning that my uncle would probably not be interested in me, as I was Robert's daughter. Robert had caused heartache and problems for my uncle and his wife by taking on my uncle's identity, so he wasn't too keen on anything or anyone to do with Robert.

Nearly two years after making contact with my cousin, she casually mentioned me to our uncle in a phone call, telling him I had found her through DNA testing, and that I was interested in talking to him. Would he mind? Surprisingly, he said he didn't.

It turned out I had nothing to worry about, and both my uncle and his wife were nothing but welcoming and kind from the moment they received my letter. I was kinfolk. They immersed themselves in our lives, and for three years until my uncle passed away in January 2023, I had a loving and close relationship with them both, despite the distance in miles from each other. I still have this relationship with my aunt.

My aunt and uncle generously helped me know my father

through their memories and stories. Maybe, since it had all happened so long ago, my uncle got tired of being angry and wasn't hurt anymore. He never said anything terrible about my father to me. He seemed to know he had problems in his life, saying, "Even with all his troubles, your father was a kind man, quiet and soft-spoken, who loved to talk about his art and who always had a smile on his face. He was a gifted artist."

I've been told my father wrote a memoir. *I hope someone finds a copy one day.* I'm thrilled to have photos of him that portray a good-looking man, which he probably used to his advantage in some situations, especially with women. Since he was also a creative person, I sometimes wonder if he was sensitive and had a deeper side to him than he portrayed to the world. It would have been interesting to have met him, though I'm not sure what I would have thought of him.

It's strange to think I love him in some way, without knowing him, but I do. He lives in my mind, heart, and dreams. Recently, I have taken up drawing and painting to connect with him in some way. If only his early life circumstances had been different or perhaps had he known the truth about who his father was, he might have turned out differently.

The photos I've been able to obtain from my paternal family add a wonderful layer to my reunion. I can say without a doubt that I favor my father, just as Frances had always told me. So now, when I look into the mirror, I see my father first before I see my mother looking back at me.

I hoped to meet my aunt and uncle in person in the spring of 2023, after several previous attempts had been thwarted due to the pandemic and my uncle's illnesses, but my uncle passed away unexpectedly three days into the new year. I was so close to meeting him and heartbroken I'd never be able to look into his eyes and hold his hand. He was eighty-eight years old and had always been loving toward me, telling me how glad he was I had found him, saying, "You are the best thing Robert ever did in his life."

I couldn't be more grateful to have known my uncle and to have heard his voice.

Epilogue

I'M LINING UP WITH OTHER PASSENGERS BEFORE entering the plane that will take me on the last leg of my journey. Tightly gripping my carry-on luggage, I'm still in awe that I am finally meeting my father's family. *My kin. My clan.* I burrow into the seat that will carry me from Los Angeles, California, to Birmingham, Alabama. We've all waited too long, but the day is finally here. My heart is full knowing my family is just as excited to meet me as I am to meet them. And this time, I have Michael by my side.

I consider how it might feel walking into my aunt's home tomorrow, seeing her bountiful collection of photos of my family, especially my granddaughters, proudly displayed on her living room "wall of love," along with the rest of the family. I feel moved by her generosity, by all of them welcoming me so warmly.

As I gaze out the plane's porthole, I think how far I've come since the first days of searching for my family so many years ago. I have known my mother and Stephanie for nearly twenty years. Frances is now ninety-one years old and still living in San Francisco. Stephanie and I remain close, and I'm still in touch with some cousins and my youngest sister, Colleen. I haven't heard from Colin since the day I met him in the coffee shop, and I haven't heard from Allison in years, though I think we'd be friendly if we saw each other. My sister Julia, whom I never did meet, passed away in 2020. I have never been able to find my older sister, Delores.

I let my head fall back into the headrest as the plane takes off. Closing my eyes and holding Michael's hand as the hum of the flying engine lifts us into the clouds, I visualize the people I know and love in Birmingham. They aren't strangers anymore. Over the years, we've gotten to know each other, so this seems more like a homecoming than anything else.

My father had three daughters. I am his middle child. My older sister was at one time in contact with the family but has since moved on. I have a younger sister, Kelly, who by good fortune also lives in the Bay Area. Along with Heather, and my granddaughters Alaina and Olivia, I met Kelly and her youngest daughter soon after we connected in 2018, and we've stayed in touch ever since. Since the start, it's been nothing but easy with her. We have a lot in common. Kelly's mother was married to my father, but Kelly didn't know him, as they divorced when she was young, so our father is an enigma to her too. We're still getting to know each other and meeting each other's families. I know we have many years ahead together.

I take a sip of coffee, handed to me by the cheerful flight attendant. The warmth soothes my nerves. I don't like flying these days. Looking out the porthole again, I wonder how it will feel visiting my father's grave a few days from now. I know it will be emotional. Moving. How could it not? Even with all his troubles, I come from him, from his people. He is a part of me, just as my mother Frances is. I feel so fortunate to have found both my natural parents.

As a Navy veteran, my father Robert Stewart is buried on

Port Royal Island at the National Cemetery in Beaufort, South Carolina. How synchronistic that both my adopted father and mother are also interred at the Los Angeles National Cemetery. My cousin Laurel has my natural father's burial flag waiting for me in Birmingham. My family will now have two military burial flags as keepsakes, from both of my fathers.

As the wide expanse of land stretches below me—geometric farms and lakes like glass—I have time for deeper thoughts. Distance and time can gift us understanding and forgiveness that can ultimately bring healing.

I love that I now have my own stories to tell and know my ethnicity. I don't feel like an impostor anymore, pretending to be someone else. As wonderful as the advantages I experienced being raised by my adoptive parents Stan and Madge were, they couldn't, no matter what, eliminate my wondering and the secret loss I felt being cut off from my family, my history, my roots.

I wish my adoptive parents had known this, as all adoptive parents need to be aware of their adoptive child's loss. My curiosity and desire to search had nothing to do with their parenting or my love for them. Adoption isn't always the best ground for becoming your true self. How can you become or even find who you are when you are missing how you began in the world, your first chapters in life? How we cringe with the thought of taking away a puppy or kitten too young from its mother yet celebrate "gotcha day"—a day that celebrates the anniversary of the day a child was adopted, which I personally find insensitive, since the celebration glosses over, or intentionally denies, the loss of the adopted child's natural family.

I am grateful Dave eventually bowed out as the trustee for

my children and passed the torch on to me in partnership with an investment banking firm. The trust was still limited to its boundaries, but we could live within it.

I have learned that I've lived with an underlying trauma from adoption. I became adaptive, a people pleaser, a chameleon, so I could fit into my adoptive family, changing into whoever you wanted me to be, because I didn't know who I was to begin with.

Yet, being an adoptee doesn't define me. It's just a word that means something that happened to me. Surely, it's a powerful undercurrent in my life, but I've learned to swim through and around the strong tide, finding myself standing strong on the sands of time.

I'm healthier today than I was before I first met my birth family. I will probably always struggle with some feelings of not belonging and abandonment, but those feelings don't happen as often as they once did as I continue to strive and evolve toward my authentic self.

Adoption is complex, messy, layered, vulnerable, and full of contradictions. It's a paradox. As Brené Brown states in her book *Atlas of the Heart*, "Paradox challenges us to straddle the tension of two conflicting elements and recognize that they can both be true." She adds, "[E]ven though the elements seem contradictory, they actually complement and inform each other in ways that allow us to discover underlying truths about ourselves and the world." This is how I feel about adoption.

I will always mourn the loss of my birth family, and I cannot fathom my life without my adoptive parents, my brother, or my grandparents. I cannot separate the two feelings. They remain unresolved and always will be, coexisting in my mind like two sides to a coin. It's as if I live between two bridges—my adoptive family and my birth family. I cannot choose between them.

They both are a link upon my path that have made me who I am.

Between the two bridges, I have found myself, collecting knowledge on this journey that helped me embrace empathy and compassion for both my adoptive parents and my birth parents. I survived acute trauma (separation from my mother), and chronic trauma (living without biological mirroring) and am fortunate to have found healing from it through loving my husband and children, finding my biological family, and forgiving my adoptive parents as well as myself.

I now live between the two bridges, beside the wildflowers and the river, feeling grounded in the earth, no longer wondering which rock I was born under. Instead, I follow the sweet scent of pine in the air, beckoning me to look up past the trees, toward the cotton-top clouds floating in the azure sky. I feel content and grateful for the mysteriousness of life and all that I've learned, grateful for the doors to my past having been opened and welcoming love along the way.

Acknowledgments

Writing this book was a labor of love, and woven between the lines for nearly a decade, healing and awareness evolved as I crafted my story, working through new connections with family as well as grief from ones lost along the way.

I have had the good fortune of working with some wonderful and inspiring people. I'd like to thank my first writing coach, author Judith Cassis, for her unfailing encouragement and support over the years to stand in my own truth.

I'm deeply grateful for having had the honor of working with Linda Joy Myers, president of the National Association of Memoir Writers, writing coach, and author of *Don't Call Me Mother*, *Song of the Plains*, and *The Forger of Marseille*. So grateful for your generous dedication to helping me find my voice and teaching me new ways to write. Your editorial eye helped bring my story to life.

To Brooke Warner, author, teacher, and publisher of She Writes Press. Brooke, you are a caring teacher and a warrior for women writers. Thank you for this opportunity to share my story. I'm honored to be published by She Writes Press, and to be a member of the She Writes Press sisterhood.

I'm grateful to the hardworking team at She Writes Press and SparkPress for helping women writers amplify their voices around the world. I especially enjoyed working with my project manager, Lauren Wise.

And thanks to author Joyce Maynard, who taught me to write shorter sentences and to embrace courage to tell my story, thank you.

An enormous thank-you to editor Sheila Trask, for her keen eye and insightful editing. You are so good at what you do.

Thank you to Nicole Neuman for your professional, kind, and knowledgeable thoughts on my manuscript. So appreciated.

Gratitude for all the people who supported me along this journey; there are too many to name, but I know who you are, and I am fortunate to have you in my life. To my dear friends and family members who lived this story with me—Ellen, Mary, Cheryl, Lynne, and Tara—as well as the recent support of friends—Cyndi, Elaine, Mags, Laura, Ann, and Sondra. I am lucky to be surrounded by such thoughtful, intelligent, and kind people. Thank you for your generous support fueled by coffee, good conversation, and, always, the good-for-your-soul laughter.

To Tracy: thank you for all the love and laughs we shared, and for being the one to embolden me to write a memoir. You are in my heart forever.

To my beloved late parents who loved me in the best way they knew how, I'm grateful for all the good things you taught and gave me in my life. We are all walking each other home. I miss you every day.

To my first mother and my natural family who welcomed me with open arms and hearts, enabling me to move forward, giving me the gift of my missing pieces, I am forever grateful for your warmth and trust.

For my daughter Heather; my son-in-law Wes; my granddaughters Alaina and Olivia; as well as my son Travis; and my daughter-in-law Molly—you are the light of my life, my world, my heart. I love you bigger than the sky, more than all the stars.

And to Michael, you are my home, my champion, and my best friend. I love you.

Sources

Brown, Brené. 2021. *The Atlas of the Heart: Mapping Meaningful Connection and the Language of Human Experience*. New York: Random House.

Fessler, Ann. 2006. *The Girls Who Went Away: The Hidden History of Women Who Surrendered Children for Adoption in the Decades Before Roe v. Wade*. London and New York: The Penguin Press.

Grace, Judi Loren. 2010. *The Third Floor*. Chico, CA: Jetstream Publishing.

Murkoff, Heidi. 2016. *What to Expect When You're Expecting: The All-in-One Guide*. Fifth Edition. New York: Workman Publishing Company.

Verrier, Nancy Newton. 1993. *The Primal Wound: Understanding the Adopted Child*. Baltimore: Gateway Press.

Verrier, Nancy Newton. 2003. *Coming Home to Self: The Adopted Child Grows Up*. Baltimore: Gateway Press.

Wilson-Buterbaugh, Karen. 2017. *The Baby Scoop Era: Unwed Mothers, Infant Adoption, and Forced Surrender*. Self-published.

About the Author

DIANE WHEATON, a reunited adoptee, is a wife, mother, and grandmother. When she's not writing, Diane enjoys spending time with her family and friends, as well as reading, painting, gardening, and swimming. She is a member of the National Association of Memoir Writers, and was a contributing author to the AN-YA Project's adult adoptee anthology, *Flip the Script*. A native Californian, Diane lives with her husband and their Alaskan malamute in Santa Clarita, California.

Stay connected with Diane at:
www.dianewheaton.com.

Looking for your next great read?

We can help!

Visit www.shewritespress.com/next-read
or scan the QR code below for a list
of our recommended titles.

She Writes Press is an award-winning
independent publishing company founded to
serve women writers everywhere.